# New "Temples" of India

# Social Sciences in Asia

*Edited by*

Vineeta Sinha
Syed Farid Alatas
Chan Kwok-bun

VOLUME 21

# New "Temples" of India

## Singapore and India Collaboration in Information Technology Parks

*By*

Faizal bin Yahya

BRILL

LEIDEN • BOSTON
2008

*On the cover*: Information Technology Park at Hyderabad, India. Photo by the author.

This book is printed on acid-free paper.

Library of Congress Cataloging-in-Publication Data

Yahya, Faizal bin.
New "temples" of India : Singapore and India collaboration in information technology parks / by Faizal bin Yahya.
p. cm. — (Social sciences in Asia)
Includes bibliographical references and index.
ISBN 978-90-04-17064-3 (pbk. : alk. paper)
1. Information technology parks—India. 2. Information technology parks—Singapore. 3. India—Foreign economic relations—Singapore. 4. Singapore—Foreign economic relations—India. I. Title. II. Series.
HC440.I55Y34 2008
338.4'70040954—dc22

2008032053

ISSN 1567-2794
ISBN 978 90 04 17064 3



PRINTED IN THE NETHERLANDS

CONTENTS

# LIST OF ILLUSTRATIONS

## *List of Tables*

## *List of Figures*



## *List of Pictures*

## ACKNOWLEDGEMENTS

No monograph is written without the help and inspiration of family, friends and colleagues over the years, despite the adage that academics live in their own 'ivory tower'. My wife Zairinah, children (Nina, Ezra and Ezriel) and parents (Yahya and Faridah) have often borne the brunt of my absence for weeks on end undertaking research in the field. I hope precious time away from them has resulted in a competent and credible monograph.

In the field of scholarship, my debts are huge; special thanks to Professor Subrata Mitra, who introduced me to India during my Masters in 1991, and Associate Professor Felix Patrikeef, who supervised my PhD at the later stages. I am lucky to have shared the PhD process with Dr Ajit Dayanandan (then at the Reserve Bank of India) who encouraged and advised me through critical stages of the PhD thesis. Having completed the PhD, my thanks go to Professor Reeves and Dean, Associate Professor, Tan Tai Yong, who provided me with a platform to research and write this monograph under the auspices of the South Asian Studies Programme, Faculty of Arts & Social Sciences at the National University of Singapore (NUS). In this regard, I am thankful to my Faculty for granting me a Writing Semester to complete publication of this monograph. My thanks to Ambassador K. Kesavapany, Director of the Institute of Southeast Asian Studies (ISEAS) which hosted me as a Visiting Research Fellow for my Writing Semester.

The Singapore Ambassador Gopinath Pillai, the Chairman of the Institute of South Asian Studies, has been very helpful and generous with his time. My increased interaction with other South Asianists and academics, especially colleagues in the South Asian Studies Programme and Faculty of Arts & Social Sciences at NUS, is thankfully acknowledged. To my research assistant and students—Arunajeet Kaur, Rodney Sebastian and Ashvin Parameswaran—your constant optimism in this area of research has been very inspiring.

Specific ministries, statutory boards and trade federations in Singapore have been helpful and encouraging in my scholarly endeavours. My thanks to friends and colleagues at the Ministry of Foreign Affairs who kept me company during my first trip to India, Ministry of Manpower officials with whom I have interacted and the Ministry of

Environment in Singapore who employed me before I joined NUS. My thanks to International Enterprises Singapore (formerly Trade and Development Board), Economic Development Board and Infocomm Development Authority for helping my research along. The Singapore India Chambers of Commerce and Industry and the Confederation of Indian Industries have also been supportive of my research. In this regard, Mr M. Rajaram and Mr Shabbir Hassanbhai provided valuable insights during the initial stages of my PhD thesis.

In the Singapore corporate world, Ascendas has to be singled out for special thanks because it has given me access not only to conduct interviews in its Singapore offices but also in its overseas operations in India in the cities of Bangalore, Hyderabad and Chennai. Gateway Distriparks, Sembawang Corporation and L&M Construction were Singapore companies that I interviewed. My special thanks to the CEO of Ascendas, Ms Chong Siak Ching, for writing the Foreword to this monograph. In the Indian corporate world IT giants, Tata Consultancy Services, Infosys Systems Limited, Wipro and Satyam Computers have kindly agreed to be interviewed for this publication. Other Indian corporates that provided the continuing belief in the dynamism of the Indian economy included, among others, Larsen & Toubro, the Aditya Birla Group, Reliance Industries Limited, ICICI Bank, IDFC Investment Advisors, Bank of Baroda, UTI Bank and Hindalco Limited.

# FOREWORD

I first met Faizal in 1997 when he, as a doctoral student, interviewed me on the International Tech Park Bangalore (ITPB) project and how it was progressing. It was a difficult time then for the IT Park, when we were taking huge risks to market an entirely new IT concept in India, against the backdrop of a global IT downcycle.

But our big gamble paid off and the rest was history. Faizal was witness to it all as ITPB struggled, sustained and then soared to become the mother of all IT Parks in India, so to speak. Over the years, he kept in touch and visited ITPB as well as Ascendas's other IT Parks in Hyderabad and Chennai. He saw first-hand how Ascendas, as well as other Singapore companies involved in our projects, translated the learnings from our business experiences to springboard onto multi-city expansion across India. So at various times, Faizal has seen through the downs as well as the ups of the IT park cluster and how India's IT outsourcing industry took off, carrying the rest of the country on its wings.

Faizal is thus one of few academics in Singapore who can actually profess to have in-depth understanding and insight into an economic phenomenon that also exemplifies the close ties and friendship between India and Singapore. He shows how the coupling of India's 'Look East' Policy with Singapore's regionalisation thrust for an 'external' wing gave impetus to the creation of 'virtual Singapores', or new 'temples' of economic strength in Indian cities. And in the process, leveraged on Singapore's brand name and employed India's vast human capital to create a classic in cross-border economic collaboration.

My congratulations to Faizal for producing this important documentation of IT and economic relations between two great nations, that has been accepted into the Brill Monograph series.

Chong Siak Ching (Ms)
President & CEO
Ascendas Pte Ltd

CHAPTER ONE

# SINGAPORE AND INDIA COLLABORATION IN INFORMATION TECHNOLOGY

## *Globalisation*

Globalisation, for all its multifaceted nature, arguably describes several processes in motion. Some of these processes reflect changing concepts of regionalism and bilateralism. The once-dominant role of the state is being challenged by influential multinational corporations (MNCs)[1] and intergovernmental organisations (IGOs). The inability of the World Trade Organisation (WTO) to deliver an acceptable multilateral approach to economic development has created a niche for alternative economic strategies, such as regional and bilateral Free Trade Agreements (FTAs). These FTAs are causing a paradigm shift among governmental agencies, MNCs and smaller medium enterprises (SMEs) because they provide alternatives to a multilateral trading agreement. In an increasingly globalised world characterised by economic integration, primary and manufacturing industries—though still important to the modern day economy—are being eclipsed by the services industry.

Various governments have intervened in numerous ways in economic development to ensure the survival of their nations, especially in periods of greater volatility in a more integrated global economy. Schmitter argued that the need for capital accumulation has forced the state to intervene more directly into the economy and to bargain with political associations that influence economic expansion (Schmitter & Lehmbruch, 1979). These political associations would include rival political parties, trade unions and other vested interests. This has given rise to corporatist theory or corporatism (Hill, 1997). States that use economic strategies based on corporatism to enhance economic development are termed 'developmental states'. According to Leftwich these

[1] The Transnational Corporation (TNC), Multinational Corporations (MNCs) or the Multinational Enterprise (MNEs) refer to a company that enters markets throughout the world by establishing its own sales and production subsidiaries, Franklin R. Root, *Entry Strategies for International Markets*, Maxwell Macmillan International, New York, 1994, pp. 252–253.

developmental states are characterised by a relatively stable economy, a powerful, competent and insulated bureaucracy, determined developmental elites and the capacity for effective economic management of private economic interests (Leftwich, 2000). Atul Kohli, in his discussion on state and development, referred to developmental states as cohesive-capitalist states. These cohesive-capitalist states have centralised and purposive institutional structures that have authority. These states were also found to equate rapid economic growth with national security and survival (Kohli, 2004). In this regard, Singapore is a developmental state or a cohesive-capitalist state but, in contrast, India could be described as a fragmented multi-class state. Kohli described a fragmented multi-class state as developing countries with plebiscitarian politics and weak institutions that pursue complex state-led agendas (Kohli, 2004).

The aim of this monograph will be to account for the expanding economic ties between Singapore and India with reference to the information technology (IT) sector. Post-1991, it will trace the factors that led to the collaboration between Singapore and India in the IT sector. However, before I begin my discussion on Singapore and India bilateral economic relations, we need to ask this: Why did Singapore choose the IT sector on which to focus its strategic economic cooperation with India? The IT sector is part of the knowledge-based economy (KBE) that Singapore is emphasising to sustain economic growth into the 21st century, but plans to develop a KBE did not materialise overnight. It has been argued by scholars like Edgar Schein that Singapore's emphasis on KBE goes back to its founding as a nation state (Schein, 1996). Prior to Britain pulling out its troops from Singapore in the 1960s, the-then Singapore Prime Minister Lee Kuan Yew had a fortuitous meeting with EJ Mayer, the director of the industrial planning department in Israel's ministry of commerce and industry. Singapore's geo-strategic concerns were similar to those of Israel, and both Lee and Mayer concluded that, 'If you are surrounded by neighbours who don't want or need your products, you must "leapfrog" (be ahead) them economically so that they will need your products' (Schein, 1996). Mayer implied that, like Israel, Singapore must skip one or more steps in the chain of economic development to get ahead of other countries that are following more traditional routes of economic development (Schein, 1996). Mayer also advised Lee to 'recognise that the only resource you have is your people, their brains, and their skills. Sort them and pick the best' (Schein, 1996). Arguably, this also sparked off the drive for the state's emphasis on meritocracy.

The main assumption the monograph will grapple with is that, in the process of developing its KBE, Singapore faced several challenges, especially the most critical element of talented human capital. Ironically, at the root of Singapore's graying population and problem of low fertility rates, was its success at curbing population growth in the early years of its independence from Malaysia. The argument was put forward by scholars like Garry Rodan, who commented on Singapore's 'stop at two' population control policy and subsequent emphasis on meritocracy (Rodan, 1989). In contrast, India has a large population of over a billion and is struggling to provide adequate employment opportunities for all its graduates. Every year, there are at least 3 million university graduates in India and, of these, about 400,000 are engineering graduates. The monograph will argue that with limited manpower, Singapore has tried to complement its strengths in infrastructure, planning and systems management with India's strengths in huge manpower potential (human capital). In this regard, Singapore has undertaken what it does best in terms of constructing and managing business and high-tech parks in India to provide the necessary infrastructure for foreign MNCs and Indian companies. These IT Parks provide the platform for foreign MNCs and Indian companies to employ thousands of knowledge workers.

How would human capital from India fit into Singapore's regionalisation policy? As described by Usha Haley, Singapore has the resources and expertise to construct industrial and high-tech parks or 'virtual Singapores' overseas (Haley, 1998). These 'virtual Singapores' provide a business climate that could attract foreign MNCs to locate in the host countries and utilise the abundant, skilled and low-cost human capital. To a large extent, Singapore has managed to procure a certain brand name with foreign MNCs due to its ability to develop and maintain good infrastructure, consistent regulations and a transparent business environment which they find attractive (Haley, 2000). Using the case study of the Information Technology Park Bangalore (ITPB) in the southern Indian state of Karnataka, it will be shown that Singapore is trying to complement India's economic priority of providing employment for its millions of new tertiary graduates every year.

Singapore's experience in nurturing research and development (R&D) clusters to attract global talent could provide pointers for India's continued development of its knowledge-based industries (KBI) (DPM Tan, 1997). As India transforms itself from third world to first world economy in the process of 'India Rising', it also needs to leapfrog economically through advances in high-technology (high-tech) industries such as information technology. As India is short of funding for infrastructure projects, it has to attract foreign investments and collaborate with foreign partners like Singapore to develop its infrastructure. How would the Singapore government and its government-linked companies (GLCs) approach the construction of 'virtual Singapores' overseas? John Dunning used the concept of 'Alliance Capitalism' to employ a more cooperative relationship between firms and governments (Dunning, 1997). Dunning explained that the concept of Alliance Capitalism is epitomised by deep structural interdependence between corporations, governments, workers, consumers, shareholders—in short, all concerned stakeholders in the wealth-creating activities of a society (Dunning, 1997). In discussing various approaches towards capitalism, especially in an era in which capitalism has seemingly triumphed over communism, Anthony Giddens used a similar concept called 'stakeholder capitalism' (Giddens, 2000). Will Hutton argued that globalisation has favoured the expansion of shareholder capitalism but that with the awareness of the need to instill better corporate governance, stakeholder capitalism has to be more transparent and behave ethically in relation to other vested interests such as the company's workers (Giddens, 2000).

In the case of Singapore and India, the Alliance Capitalism concept promulgated by Dunning could be used to explain the relationship between the Singapore GLCs and the state in the process of creating an external economy through the process of regionalisation. How would new forms of capitalism such as Alliance Capitalism connect to IT? Manuel Castells argued that productivity and competitiveness are a function of knowledge creation and information processing (Castells, 2000). In the area of developing high-tech parks, both India and Singapore have complementary strengths in developing the IT industry in India. In this context, Singapore's strengths, which include financial capital for investments overseas, building and management expertise of high-tech parks will offset India's infrastructural weaknesses and lack of capital for investment purposes. This monograph will argue that the deep structural independence between the Singapore state and GLCs is a key feature of Singapore's regionalisation strategy.

A more integrated global economy with an expanding services sector has also led to greater labour mobility. Greater labour mobility spurred by declining birth rates and a shortage of skilled and professional workers in developed economies will likely influence employment patterns leading to institutional changes and demographic shifts (Lavoie, 2003).

What are the likely trends of future economic growth and development? Apart from the developed OECD economies, more advanced developing economies like Singapore with a small population base of around 4 million will be competing with the developed economies for skilled and professional foreign talent. Of the 4 million, about 1 million are expatriate workers and the Singapore government intends to increase the population to 6.5 million. This projected increase in population, together with the desire to 'move up the value chain', has made it critical to deal with more valued high-tech industries. When in the 20th century mankind made the transition from resource-based economies to those based on ideas, the tools relevant for the new economy were predicated upon thought, design and organisation (Lavoie, 2003). How different are knowledge-based economies from those focused on manufacturing and primary industries?

The core activities of KBEs revolve around knowledge industries such as software development, biotechnology and nanotechnology. This seems to be the crux of the matter and why various countries are obsessed with accumulating human capital. Singapore Defence Minister Teo Chee Hean has emphasised the importance of knowledge for the Singapore economy (*The Straits Times*, 20 April 2007). This is manifested in the state's commitment to high levels of education, skills, complex manufacturing, high value-added services, competency and IT among others (*The Straits Times*, 20 April 2007). While the state in Singapore strives to be a KBE, its shortcomings are primarily human capital and land area. Could Singapore be a KBE by leveraging on the strengths of emerging markets such as India?

From the perspective of internationalisation theory, the more knowledge intensive the industry, the lower the propensity to form alliances[2] because of the fear of misappropriation of knowledge by allies who could become competitors (Contractor & Lorange, 2002). The early history of software development in Silicon Valley is a case in point. This monograph takes the argument in a different direction and will prove that economic alliances are necessary in the event that companies and/or national economies do not possess the human capital and business environment required to stimulate innovation, such as in the case

[2] An alliance is usually defined as any inter-firm cooperation that falls between the extremes of discrete short-term contracts and the complete merger of two or more alliances: Ibid., p. 486. In this monograph, the concept of an alliance refers more broadly to the cooperation between two economies.

of the IT industry. Using the concept of Alliance Capitalism, it could be refined here to examine the economies of Singapore and India in terms of complementarity. Is Alliance Capitalism between Singapore and India in developing the IT sector leading towards an economic alliance between the two economies?

Singapore and India differ in terms of their physical size and economies. India is over 3 million square kilometres in size and Singapore barely makes up 647 square kilometres.

Singapore, the developed island city-state with enviable infrastructure and per capita income, is the antithesis of India. India is often seen as a disorganised but lively democracy with inadequate infrastructure and low per capita income. Despite their seeming differences from tiny-island state Singapore to India's subcontinental land mass, both economies have underlying complementary strengths. Nonetheless there will be challenges confronting Singapore companies venturing into India, and one of the main problems is economies of scale due to the immense size of projects in India. In this regard, it will be shown that Singapore GLCs have resorted to the consortium approach to develop the ITPB. In terms of organisational pattern, Manuel Castells coined the concept of 'corporate strategic alliances', which is the intertwining of large corporations (Castells, 1996). According to Castells these alliances are different from traditional forms of cartels because they concern specific times, markets, products and processes. Moreover, strategic alliances do not exclude competition in all areas that are not covered by the agreements. This is especially true in the case of high-tech industries where complex linkages and joint ventures do not preclude stepped-up competition (Castells, 1996). However, collaboration as a result of strategic alliance also stands in contrast to the competition for market share in another sector or region in the world.

A new global competitive environment is emerging; how will Singapore adapt to this change? The new global competitive environment after 9/11 has created greater uncertainty and volatility in the global economic environment.[3] Smaller economies, like Singapore, that rely on the international market and exports for their livelihood need to

[3] In 2001, due the volatile global economy and after 9/11, the Singapore economy experienced negative growth after 9% growth in 2000: Leslie Koh, 'Reinventing the Singapore economy', *The Straits Times*, 24 November 2001.

adopt strategies that would prevail against negative effects of volatility and instability.

Historically, Singapore was ahead in economic development among the regional economies of Southeast Asia. However, Singapore faces growing competition not only from its Southeast Asian neighbours like Malaysia and Thailand, but also from China and the other New Industrialising Economies (NIEs).[4] Why does Singapore need to diversify and reshape its economic policies? Over-dependence on regional economies in Southeast Asia has resulted in an adverse impact on the Singapore economy. For example, during the Asian Financial Crisis of 1998, the Singapore economy experienced contraction because it was strongly linked to regional economies, especially in the financial sector and investments in various projects. Singapore has also come to realise that it has to benchmark its development beyond the Southeast Asian region and achieve international standards (Yeo, 2001). Former Nominated Member of Parliament Dr Lee Tsao Yuan also pointed out that with overall economic growth slowing down in the ASEAN (Association of South East Asian Nations) region, Singapore should focus on opportunities in other regions including India (Campbell, 2001). While the economic growth in the ASEAN region has slowed down to 5%–7%, India's economic growth reached 9.2% by the end of 2006 and will have a sustained economic growth of 6%–8% until 2009.

The reinvention of Singapore Incorporated (Inc) to Singapore Unlimited by the Economic and Development Board (EDB) was to accommodate the regionalisation drive of the Singapore economy in the early 1990s. As described by former EDB Managing Director Tan Chin Nam, EDB's prime aim of attracting foreign investments to Singapore had to be reconfigured into concentric circles (Tan, 2002). The EDB's focus on attracting foreign investments from the developed world became its 'outer globalisation' strategy while its 'inner globalisation' strategy was directed at driving Singapore's investments into the region (Tan, 2002). Another potential challenge for the Singapore economy was that its regionalisation drive should not be focused on a single economy. Over-exposure in terms of trade and investment in a single large economy like China could also have a negative impact should the Chinese economy falter. Therefore, in hedging its risks overseas, Singapore began to diversify its investments and external economic linkages

---

[4] 'Global City, Best Home', National Day Rally Speech, 1997, Ministry of Education.

to include the South Asian region, especially the Indian economy. In the South Asian region, India is the largest economy, larger than all the other South Asian economies combined. Singapore has been trying to expand economic linkages with India from the early 1990s. After two years of negotiations, 13 rounds of talks and changes in government and prime ministers, Singapore and India finally signed their bilateral Free Trade Agreement (FTA) called the Comprehensive Economic Cooperation Agreement (CECA) in June 2005.

What is the significance of CECA? The CECA is more than just an FTA because one of the key features of CECA is the provision for Indian skilled workers and professionals in 127 categories to seek employment in Singapore. Greater attention has been given towards collaboration in education, science and technology between the two economies. Central to the emergence of knowledge-based economies of the future will be the need to create competencies or capabilities through the process of knowledge accumulation (Van Gils & Zwart, 2004). The Singapore government realised in the 1990s that to be a successful knowledge-based economy, the critical resource is intellectual capital which is in short supply in Singapore. The problem that confronted Singapore was twofold. Already short of a critical mass of creative and innovative talent, the problem was aggravated as labour mobility becomes a facet of the IT age. In this context, Singapore needed to open its doors wider to skilled foreign talent because Singapore was likely to lose more of its talented individuals overseas.

The global war for talent means that Singapore has to be prepared to lose some talented Singaporeans to other countries as well (*The Straits Times*, 12 March 2007). When MNCs start up or expand their operations in the region and especially in China they tend to look for Singaporeans, particularly those studying overseas, to recruit (Van Gils & Zwart, 2004). Senior Minister Goh Chok Tong commented that if Singapore were to lose even 0.5% of its brightest talent, it would have a much lower peak of talent; he said, 'while the country had a promising future...issue we are most concerned with is the loss of our own people at the very top' (*The Straits Times*, 15 March 2007). SM Goh pointed out that bright young Singaporeans studying overseas of very well-educated parents are immediately 'green harvested' by companies (*The Straits Times*, 15 March 2007). Green-harvesting refers to recruitment by top firms at universities before students graduate. There are an estimated 140,000 Singaporeans living overseas, or 230,000 if Permanent Residents are included. This would further aggravate the shortage of talent within the Singapore economy. The response from the Singapore authorities to the lack of human capital is a twofold strategy to recruit good foreign talent and to invest overseas in economies where there is availability of talent, such as in India. Singapore educationists have also visited some of India's top private schools, such as Dehradun's Doon School, to study how top Indian schools educate their pupils. They were impressed and recruited two well-regarded teachers from the Doon School, one in English and the other in mathematics to work in Singapore (*The Straits Times*, 31 March 2007). This approach will link to Singapore's overall regionalisation[5] strategy to create an external wing for its domestic economy.

As argued by Ian Austin, with a small internal economy, Singapore had no choice but to seek free trade to ensure its economic survival (Austin, 2001). One of the main tools of state policy to ensure Singapore's economic survival was to be involved in entrepreneurship by creating state-owned enterprises (SOEs) that are better known as GLCs. The GLCs paid particular attention to sectors that were neglected by the private sector companies but essential if Singapore were to meet the challenges of an open economy (Austin, 2001). Garry Rodan commented that the need to create an open economy and promote free trade was essential and important because the state had to depend on foreign investments especially from large foreign MNCs for technology, expertise and access to overseas markets (Rodan, 1989). This policy to ensure economic survival has been labelled by scholars such as Ian Austin and Edgar Schein as Singapore's strategy of pragmatism or strategic pragmatism (Schein, 1996). When Singapore started on its path of economic development after independence in 1965, the government encouraged local companies, especially GLCs, to venture abroad to enable the expansion of domestic capital. Private companies in Singapore were also encouraged to invest in the established markets of Europe and North America. However, only a few Singapore companies, mostly GLCs, managed to secure a foothold in those industrialised countries (Yeung WC, 2000). In the early 1990s the focus shifted to regionalisation on the assumption that Singapore companies were likely to better

[5] The process of regionalisation involves the state seeking partnership with domestic capital to extend the economy across national boundaries in order to legitimise the role of a strong state in economic development: Henry Wai-chung Yeung, 'State intervention and neoliberalism in the globalising world economy: lessons from Singapore's regionalisation programme', *The Pacific Review*, Vol. 13, No. 1, 2000, p. 141.

understand the Asia Pacific region and there would be more opportunities in emerging Asian economies like China and India. The Singapore government has taken regionalisation further by a process of political entrepreneurship. Essentially, this process involves the state opening up overseas business opportunities for private capitalists by negotiating the institutional framework for such projects for Singaporean firms. An example of this is the International Technology Park Bangalore (ITPB), Singapore's flagship investment project in India.

What is the state of infrastructure in India? In 2003, consultancy firm Morgan Stanley estimated that China spent approximately US$325 billion on infrastructure, while India spent only US$35 billion. With India's limited resources and infrastructure, initiatives to expand the manufacturing sector will be costly and unviable compared to lower-cost countries like China. However, in certain production areas such as automotive parts, India is competing well with China. Nonetheless, based on its comparative advantage of a huge labour force trained in English and engineering, India is competing for a larger share of the global IT market. Increasing global labour mobility suggests that economies like Singapore and India could benefit from this growing trend to expand their respective economies. An argument could be made that India has yet to meet its economic potential but for a maturing economy like Singapore, the issues are no less pressing in how it should ensure further economic growth with its own inbuilt constraints.

### *Multinational Companies*

When they became independent, India and Singapore chose two different paths to economic growth and development. India opted for self-reliance and self-sufficiency in a closed mixed economic model since its independence in 1947. Singapore, in contrast, pursued the alternative capitalist choice as it embraced a free market economy after its forced separation from Malaysia in 1965. While India has a large market, labour and natural resources to develop heavy industries, Singapore had none of these advantages. Singapore had to turn towards the international market for its survival and invited multinational companies (MNCs) to invest in the country. In comparison, India was distrustful of MNCs and foreign investors after its experience with the British East India Company. India adopted Import Substitution Industrialisation (ISI) policies but these did not reap the same rewards as the Export-

Oriented Industrialisation (EOI) policies that were adopted by the Asian 'Tiger' Economies such as those of Singapore, Hong Kong, South Korea and Taiwan, which experienced double-digit economic growth in the late 1960s and 1970s. India expelled both IBM and Coca-Cola in the 1970s. Both MNCs were iconic symbols of Western capitalism and this branded India as hostile from the perspective of potential foreign investors. As India's own economy was straight-jacketed by regulations with the state assuming the commanding heights of the economy, Singapore in contrast adopted free market principles and established policies that were friendly to foreign investors and MNCs. Unable to survive without a natural economic hinterland, the Singapore government decided to expand economic growth and development by enhancing ties with the global economy. The Singapore government, like the Indian government, did intervene in economic development but their policies have produced very different results for both economies.

While both economies diverged in terms of ideology during the Cold War, post-Cold War conditions had improved prospects for convergence. During the Cold War, Singapore's economy became more integrated into the global economy but India became more closed and insular. However, after the Cold War several factors forced India to liberalise its economy through reforms (Thornton, 1992). Post-Cold War, India was cast adrift economically and strategically, and had to purchase oil imports at market prices and not at discounted or 'friendship' prices it had paid before to the former Soviet Union (Ganguly, Winter 2003/2004). Then the first Gulf War caused the repatriation of thousands of Indian workers in the Gulf region, resulting in losses of billions of US dollars in remittances to India. These factors contributed to India's severe financial crisis because its foreign currency reserves were drawn down to about two weeks' worth of imports and it was in danger of defaulting on its loan payments to international lending institutions like the World Bank (Anderson & Lanen, 1999). To secure fresh short-term loans, India had to mortgage its gold reserves for the first time in its history. The financial crisis spurred India's late Prime Minister Narasimha Rao and Finance Minister Dr Manmohan Singh to reform and liberalise the Indian economy towards a more market-oriented model.

In 1991, India started to undertake and implement bold economic reforms to liberalise its economy and, at the same time, to realign its economic links with the Southeast Asian region (Vaghul, 1994). India has also come to realise that its ambition to become a major power has been constrained and limited to concerns in South Asia, while its main rival China has grown in standing in the region as well as globally. China and India are often compared because of their physical size and billion-strength populations. The entry of China as a member of the World Trade Organisation (WTO) at the end of 2001 indicated more challenging times for regional economies in Southeast Asia. Among the members of ASEAN, the delay in implementing an ASEAN Free Trade Area (AFTA) to create a common market among the grouping's members has led to increasing concerns over its ability to compete with emerging economies like China. For some members such as Singapore, China has been portrayed as ASEAN's main competitor for foreign direct investment (FDI) in the region (*Business Times*, 13 May 2002).

### *China and India Trade*

Historically, China and India have had centuries of economic, political and social interactions. Even before the spread of Buddhism to China around the 1st century AD, China and India were already exchanging emissaries and engaged in trade, particularly of silk and cotton textiles (Shanker, April 2003). The Sino-Indo War in 1962 had derailed the process of bilateral engagement between both economies but post-1991, bilateral ties seem to be improving. The visit by Chinese Premier Wen Jiabao to Delhi in April 2005 followed by Indian Prime Minister Dr Manmohan Singh's visit to Beijing in November 2006 increased expectations all around that Sino-India bilateral trade was set to take off. In 2005, more than 100 trade delegations from India visited China seeking business opportunities. Approximately 80 Indian companies have established operations in China and some 45 Chinese companies have operations in India (*The Hindu*, 7 September 2006).

Table 1.1: Comparison between China and India in 2003

| | Population | Population growth rate (%) | Size of economy (GDP) | Purchasing power parity (PPP) |
|---|---|---|---|---|
| China | 1.3 billion (January 2005) | 0.57% | US$1.4 trillion (2004–7th largest) 9.1% annual growth | US$5,000 per capita |
| India | 1.06 billion (2004) | 2% (1975 to 2001) | US$496.8 billion (2002) 7–8% annual growth | US$2,880 per capita |

Source: Country Study of China, the US Library of Congress, February 2005. Country Study of India, the US Library of Congress, December 2004.

China and India agreed to reopen the Nanthu La Pass in July 2006 after it was closed for 44 years from 1962 because of border conflicts (*Asia Times*, 20 June 2006). Table 1.1 provides a basic comparison between China and India in 2003, in terms of their respective populations, population growth rate, size of their economies and the purchasing power parity per capita of their respective markets. Both are billion-dollar economies that have the potential to power global economic growth. The total bilateral trade between China and India has increased from US$250 million in the early 1990s to reach US$18.7 billion at the end of 2005 (BBC News, 21 November 2006 and *The Hindu*, 7 September 2006). Sino-India bilateral trade is expected to cross US$20 billion by 2008 or earlier and reach US$30 billion by 2010 (*Business Line*, 16 April 2005).

Table 1.2 shows the steady increase of bilateral trade between the two Asian economic giants from 1999 to 2005. However, the picture is not as encouraging as it looks. The initial euphoria over the visit of Premier Wen Jiabao did not last long because the recommendations of the India-China Joint Study Group (JSG) for a Task Force to examine the feasibility of a Regional Trading Arrangement was mainly driven by China (Sridhar, 20 May–2 June 2005) and was not supported by Indian industry. Indian and Chinese investments in each other's markets have not been impressive. In 2005, India invested US$130 million in China while Chinese investments in India was approximately US$2.03 million (*The Hindu*, 7 September 2006). Former Indian Consul in China, Sujan Chinoy, explained that China did not invest in India to a large extent because it was not seen as a high-value market. Moreover, Chinese investments in Indian infrastructure projects have been repeatedly blocked because of security concerns (*The Hindu*, 7 September 2006).

Table 1.2: Bilateral Trade between China and India (US$ million), 1999–2005

| Years | 1999 | 2000 | 2001 | 2002 | 2003 | 2004 | 2005 |
|---|---|---|---|---|---|---|---|
| Imports | 1,161.9 | 1,569.5 | 1,896.3 | 2,671.7 | 3,345 | 5,927 | 6,200 |
| % increase | 14.3 | 34.3 | 21.5 | 40.8 | 25.1 | 77.3 | 32 |
| Exports | 825.8 | 1,350.4 | 1,670 | 2,274.2 | 4,252.8 | 7,677 | 12,500 |
| % increase | –8.8 | 63.9 | 25.6 | 33.7 | 86.9 | 80.6 | 67 |
| Total trade | 1,987.68 | 2,914.2 | 3,596.2 | 4,945.9 | 7,597.8 | 13,604.1 | 18,700 |

Source: 'The Road Ahead, India-China', Confederation of Indian Industry.

Table 1.3: India's Exports and Imports to China, 2001–2006 (Rs lakh)

| Country | 2001–2002 | 2002–2003 | 2003–2004 | 2004–2005 | 2005–2006 |
|---|---|---|---|---|---|
| China | | | | | |
| Export | 454003.59 | 956039.19 | 1357905.88 | 2523297.00 | 2992491.50 |
| Import | 971192.38 | 1351215.13 | 1862513.75 | 3189230.75 | 4811665.00 |
| Balance of Trade | −517188.79 | −395176 | −504607.9 | −665933.7 | −1819173.5 |

Source: EXIM Data Bank, Dept of Commerce, Ministry of Commerce, 16 January 2007.

Table 1.3 shows India's trade with China from 2001 to 2006. The trend shows clearly that India's imports are greater than its exports with China, indicating that its overall trade with China is in deficit. This would account for complaints from the private sector in India accusing China of 'dumping' subsidised goods into the Indian market.

The pattern of bilateral trade also revealed some trends of concern to India. Indian exports to China have been mainly primary commodities such as ores, minerals, iron and steel, accounting for 57% of total exports to China. In contrast, Chinese exports to India have been more diversified and dominated by manufactured goods (Sridhar, 20 May–2 June 2005). Nonetheless, India's Chinese engagement has been important for Indian industry in several ways. The competition from China has forced several Indian companies to upgrade their operations and productivity (Khanna, 6 December 2006). Competition between China and India will also be influenced by differences in their economies. These differences include business environment, infrastructure, inflow of foreign direct investments, business strategy and population structure.

### *Foreign Direct Investments*

Table 1.4 illustrates the foreign direct investment (FDI) inflows for China, India and Singapore from 2002 to 2004. In 2004, China's rate of FDI inflows is more than 10 times that of India in 2004 and, more significantly, China has grabbed a 10% share of total global FDI inflows. In US-dollar terms, India attracted US$4 billion in FDI compared with China's US$60 billion of FDI in a year (*Asia Times*, 14 April 2005). Singapore, with a much smaller domestic economy, also received more than three times India's share of FDI in 2004. However, there is growing debate over the role of FDI in the development and

Table 1.4: Foreign Direct Investments in China, India and Singapore, 2002–2004

| Country | FDI Inflows (US$ billion) | | | Share in World FDI Inflows (%) | | |
|---|---|---|---|---|---|---|
| | 2002 | 2003 | 2004 | 2002 | 2003 | 2004 |
| China | 52.74 | 53.51 | 60.63 | 7.36 | 8.46 | 9.35 |
| India | 3.45 | 4.27 | 5.34 | 0.48 | 0.67 | 0.82 |
| Singapore | 5.82 | 9.33 | 16.06 | 0.81 | 1.47 | 2.48 |

Source: World Investment Report 2005, UNCTAD.

growth of economies. In terms of FDI in infrastructure, progress in education and health, China seems better poised to further economic growth compared with India. However, some analysts argue that overall, capital is used less efficiently in China than in India (Bardhan, 25 October 2005). Indian companies are also more commercially driven than their Chinese counterparts (Chaze, 2006). Academics Tarun Khanna and Huang Yasheng have argued that India's economic development is more sustainable because it relies mainly on growth from within. In this regard, Indian companies make fuller use of resources and are more autonomous than Chinese companies that are dependent of FDI for economic growth (Huang & Khanna, July/August 2003).

Since the early 1990s, India has invested about 23% of its GDP on infrastructure and has seen economic growth averaging 6%. China had invested about twice as much of its GDP on infrastructure in the same period but its rate of economic growth has been about 9% (Huang & Khanna, July/August 2003). For example in 2004, China posted economic growth of 9.5% after investing US$850 billion or half of its GDP into infrastructure. China's factories burn five times more fuel than Western factories and 20% of China's bank loans are unrecoverable (Engardio, 6 September 2005). An estimated 57% of China's exports are from foreign-invested factories indicating that its march towards industrialisation is not driven by indigenous firms. Moreover, of the 1,300 public listed companies in China in 2004, two-thirds do not earn back their true cost of capital. In comparison, Indian companies with much less resources and foreign investment have no room for wastage and are compelled to recover their capital costs because it has Western legal institutions, a modern stock market and a better-managed banking sector (Engardio, 6 September 2005).

Furthermore, India has managed to produce a number of companies in the IT manufacturing and pharmaceuticals sectors, among others, that are competing with the best companies in Europe and the US. Apart from large IT companies (Infosys, Wipro) or pharmaceuticals companies (Dr Reddy's, Ranbaxy), smaller Indian companies are also being transformed into mini MNCs by acquiring foreign companies to gain expertise and entry into foreign markets (*International Herald Tribune*, 2 September 2005). In contrast, the wastage in China's manufacturing sector continues into its R&D sector. China's huge state-run R&D institutions are close to cutting-edge technologies at the theoretical level but they have yet to yield commercial breakthroughs. The lack of intellectual property protection and the state's heavy influence in building up its own technology companies make foreign MNCs and SMEs wary of doing serious R&D with China (Engardio, 6 September 2005).

A difference in strategy is also detected among Indian and Chinese companies seeking to become global companies. An Indian company called Bharat Forge, which is a manufacturer of steel car components, has acquired forges in the US and Germany as part of its 'multishore model'. According to the company's chief executive, Baba Kalyani, 'Being a global auto-component player does not only mean growing exports, it also requires a strategic vision that skillfully combines the comparative advantages of each location so that the whole is significantly greater than the sum of its parts' (*International Herald Tribune*, 2 September 2005). In contrast, Chinese companies are leveraging on lower-cost manufacturing in China by acquiring foreign companies and hollowing out its manufacturing. Which competing strategy would be preferred by ASEAN members? Furthermore, in terms of state influence, Indian companies that invest overseas are relatively more entrepreneurial than Chinese companies. Chinese companies that expand overseas might not necessarily undertake the state's bidding but they are fostering the state's national sovereign desires around the world (*International Herald Tribune*, 2 September 2005). The Chinese government has also flexed its influence domestically to prevent foreign firms from acquiring Chinese companies in strategic sectors such as ports and telecommunications.

### *Financial Sector*

The financial sector for both China and India are playing key roles in the growth and development of their respective economies. As China starts to loosen its foreign currency controls and restructure its banking system, some analysts are predicting that there is a danger that its financial market liberalisation will go wrong (Engardio, 2007). Critics point out that the Chinese equity market is not well regulated and rampant speculation continues (Chaze, 2006). The Indian equity market, on the other hand, is better regulated and more sophisticated. Since 2001, India has been part of the global process of regulatory convergence. The tightening of domestic compliance in India has been useful for Indian companies because it has facilitated a faster response whenever these companies decide to go for cross-border listings. The stocks of listed public sector banks in India has seen increasing valuation, indicating that the sector is not only healthy but shows great growth potential. The banking sector in India has seen a huge expansion of earnings and has used profits to clean its accounts of non-performing loans (Chaze, 2006). Indian banks have also used capital infusion from the domestic equity and international debt market to reduce non-performing loans and raise capital adequacy. The level of non-performing loans in the Chinese banking system was estimated at 15% of total assets compared to about 5% in India. In some Southeast Asian countries, the level of non-performing loans could be as high as 30% of total assets (Chaze, 2006).

### *Governance*

The 'bottom up' model of policy implementation in India has often been criticised by foreign investors as taking too long to deliver and many prefer the Chinese 'top down' model. However, there is growing consensus among China and India analysts to suggest that the Indian model of policy implementation, while slower than China's, would be more stable and sustainable in the long run because it has consensus from a wide spectrum of stakeholders. For example, in the run-up to the Olympic Games in Beijing in 2008, the media has reported news events highlighting the harsh tactics used by state authorities in developing facilities for the games. Reports are increasing about the forcible eviction of inhabitants from dwellings and the lack of adequate compensation and resettlement schemes (BBC News, 25 November 2006 and Gulf News, 7 August 2007). In this regard, the Indian system could also be argued to be more transparent than the Chinese system. The Chinese government implements policy decisions based on a 'top down' approach while the Indian government seeks consensus from the ground up and implements policy decisions from a 'bottom up' approach. The Chinese Communist Party harshly represses dissent and does not stand for interference in its drive towards economic growth (Engardio, 2007). Serious challenges await the Chinese ruling elites as the disparity gap widens between the rich and the poor, as well as between the different provincial states. In India the system of governance, despite its critics, enables multiple issues and perspectives to be heard. The press and media are relatively more liberal and are able to represent a large spectrum of views. Which model would better integrate into an overall model of Asian economic development to include the ASEAN region? In some sense the Singapore model, highly interventionist state policy in economic development, is closer to the Chinese model but it could provide pointers to India because it has encouraged discipline yet is based on free market principles.

### *Human Capital*

Singapore's drive towards a KBE apart from training its own human capital especially its creative talent would involve its ability to attract creative human capital from countries like India. Singapore has limited human capital especially creative human capital. Former Deputy Secretary of the National Trade Union Congress in Singapore, Mr Lim Swee Say, mentioned that the drive towards innovation could include attracting leading experts worldwide from various disciplines to form the core of a creative group (Mahiznan & Lee, 1998). This would then be supported by young local and foreign scientists and engineers. Where would Singapore tap for creative human capital? China's working age population will hit its peak at 1 billion in 2015 and then start to decline as China becomes a graying economy (Engardio, 22 August 2005). The 'one-child policy' has averted over 300 million births since the early 1980s. While this translated into 300 million fewer mouths to feed it also would mean 300 million fewer workers to prop up an ageing population (*The Economist*, 5 March 2005). With an average age of 26 years, India will be a younger country than China with an average age of 33 years (*The Economist*, 5 March 2005). India currently has 500 million people under 19 years of age and by 2050 will have a population of 1.6 billion, which would translate to 220 million more workers than China (*Businessweek*, 6 September 2005). The possibility of allowing skilled labour to move freely among the ASEAN countries may help regional economies to restructure their own economies to remain competitive (Mohanty, Pohit & Roy, September 2004). Encouraging and leveraging on the Indian diaspora could be a strategy for some ASEAN countries to strengthen their own linkages with India (Asher & Sen, March 2005). As more skilled workers and professionals stay in India after graduation, this younger and more skilled working population in India will also have more influence on consumption patterns that could expand the Indian economy in several other areas such as real estate and retail. This is something that ASEAN economies need to consider as they engage India and China as potential markets and sources of investments.

The pool of technical and managerial talent is staggering in India. The Indian Institute of Management (IIMs) trains thousands of much sought after MBA post-graduates every year who are headhunted by every known company, both Indian and foreign. Likewise, the Indian Institute of Technologies (IITs) trains technical talent especially in engineering who are also sought after by corporate bodies the world over.[6] The well-developed technical and managerial talent combined with the entrepreneurial spirit and access to capital will drive the growth of the Indian economy (Chaze, 2006). There is an abundance of human capital in India of varying types and quality for all companies. One trend to note is that as the developed economies having already experienced a graying population and now China set to face one by 2015, human capital from India looks set to power the world's global corporate bodies. A quick glance of top US corporations on Wall Street consultancies will reveal human capital of Indian origin or Indians among their ranks. The ASEAN members like Singapore and possibly Malaysia and Thailand will need to recruit foreign talent from India to varying degrees to sustain their economic growth and prospects.

### *Southeast Asia and FDI*

The rise of the two Asian giants—China and India—will have an impact on the Southeast Asian region. China has also altered the flow of FDI to Southeast Asian countries and has benefited at the expense

---

[6] Interviews with companies, IITs, IIM and recruitment agencies in Chennai, Mumbai and Delhi from 11 December 2006 to 9 January 2007.

of Southeast Asian countries (*Washington Quarterly*, Summer 2002). For example, in the early 1990s, three-fifths of FDI moving to Asia were channelled to Southeast Asia. By the end of the 1990s, two-fifths of FDIs flowing to Asia went to China and only about one-fifth went to Southeast Asia (Rajan, June 2003). In 1996, Southeast Asia received US$27 billion as FDI, in 1998 the figure was US$19 billion and this declined to US$16 billion in 1999 and US$10 billion by 2000 (*Asia Times*, 8 October 2002). Other ASEAN political leaders such as former Malaysian Prime Minister Mahathir have also commented that China is a threat to the economies of Southeast Asia (*Asia Times*, 2 August 2003). At the end of November 2002, overseas investments in China reached US$48 billion, a 14.6% rise over the same period in 2000 (*The Straits Times*, 28 December 2002). Concurrently, the inflow to ASEAN members such as Singapore, Malaysia, Thailand, Indonesia and the Philippines fell from US$27 billion in 1997 to US$11.4 billion in 2001. China's exports will also compete with ASEAN exports in other regional markets (Shafaeddin, 2003). In some sense, the ASEAN region has tried to benefit from, and cushion the impact of, a rising China by establishing strong links with the Chinese economy and others through FTAs.

India could potentially act as a counterbalance from ASEAN's perspective to a fast-rising China in strategic and economic terms. In this context, Singapore was a strong supporter of India's engagement with ASEAN. India's interaction with ASEAN through its 'Look East' Policy has steadily progressed from a sectoral dialogue partnership in 1992 to a major or full dialogue partner in 1996 and gained membership into the ASEAN Regional Forum (ARF). In 2002, India's status and recognition within ASEAN increased further when it was accorded a Summit-level status and the first ASEAN-India Summit was held in November 2002 in Vientiane, Laos. Within ASEAN, Singapore was one of the original founding members in 1967 and was quick to realise the potential of enhancing strategic and economic linkages with India. In a post-9/11 world, India has gained rapid recognition as a stabilising influence and its membership in the ARF has widened its experience of dealing not only with ASEAN members but all the ASEAN dialogue partners. The engagement of India within the ASEAN context was a sign of the changing strategic imperative for the regional organisation. During the Cold War, India was viewed with suspicion from ASEAN's perspective because it was modernising its blue water navy, but post-9/11 India began conducting joint naval exercises with counterparts from Singapore, Thailand and Malaysia. India and Singapore have also conducted air exercises in Guwahati, India, and this cooperation could be extended to India providing military facilities for Singapore's army to train in southern India. India has been accepted as an American ally in the war against terror and conducts maritime patrols in the Straits of Malacca, alternating with the US navy on a six-monthly basis. India also realises that as it engages with ASEAN, the US, Japan and South Korea, it has effectively expanded its sphere beyond the confines of South Asia and has 'broken out' from its South Asian stranglehold.

The global economy has not stood still and a city-state such as Singapore without natural resources faces numerous challenges. At one time, Singapore considered its main resource to be its people but given the challenges presented by knowledge-based economies (KBEs) and increasing global labour mobility resulting in the loss of local human talent, Singapore tried to offset this by attracting foreign talent. The main strategy was to provide good infrastructure and facilities, especially in R&D. In contrast, India lacks good infrastructure but has managed to cope with this immense problem and still produces bright and innovative talent in the thousands. However, not all of this talent is content to stay in India and the attraction of working abroad still holds great promise for most of them. While the US and Europe, particularly Britain, lured most of them, increasing numbers have also heard about Singapore. This works in favour of Singapore that had actively recruited foreign talent from India.

In the knowledge-driven global economy, India has become synonymous with information technology, especially software exports, and is the favoured destination for business process outsourcing (BPO). While China has become the world's factory in terms of manufacturing goods, India is rapidly becoming a global hub in terms of services. There are about 7,000 MNCs in Singapore and Singapore has links with various producers in the region. In this regard, potential opportunities exist for Indian IT companies to promote their skills in software for designing, manufacturing, distribution and trading (Mehta, February 2003). Singapore has also become aware that it has to diversify its regional investments and trade relations away from China to preempt the possibility of being adversely impacted should the Chinese economic engine falter. India has become more of an alternative to Singapore because of the former's economic liberalisation and reforms in 1991. Singapore also needs to factor the impact of a dynamic China in the short term and the economic fallout to itself and other ASEAN member countries in the longer term. The rise of China and India as the emerging giant economies of Asia highlighted the need for ASEAN, including Singapore, to develop a regional strategy to prevent marginalisation by these giant Asian economies.

It is against this backdrop that this monograph examines the relationship between Singapore and India. The monograph examines the relationship at the regional and bilateral perspectives. Singapore is a part of ASEAN and economic competition from the region especially from Malaysia and Thailand has intensified since the 1980s. The monograph focuses on knowledge-based services because the Singapore economy needed to progress to higher-end economic activities and was encountering structural problems as a maturing economy. India has focused on IT and services because it planned to leapfrog ahead of competing economies and leverage on its enormous pool of manpower. Moreover, India's infrastructure and domestic economic constraints such as bureaucracy and unions indicate that it could not rival China in terms of manufacturing. Singapore has also developed excellent infrastructure and increased its connectivity to the global economy. Against this background, the Singapore government realises that it has to compete and attract the best foreign talent that it can find to enhance its economic growth. Consequently, Singapore is wooing foreign talent from India and elsewhere.

Singapore has largely been displaced in manufacturing by lower-cost competitors but has tried to reinvent itself as a services hub. Singapore's brand of efficiency, transparency and management has increased its credibility as a regional hub for services. Singapore is also relying on the 'hubbing' strategy to expand its economic development by inviting foreign MNCs, such as those in the IT sector, to establish their R&D base in Singapore. Working on the premise that Singapore could be used as a stepping stone or launching pad to the Chinese market or the wider market of Southeast Asia, foreign MNCs are being attracted to establish a base and/or their regional OHQs in Singapore (Dunning, 2000). Through its GLCs, Singapore has invested in several emerging markets to secure not only a foothold in these markets but also to exploit potential synergy between Singapore companies and their foreign counterparts such as those in India (Mani, 2002). Singapore has land constraints and its homegrown companies, GLCs, could not be transformed into MNCs if they were rooted to the domestic economy. Its GLCs were also compelled to venture overseas because Singapore was committed to liberalising its domestic industry to foreign competition such as in the telecommunications sector given its various treaty obligations such as those to the World Trade Organisation and the various Free Trade Agreements.

Due to increasing competition in its own domestic market, the Singapore GLCs and small medium enterprises (SMEs) have to regionalise and expand overseas. To increase its economic advantage in a very competitive international market, Singapore is developing a regional and international strategy that is based on the process of linkage, leverage and learning (3Ls) (Mathews, 2002). Linkage is defined as 'an outward-oriented concept'. It refers to the methods in which a firm may extend its influence into new markets or businesses. In the international market, it refers to a firm's capacity to extend into new cross-border activities via inter-firm relations. The denser these inter-firm connections are, the more opportunities there are for the firm to be drawn into the international economy. The Singapore government has invested heavily in an innovative environment by lavishly funding higher education and promoting public policy choices to increase patents while boosting copyright laws (Furman, Potter & Stern, 2002). However, Singapore still lacks the human talent and the critical pool of scientists and engineers that it needs to dedicate for the production of new technologies. Therefore, Singapore needs to leverage in order to accumulate the critical pool of human talent. The process of leverage refers to both an outward- and inward-oriented concept. It refers to the outward reach by the firm for resources it lacks and which may be found in other firms and institutions in the global economy; hence, it must form linkages of one kind or another. The inward process refers to capability enhancement that the firm engages in after the absorption of new resources.

Through the enhancement of capabilities that resulted from repeated application of linkage and leverage strategies, the process of learning takes place so that latecomers or newcomers into high-tech fields like IT and biotechnology (BT) can create a niche for themselves. The Singapore government has to develop its national innovative capacity as both an economic and political entity so that it can produce a stream of commercially relevant innovations (Furman, Potter & Stern, 2002).

How can innovative capacity be expanded? Singapore companies need to explore emerging economies such as India either for investment or go into joint ventures in specific areas with Indian companies. Homegrown Singapore companies face a number of difficulties if they are to compete successfully overseas and some of the main problems are in terms of their size, financial reserves and familiarity with overseas markets. Not all of Singapore's companies have the financial reserves, networking and technical know-how of the well-known GLCs, Singapore Telecoms (SingTel) and Singapore Airlines (SIA). In this context, Singapore companies are encouraged to initially explore the region and look at emerging economies like India. This process of establishing Singapore companies as regional MNCs was derived from the assumption that Singapore, because of its ethnic diversity, was better able to appreciate and understand the varied historical and socio-cultural make-up of a country such as India. The IT industry was chosen as a case study to showcase Singapore's growing trade alliance with India because of the cluster-specific strategy that could be implemented to overcome economic impediments in India.[7]

### *Structure*

Chapter One has outlined the challenges that Singapore as a developmentalist state is facing to sustain economic growth. As a maturing economy, Singapore has to create an external economic wing to ensure its continued economic survival. The Singapore government is encouraging its own GLCs to invest overseas, especially in emerging Asian economies. India has a large talent pool and resources, such as land, but poor infrastructure. Singapore has developed excellent infrastructure over the decades, has good systems and management in place. In this regard, both the Singapore and Indian economies complement each other because they could collaborate for their mutual benefit.

Chapter Two sets the background for the study by looking at the economic challenges facing India and Singapore in a post-Cold War setting. Was there a need for Singapore and India to realign their eco-

[7] Michael Porter had identified four key features of a cluster strategy. They include the availability of high-quality and specialised innovation inputs. This could lead to more intense competition among local companies but also rewards successful innovators. Another criterion is the domestic demand for cluster production and services. Finally, the density and interconnectedness of vertical and horizontal relations. Jeffrey L. Furman, Michael E. Porter and Scott Stern, 'The determinants of national innovative capacity', *Research Policy*, 31 (2002), pp. 903–905.

nomic polices? Moreover, if there was a need for economic realignment, what were the likely forces that shaped this realignment? The chapter will present a case that as India was shackled to the South Asian region due to the Cold War ideological divide, this gave its closest rival, China, free reign to enhance its relations with the ASEAN region. However, despite its late entry, India's steady progress within ASEAN has been impressive. India has engaged ASEAN at the regional level as well as the bilateral level with individual ASEAN members. Through its 'Look East' Policy, India also hoped to engage ASEAN at the social and cultural context.

Chapter Three examines the regional context of India and Singapore economic linkages. The emergence of trading blocs will be explained as an influential factor in India's 'Look East' Policy. The chapter then examines how Singapore aims to collaborate with India to offset future trends that depict a worrying picture for its economic growth. There is a pressing need for Singapore to foster homegrown companies to venture overseas. For most of these Singapore companies, the risks of investing and doing business overseas could be reduced by exploring regional economic opportunities. A section on literature review will examine scholarly work on the development of clusters and knowledge-based economies to see whether Singapore could emerge as a KBE. However, due to a shortage of natural resources, especially human capital and land, Singapore's ambition to be a KBE will involve an external dimension. It will involve the concept of regionalisation to expand the Singapore economy overseas. In order to promote regionalisation, Singapore has to persuade its companies, especially the GLCs which are also known as Temasek-linked companies (TLCs), to move overseas.

Chapter Four looks at the state capitalism approach as used by the Singapore government to create an external economic wing. Discussion on the Asian Financial Crisis in 1998 and the creation of innovative clusters leads to the investment of focal growth areas in India. Initial exploratory business forays into India by International Enterprises (IE) Singapore leading business delegations has become more focused and specialised in areas such as IT, telecommunications, real estate, ports and tourism development. Singapore GLCs are the main tool being used by the government to venture into India. After exploring several economic sectors in India, the Singapore government and GLCs decided that the IT sector had the most promise in terms of leveraging economic complementarities between both economies. Singapore examined several locations in India to concentrate its investments and evaluated their strengths and weaknesses. The implementation of CECA will also be discussed, especially in relation to technology and human capital in the IT sector.

Chapter Five looks at the fostering of a knowledge-based economy by the Singapore government. The flagship investment project decided by Singapore's capabilities and India's strengths was to be in IT. Bangalore in the state of Karnataka in southern India was chosen to host Singapore's flagship investment in India, the IT Park Bangalore (ITPB). Using the 'flagship' project approach, it will be argued that Singapore needed a successful model to demonstrate to Singapore companies that it was possible to achieve success by venturing into the Indian economy. Among the Singapore companies involved in the project, a consortium approach was used to illustrate how Singapore companies were able to leverage on their respective expertise, experience, and financial and technical capabilities to develop the Bangalore IT Park. The chapter will also argue that the initial phase of the Bangalore IT Park was completed just in time before the Business Process Outsourcing (BPO) boom hit India in early 2000.

Chapter Six looks at the challenges faced by the Singapore consortium and the Indian counterparts in the construction, management and marketing of the Bangalore IT Park. The chapter also argues that factors such as cultural similarities and especially the role of Non-Resident Indians (NRIs) in Singapore have managed to enhance economic links with India. The Bangalore IT Park project also received strong political support and endorsement from both the Singapore and Indian governments at a critical junction of its construction and expansion. As much as Singapore could be a conduit for more FDI into India, in the manner that Hong Kong was to China's economic development, Indian companies have also started to venture into Singapore. It will be argued that they are in Singapore for various reasons such as a hub for the Southeast Asian region and a staging post for onward foray into China and other economies in East Asia. At the end of 2005, there were 1,700 Indian-owned companies in Singapore but this had increased to 2,600 at the start of 2007.

Chapter Seven shows that the Bangalore IT Park was not a 'one-off wonder' for the Singapore investors and companies as they ventured into other Indian states to invest in IT and other economic areas.

Singapore GLC Ascendas has branched into other Indian cities such as Hyderabad. Ascendas is involved in the third phase of the IT cluster in Hyderabad called Hitec City. Ascendas with L&T Infocity has developed CyberPearl, an IT Park in Hyderabad's Hitec City. This showed other investors that the IT Park concept could be replicated elsewhere in India. Continuing global interest in India in terms of IT and Business Process Outsourcing (BPO) will fuel further economic growth that, in turn, will increase the demand for Grade 'A' office space.

Chapter Eight concludes the monograph with a discussion on continuing and future bilateral challenges that Singapore and India face in fostering greater economic collaboration. These challenges could be future areas of studies for scholars interested in this topic. It looks at the efforts by the Singapore government to expand and broaden the areas of economic cooperation with India. India is benefiting from Singapore investments and the tie-up between Indian and Singapore companies. Singapore is also enticing foreign Indian talent either to study in Singapore through scholarships provided or to work in Singapore.

Whether there are emerging economic linkages[8] between Singapore and India will ultimately depend on a number of factors. From the perspective of bilateral trade that has reached S$12 billion, surpassing the target of S$10 billion in 2004, there is an economic alliance in the making. Whether Singapore could function as a 'Hong Kong' for India by bringing foreign investments and expertise, especially in infrastructure development, will depend on the level of cooperation between both economies. As the Indian brand becomes stronger, particularly in the IT sector around the world, it will pay less attention to Singapore and the need to link up with a Singapore brand that connotes competency and reliability. The emerging economic relations between Singapore and India could possibly be curtailed if India and China were to forge closer economic ties. In addition, Singapore companies proposing to be the middle-men players between these two Asian giants could be marginalised if India and China were to enhance economic relations

[8] Alliances could also be categorised into different types such as Tactical Alliances and Strategic Alliances. Tactical Alliances are defined as agreements, the main goal of which is to gain scale advantages. Strategic Alliances are long-term cooperative agreements. Anita Van Gils & Peter Zwart, 'Knowledge Acquisition and Learning in Dutch and Belgian SMEs: The Role of Strategic Alliances', *European Management Journal*, Vol. 22, No. 6, 2004, p. 687.

especially in the field of IT. The political leaders in Singapore estimated that by 2015, the Chinese and Indian economies will have forged such strong linkages that they will not need 'intermediary' countries such as Singapore to advance their bilateral economic initiatives. The challenge then would be how Singapore reinvents itself to be continually useful to its economic partners, such as India.

CHAPTER TWO

# POST-COLD WAR: TOWARDS REGIONALISM AND INDIA'S 'LOOK EAST' POLICY

## *Economic Regionalism*

The main impetus for India to realign its foreign economic policy eastwards through the 'Look East' Policy (LEP) was based on its insecurity of being excluded from major trading blocs. The South Asian Association of Regional Cooperation (SAARC) grouping of which India is a member has not been able to effectively promote intra-regional trade. In comparison, trade within the North American Free Trade Area (NAFTA) was approximately 60% of the total trade for members in that trading bloc which included Canada, Mexico and the US. Similarly, 55% of total trade of the members in the European Union were intra-regional. Closer to the South Asian region, members of the Association of Southeast Asian Nations (ASEAN) had 30% of their total trade with each other. In contrast, SAARC members traded only 5% of their total trade within the South Asian region (Himal, February 2004). To facilitate intra-regional trade in South Asia, the following should be emphasised: free movement of people, trade in services, improved physical infrastructure and the need to harmonise customs regulations, banking systems, insurance and quality standards especially on safety (Himal, February 2004).

India was not keen on the formation of SAARC because it viewed SAARC as a coalition of smaller nations in the South Asian region to curb its own regional influence. The smaller economies in SAARC, especially Bangladesh and to a lesser extent Sri Lanka, were spearheading the formation of the regional organisation. Under the agreement founding SAARC, bilateral problems such as the 'Kashmir' dispute were not to be aired within SAARC. However, the Kashmir dispute has featured in SAARC forums and has often derailed non-security meetings such as those dealing with trade issues. From the Indian perspective, improving trade relations in SAARC was a political gesture. As the largest and most diverse economy in the South Asian region, India has to accede to providing trade concessions to its smaller neighbours for regional economic initiatives to progress (Khosla, 2006). Without tangible improvements in South Asian intra-regional trade, India, especially after its 1991 economic liberalisation and reforms, began to look more towards the East Asian and Southeast Asian regions for economic linkages.

India's interests in the process of economic regionalism and trade blocs as opposed to multilateralism as symbolised by the World Trade Organisation (WTO) was also tempered with the perception that the WTO had been unable to forge ahead with a multilateral trade agenda. ASEAN as a regional body, especially its member Singapore, also started to promote more bilateral and regional trading agreements (RTAs) that would include Free Trade Agreements (FTAs) as an alternative strategy to counter the inability of the WTO to forge a multilateral trade agreement among its 190-odd members. Moreover, as the East Asian countries recovered from the devastating effects of the Financial Crisis of 1997, there was a growing belief among ASEAN political leaders that they could rely only on themselves to overcome their regional problems and need not depend overtly on multilateral institutions such as the World Bank (WB) and the International Monetary Fund (IMF) to come to their rescue (Dieter & Higgott, January 2002). In the aftermath of the Asian Financial Crisis, the lack of support from the US, in particular for Asian countries to have their own Asian Monetary Fund (AMF), indicated to Asian countries that diluting the influence of the IMF and the WB was contrary to the national interest of the US. With the rise of China and India as the second and fourth-largest economic powers in the world, respectively, it also became evident to ASEAN that moves towards securing Free Trade Agreements with these two Asian economic giants would be favourable for their continued economic growth and development.

Reciprocally, both China and India had also signed several agreements with ASEAN to enhance their ties with the regional grouping. These agreements included cooperation to eradicate drug trafficking, promotion of agricultural cooperation, dialogue on territorial disputes in the South China Sea and potential Free Trade Agreements. China's initiatives to conclude an FTA with ASEAN by 2012 have put it ahead of another rival, Japan which was a model for economic development in Southeast Asia (*Asia Times*, 6 November 2002). With ASEAN member countries being able to source lower-cost manufactured goods from China and the potential for ASEAN to increase its own exports to China after its entry into WTO, India could be increasingly marginalised in terms of trade with ASEAN if it does not respond by strengthening its own ties with the grouping.

### *Regional Trading Arrangements*

As part of the SAARC region, India's total trade with the other six members of the South Asian region, excluding Afghanistan, in 2003–2004 reached US$4.8 billion (Mehta & Narayanan, August 2006). From 2004 to 2005, India's total trade with the SAARC region rose to US$5.2 billion (Mehta & Narayanan, August 2006). While these increases looked impressive, they were relatively much less than India's total trade with the ASEAN region. India's trade with the ASEAN region has gone up from US$2.4 billion in 1990 to US$23 billion in 2005. According to India's Minister of Commerce Kamal Nath, India and the ASEAN members were supposed to conclude an agreement for the India-ASEAN FTA by July 2007. However, a key obstacle in the negotiations for an India-ASEAN FTA was the list of goods in which India wishes to maintain trade tariffs. Although the Indian government has reduced the negative list of goods from 1,414 items to 489, the list still contains four very sensitive items on which India refuses to reduce customs tariffs but which is of great interest to ASEAN producers and exporters (*The Straits Times*, 18 April 2007). These four items are palm oil, black tea, pepper and coffee.

The world's largest producers of palm oil are Indonesia and Malaysia, while Indonesia and Vietnam are leading exporters of pepper and black tea (*The Straits Times*, 18 April 2007). The Joint Secretary of India's Commerce Ministry PK Dash commented that India had significantly reduced the negative list and if the ASEAN negotiating team headed by Malaysia agreed, they could have an India-ASEAN FTA in a matter of months. However, if ASEAN were to reject the offer, the negotiations could drag on indefinitely (*The Straits Times*, 18 April 2007). India is unwilling to offer more cuts over tariffs because it has a large agrarian sector, and lower tariffs on those four goods could bring added distress to its own farmers. PK Dash added that if an India-ASEAN FTA were concluded, both sides could begin negotiating on a free trade in services. After India and ASEAN missed the July 2007 deadline to conclude an FTA, Indian Commerce Minister Kamal Nath commented that negotiations for an FTA were continuing. The ASEAN grouping were also keen to firm up an FTA with India in time for its November Summit in November 2007 (*Business Line*, 15 August 2007). However, officials were unable to reach consensus on several issues and discussions are still ongoing with a revised completion target in May 2008.

Given the challenges, what mooted India to propose an FTA with the ASEAN region? The launching of the ASEAN Free Trade Area (AFTA) in Singapore in 1992 and China's efforts to have a free trade agreement with ASEAN by 2012 spurred India's engagement with ASEAN (Green, 1994). To counter China's economic initiatives in ASEAN, India hosted the first India-ASEAN Business Summit in the Indian cities of New Delhi and Hyderabad in October 2002 (*The Hindu*, 8 November 2002). Realising that it was unable to compete with China to produce lower-cost manufactured goods, India has tried to entice ASEAN in the area of technological cooperation and high-tech services such as software development. India believes that there is great scope for it to enhance technological cooperation, especially in the IT sector with the ASEAN member states (*The Hindu*, 28 July 2001). India's growing capabilities and reputation for business process outsourcing (BPOs) in IT-enabled services (ITES) work, such as call centers, would also attract companies in the ASEAN region.

Relations between India and the ASEAN nations have visibly improved since the India-ASEAN Summit meeting in Cambodia in November 2002. India's role has grown within ASEAN from a sectoral dialogue partner to a full dialogue partner including membership into the ASEAN Regional Forum (ARF). India is also keen to enhance its ties with ASEAN as a means towards improving relations with larger regional groupings such as the Asian Pacific Economic Cooperation (APEC) forum and the Asia-Europe Meeting (ASEM) (Chirathivat, 1996). The APEC moratorium on new membership expired in 2007; the strengthening of economic linkages between India and ASEAN will garner India with crucial support if it does apply for APEC membership. Other moves have been made towards increasing trade linkages between India and ASEAN initiatives, like the establishment of a Regional Trade and Investment AREA (RITA) at the ASEAN Economic Ministerial Meeting (AEM) in Brunei in September 2003.

### *'Look East' Policy*

Indian relations with the ASEAN nations began in earnest with the 'Look East' Policy. The 'Look East' Policy was implemented just after

India's economic reforms in 1991. However, the first phase of the 'Look East' Policy did not fulfill its objectives of developing close links with the Southeast Asian region because of several developments in India (Baru, 2006). These developments included: frequent change in governments at the federal level, the economic sanctions imposed on India after the testing of its nuclear device in May 1998, and the unfamiliarity of Indian companies with the Southeast Asian region. The ASEAN region, too, had to deal with its own problems which took its attention away from enhancing links with India. These problems included the Asian Financial Crisis in 1997–98 and the enlargement of the ASEAN organisation from six to ten members by the end of 1999.

India embarked on its 'Look East' Policy in the post-Cold War era because geo-strategic considerations made it more conducive to foster closer relations between India and Singapore. As Singapore is a member of ASEAN, its bilateral relations to India was influenced by ASEAN's overall strategic view on forging relations with India. Closer ASEAN-India relations became possible because of the Soviet withdrawal from Afghanistan, Vietnam's withdrawal from Cambodia, and the dissolution of the Soviet Union (Thakur, 1994). Since the demise of the Soviet Union, India perceived that there would be greater willingness on the part of the ASEAN members to judge Indian economic policy based on its merits without distractions from a Cold War environment (Thakur, 1994). Although doubts remained among some ASEAN members regarding India's strategic intentions, it was also felt that ASEAN as a regional organisation could look favourably upon Indian intentions of extending an 'olive branch' after being encamped on the opposite side of the Cold War ideological divide (*The Hindu*, 11 March 1996).

India felt that a trade pact with ASEAN was its best option of gaining economic and strategic security (*The Hindu*, 8 November 2002). While the ASEAN Free Trade Agreement is still to be fully implemented, individual ASEAN members such as Malaysia, Singapore and Thailand have managed to increase their bilateral trade with India. India as a regional power also shared similar strategic concerns by ASEAN over the rise of China's regional ambitions (Shaumian, November 1988). In response to the growing influence of China in the Southeast Asian region, in the early 1990s, India's Ministry of External Affairs (MEA) initiated India's 'Look East' Policy (Kuppuswamy, April 2002). As a precursor to the LEP, Indian Prime Minister Narasimha Rao initiated closer interaction with ASEAN leaders through the first phase of India's 'Look East' Policy when he participated in the Commonwealth Heads of Government Meeting (CHOGM) at Langkawi, Malaysia, in 1989. PM Rao said that the Asia-Pacific could be India's springboard for its leap into the global market place (Rao, 1996). India has also noted with growing concern that while it has remained embroiled in, and shackled to, problems in the South Asian region, China has steadily increased its influence among the Indo-Chinese states, particularly in Myanmar. To counter China's advances in the region, India has increased its initiatives under its 'Look East' Policy to extend its own influence towards the South China Sea (Naidu, 2005).

The motivation behind India's 'Look East' Policy included the economic dynamism of the Southeast Asian economies since the 1970s, coupled with lower transport costs and shorter delivery times for shipping goods because of the region's geographical proximity to India. The inclusion of Myanmar into the ASEAN grouping in 1997 means that India now shares a common border of 1,647 kilometres with the ASEAN region. Furthermore, there are large minorities of Indian Diaspora among the populations of Southeast Asia. The largest concentrations are in Malaysia (with over two million Indians) and Singapore (with over 335,000 Indians). Apart from the ethnic Indian migrants who had migrated to Southeast Asia in the 19th and early 20th centuries, a new breed of Indian professionals, especially those in the IT industry, is also emerging. These inflows of human capital from India were manifestations of the potential for India and ASEAN economic cooperation (*Business Line*, 16 October 2002). The ASEAN economies are steadily recovering from the Asian Financial Crisis of 1997–98 and are regaining their former vigour (*The Hindu*, 8 November 2003). India should take advantage of the cultural footprints that it has bestowed on the Southeast Asian region through Buddhism, Hinduism and social influences it has in the region (*Business Line*, 2 June 2001).

In the early 1990s, ASEAN responded positively to India's diplomatic advances and India was made a sectoral dialogue partner of ASEAN in 1992. India realised that part of the key to developing better relations with ASEAN was to build strong bilateral ties with its individual members (Rao, 1996). Prime Minister Narasimha Rao visited several ASEAN countries between 1992 and 1995. At the fifth ASEAN summit in Bangkok in December 1995, India was elevated to full dialogue partner status. The 'Look East' Policy had an overall positive effect on India's trade links with the region. In the 1990s, investments from ASEAN countries in India rose by 15% of the total amount of FDI flowing into India. In 1997, trade between India and ASEAN was valued at US$7 billion and this rose to US$10 billion by 2001. In 2001, in terms of two-way trade, India's exports to ASEAN countries was worth US$3.6 billion and imports were worth US$6.4 billion (*Economic News*, 16 October 2003), or the equivalent of 12% of India's total global trade (*Business Times*, 24 September 2002). This represented a 30% increase from the US$7.6 billion bilateral trade between ASEAN and India in 1999 (*The Straits Times*, 26 September 2002). In 2004, trade between ASEAN and India reached US$13.25 billion and this figure rose further to US$23 billion at the end of 2005. Nonetheless the-then Indian Finance Minister Yashwant Sinha also made the point that India are 'latecomers in the field' and acknowledged that East Asian countries, such as South Korea and China, had made further advances in enhancing closer ties with ASEAN. A report from financial consultants McKinsey, which is supported by the Indian government, indicated that India has the potential to raise its trade with ASEAN from US$24 billion to US$30 billion by 2007 (*The Hindu*, 18 October 2002).

India's 'Look East' Policy is also viewed by Delhi in terms of economic opportunities for its north-eastern region which comprises the states of Assam, Arunachal Pradesh, Nagaland, Mizoram, Meghalaya, Manipur, Tripura and Sikkim. These states share borders with China, Myanmar, Bhutan and Bangladesh. Although this area has been rife with insurgent activities, it still accounts for more than half of India's oil and tea production (*The Straits Times*, 17 April 2007). Its potential lies not only in vast oil and gas reserves but it also has hydroelectric power potential of more than 70,000 megawatts. The Indian government believes that the key to developing the north-eastern states so that they do not lag behind in economic development would be to integrate the region with the ASEAN economies. India's Commerce Minister Kamal Nath commented that the involvement of the Southeast Asian nations in the development of the Indian north-east region would add a new dimension to the 'Look East' Policy. He added, 'We will have a road across Myanmar into Thailand and from Thailand right into Singapore' (*The Straits Times*, 17 April 2007). Minister Nath believed that 'the new architecture of business will not be between the north-east and the rest of India. It will be between the north-east and the countries to its east' (*The Straits Times*, 17 April 2007). He urged Indian and Southeast Asian companies to take note of the new architecture of business that is evolving in the region. Thailand has been a leading partner for India in this new framework and both countries are members of the sub-regional cooperation called BIMSTEC (Bay of Bengal Initiative for Multi-Sectoral Technical and Economic Cooperation). BIMSTEC has evolved from its original members comprising Bangladesh, India, Myanmar, Sri Lanka and Thailand. BIMSTEC was established on 6 June 1997 at the meeting of the Foreign Ministers of the respective countries in Bangkok. BIMSTEC is working towards enhancing economic linkages between South Asia and Southeast Asia.

### *Growth Triangles*

Intra-regional economic cooperation among the ASEAN member countries have produced a number of regional initiatives such as the Growth Triangles. Growth Triangles emerged as a result of the convergence of regional economic cooperation and large inflows of FDI (Tang & Thant, 1994). Regional cooperation efforts in Asia have led to an increase in economies of scale, exploitation of complementarities in production processes and have enlarged the size of markets (Tang & Thant, 1994). Foreign investment in Asia started with the extraction and exploitation of natural resources and proceeded towards manufactured goods in the early 1960s (Tang & Thant, 1994). This was facilitated by the similarities of language, religion and culture between different countries.

The Growth Triangles that have emerged in Asia include the Johor-Singapore-Riau Growth Triangle also known as the 'Southern Growth Triangle' or 'SIJORI', the Baht Economic Zone, the Southern China Growth Triangle and the Tumen River Delta Economic Zone (Kakazu, 1994). These zones were mostly located within Free Economic and Trade Zones established by the governments involved to promote economic development in chosen regions. These zones were designed to be export-oriented and to attract foreign capital. In terms of comparative advantage, these zones have a clear lead over their competitors either in terms of location, labour or natural resources. Moreover, the development of these zones has been pursued by the national or provincial development policies of the governments concerned (Kakazu, 1994). Within the parameters of ASEAN, the Growth Triangle is seen as a form of cooperation between member countries (Kamil, Pangestu & Fredericks, 1991).

The Growth Triangle as a model of economic development emphasises economic complementarity, which was derived from the various countries involved in different stages of economic development or from differences in resource endowments (Tang, Thant & Kakazu, 1994). For example, if a country has a limited supply of labour and scarce land, its competitiveness will decrease, thus necessitating a need to look for new areas where it could invest with abundant labour and land in which it could invest. Economic complementarity within a Growth Triangle is also characterised by differences in technology and the quality and experience of personnel. For example, labour-intensive industries are usually phased out in one party and transferred to another party. This conforms to the 'flying geese'[1] theory. However, there is also flexibility in the idea of economic complementarity, for example, contributions such as capital need not come only from the countries that are physically in the Growth Triangle because investment funds could also come from more distant sources (Tang, Thant & Kakazu, 1994).

Political commitment is the second criterion of the Growth Triangle Model. This is reflected through the extent of governmental support a project receives within the Growth Triangle (Chen & Ho, 1994). Governments involved in the Growth Triangle have committed their support to economic projects and policy coordination among the different countries. Min Tang, Myo Thant and Hiroshi Kakazu argue that at the national level, there is a need to implement appropriate policies but these policy directives and initiatives should be supported and implemented by both central and local governments (Tang, Thant & Kakazu, 1994). For example, the economic reforms and 'open door' policy of the People's Republic of China laid the foundation for the economic success of its Special Economic Zones (SEZs). In India, this is similar to the process of economic reforms and liberalisation of 1991, which emphasised the process of decentralised economic development.

Development of infrastructure is the third criterion of the Growth Triangle Model. Min Tang and Myo Thant argue that infrastructure development is the single most important factor in the creation of an economic environment conducive to the development of a Growth Triangle (Tang, Thant & Kakazu, 1994). For example, the Southern China Triangle involved large-scale development and capital construction. In India certain provincial states, such as Tamil Nadu and Karnataka, are constructing large-scale infrastructure in the form of

[1] The flying geese theory likens industries to geese that migrate from continent to continent in search of better prospects. This is especially the case of labour-intensive industries that continually shift from high- to low-wage countries.

electricity-generating assets, telecommunications and port facilities to attract foreign investment. The fourth criterion of the Growth Triangle Model is geographical proximity. The importance of geographical proximity implies that the relocation of capital would be enhanced between transnational boundaries from relatively well-developed countries to their less developed neighbours, for example, the flow of financial capital from Hong Kong to Guangdong, and from Singapore to Johor. However, the situation in India is somewhat different in that it has not received substantial investments from other South Asian countries and is itself a large investor in the South Asian region. In this regard, India is exploring further afield and is enhancing links with the East Asian region to attract foreign investments and as potential future markets for Indian goods and services.

### *Strategic Considerations*

India's engagement with Southeast Asia has several dimensions. In the strategic security dimension, India came to share a border with ASEAN when Myanmar joined ASEAN in 1997. Pakistan's special friendship with China is also a major concern for India, as there are fears that this will limit India's influence to South Asia and keep India contained in that region. India has also realised that its own regional organisation, namely, the South Asian Association for Regional Cooperation, is not as dynamic as ASEAN despite the challenges facing ASEAN (such as the Asian Financial Crisis in 1997–98). For these reasons alone, it is imperative that India engages with countries in the Southeast Asian region, break out of its strategic confines in South Asia and challenge China's dominance in the region. The First ASEAN-India SOM was held in 1998, while the second SOM was held in 1999. One area in which India could cooperate with ASEAN members in relation to the technological sector is the IT industry. For example, India successfully organised a training programme for ASEAN candidates in advanced software techniques in 2000 and various ASEAN members have asked for the continuation of this programme (*The Hindu*, 28 July 2001).

As part of the process on engagement with ASEAN, former Indian Prime Minister Atal Bihari Vajpayee visited Vietnam in July 2000, Malaysia in May 2001 and Thailand in July 2001. In addition, India's Minister for External Affairs Jaswant Singh visited Myanmar in February 2001. In an address to the Institute of Diplomatic and Foreign

Relations, entitled 'India and ASEAN—Shared Perspectives', in Kuala Lumpur, Malaysia, Indian PM Vajpayee said, 'We are conscious that in the first few decades after our independence, we did not attain the full promise of our relationship... the full scope of our partnership was constrained by divergences in economic ideology, political outlook and security assumptions, which the Cold War imposed on us' (*The Hindu*, 17 May 2001). PM Vajpayee emphasised India's interest in ASEAN by saying that as India was developing its 'Look East' Policy, ASEAN had moved west by drawing Myanmar into its regional grouping, thereby creating an opportunity for enhanced economic convergence (*The Hindu*, 17 May 2001).

Prime Minister Vajpayee had underlined the importance of ASEAN in India's economic and strategic considerations because economic linkages with ASEAN member countries encompassed a range of varied strategic interests. He commented that, 'ASEAN has always been very close to us in terms of history, geography and cultural association. The Ganga-Mekong Cooperation Programme, India's dialogue partnership with ASEAN and our ARF (ASEAN Regional Forum) partnership all underlie our linkages'. Brajesh Mishra, Principal Secretary to the-then Prime Minister Vajpayee, echoed the same sentiments and said, 'ASEAN is a very important entity to us. Trade-wise, economic cooperation-wise... don't forget that the sea lanes here are as important to us as they are to any other country. Our trade through the sea lanes to Japan etc... is an important factor' (*The Hindu*, 10 January 2001). Mishra also added that if India wanted to import crude oil from Vietnam, which is a member of ASEAN, then India would want security of the sea-lanes in ASEAN for the crude oil to reach India (*The Hindu*, 10 January 2001). According to Mishra, this is part of India's security strategy (*The Hindu*, 10 January 2001).

### *New Asian Regionalism—East Asian Integration*

The trend towards new Asian regionalism in terms of how it would impact on India and Singapore indicate the following: the existing sub-regional cooperation initiated under the ASEAN or the SAARC frameworks were unlikely to exploit the full potential of regional economic integration across the Asian region (Asher & Srivastava, May 2003). Countries that are not participant in any of the new regional trading arrangements (RTAs) will be adversely affected because diversion of trade and investments will affect their balance of trade (Rajan, February 2003). The ASEAN intra-regional trade accounts for approximately 30% of its total trade, while in the SAARC region intra-regional trade is less than 5% of the region's total trade. In the process of realigning its foreign trade focus, since the 1990s, India has attained a higher degree of integration with the global economy (Rajan & Sen, December 2002). Nonetheless, India has remained relatively inward-looking compared to its East Asian neighbours. However, India has launched initiatives to enhance economic and trade links with the East Asian region. Within this region, capital flows and technology transfers have continued to rise—Japan continues to be the main source of capital and technology within the region, but China will increasingly compete for this role (Lau, January 2004).

The emergence of an East Asian economic region and the potential influential role that India could play will be the ultimate test as to whether India has managed to realign its economic foreign policy with that of the region. In the early 1990s, Malaysian Prime Minister Mahathir Mohamed mooted the idea of an East Asian economic grouping but this initiative did not take off (Teo, March 2005). However, the idea of an East Asian economic grouping never died out and the enlarged framework of an ASEAN + 3 could form the backbone of a new Pan-Asian economic grouping. Which economies would such a grouping encompass? A Pan-Asian economic grouping could come in the form of JACIK (Japan, ASEAN, China, India and South Korea). These 14 economies have a combined population of 3 billion and a purchasing power parity of US$16 trillion, which is much larger than those of either NAFTA or the EU (Kumar, November 2005). The potential of JACIK is clear because it has a combined export of US$1.66 trillion compared with US$1.48 trillion for NAFTA. In 2003, the combined official reserves of the JACIK economies—US$1.6 trillion—were much larger than those of the US and the EU combined (Kumar, November 2005).

While China and India dominate the news as emerging economic giants, some analysts have forgotten that Japan's GDP is larger than all of the East Asian economies combined (Kumar, November 2005). In 2005, in terms of per capita among the East Asian economies, Japan led the way with almost US$38,980 followed by Singapore at US$27,940. At the end of 2005, China's per capita income was US$1,740 and India's was below US$720 (World Bank Website). The new drive towards East

Asian regionalism received strong support from major Asian economies, especially after the Asian Financial Crisis. China, which was to a large extent suspicious of East Asian initiatives because it suspected the overarching influence of the US, took a more active part in these regional initiatives after the US opposed calls from Japan to create an Asian Monetary Fund (Akira, February 2005). Despite closer economic integration between the major economies in East Asia and ASEAN, analysts also noted that bilateral political differences, especially between China and Japan, could indefinitely delay the realisation of an East Asian economic grouping (*Japan Times*, 13 December 2005). However, China and Japan bilateral trade is heading for rapprochement with the appointment of Japanese Prime Minister Shinzo Abe in September 2006 (BBC News, 23 July 2007). In August 2007, Chinese and Japanese defence officials held talks to improve cooperation and revive defence dialogue (BBC News, 30 August 2007).

What role could India play in the establishment of a Pan-Asian regional cooperation group? The ASEAN + 3 framework including India could become a building block for a wider Pan-Asian economic community (Kesavapany, May 2003). There is potential for India to have a large role and be a main part of a China-ASEAN partnership. India's impressive sustained economic growth could centre Asian economic growth and share this role with China in the region (Teo, March 2005). India should seriously pursue a broader Asian integration plan and it could contribute in several ways (*The Hindu*, 25 November 2005). India's strong financial regulations and banking experience would be critical for the sound expansion of the East Asian region. Moreover, India's strong historical, social and cultural links with the Southeast Asian region suggests that it could also bridge the gap between the older and newer ASEAN members. This is because India is still an agrarian economy and could assist similar economies in the ASEAN grouping. Singapore's Prime Minister commented that both China and India could act as catalysts around which a larger trans-Asian grouping could mesh together (*Economic Times*, 20 September 2005). The Indian economy is becoming increasingly integrated with the East Asian economies. To compare, India's trade with ASEAN was US$13 billion in 2003, while its trade with SAARC was only US$7 billion (Ong, May 2005). India is also eyeing the possibility of integrating into the value chain of MNCs that are thriving in the ASEAN region (Ong, May 2005). Moreover, India is attracted to the economic activities of the ASEAN region as a whole, which is estimated to be around US$500 billion. India's strengths in services and software would complement the East Asian region's strengths in hardware and manufacturing (Ong, May 2005).

However, while India-ASEAN trade has grown rapidly since the 1990s, it still constitutes to less than 2% of ASEAN's total trade. One of the impediments to greater trade is the knowledge gap that exists between the business communities and the business opportunities available in India and their respective ASEAN economies. To address this issue, the business communities from India and ASEAN have to interact more closely. In this regard, ASEAN will form working committees to look into enhancing trade ties in various economic sectors with India. Singapore has overtaken Malaysia as India's largest trading partner in the region. Singapore and India bilateral trade at the end of 2004 was less than US$7 billion (*Business Line*, 1 July 2005) but this rose to more than US$13 billion by the end of 2006 (Iswaran, 2007), which is more than half of ASEAN's total trade with India at US$23 billion (*Hindustan Times*, 28 August 2007). India and Malaysia bilateral trade was US$4.5 billion at the end of 2004, and bilateral trade between India and Thailand was around US$2 billion at the end of 2004 (*The Hindu*, 11 July 2004). The three ASEAN countries' trade with India formed the bulk of ASEAN's trade with the country.

While ASEAN members have considered alternatives to the FTAs such as the 'Growth Triangles' or transnational investment zones, the FTAs are likely to create better synergy between India and ASEAN economies. The Indian Ministry of External Affairs (MEA) and the Indian Ministry of Commerce have been very proactive in their efforts to enhance India's links with ASEAN. India was promoted as an ideal place for investments from ASEAN countries and the Indian government welcomes the idea of an ASEAN-India free trade area. In this regard, former skepticism among ASEAN members has given rise to optimism. For example, former Malaysian Prime Minister Mahathir was rather skeptical about the idea of an ASEAN-India FTA. The First ASEAN-India summit was held in Cambodia in November 2002. At the 5th ASEAN-India Senior Officials Meeting (SOM) in New Delhi in May 2003, Malaysia as co-chair mentioned the ongoing work and potential of India and ASEAN trade linkages that was progressing towards a Framework Agreement on Economic Cooperation. Although the issue was raised at the 2nd ASEAN Summit in Bali, Indonesia in October 2003 there has been no conclusion to the discussion. The 2nd ASEAN-India Summit was a 'watershed' for India-ASEAN relations because

Table 2.1: Indian Exports to ASEAN Countries in Rs lakh (100,000)

| Country | 2001–02 | 2002–03 | 2003–04 | 2004–05 | 2005–06 |
|---|---|---|---|---|---|
| Brunei Darussalam | 1,363.41 | 2,155.00 | 2,109.37 | 2,275.46 | 19,010.55 |
| Cambodia | 5,385.89 | 9,600.21 | 8,546.90 | 8,148.07 | 10,710.02 |
| Indonesia | 254,535.19 | 399,773.69 | 517,967.66 | 598,756.63 | 611,063.25 |
| Laos | 1,508.85 | 763.17 | 199.04 | 1,190.39 | 2,422.73 |
| Malaysia | 368,989.44 | 362,661.06 | 410,238.16 | 487,084.69 | 514,398.00 |
| Myanmar | 29,040.79 | 36,331.91 | 41,192.50 | 50,859.74 | 49,009.53 |
| Philippines | 118,174.79 | 228,425.63 | 147,747.91 | 185,219.61 | 219,005.41 |
| Singapore | 463,712.59 | 687,977.69 | 976,392.94 | 1,797,534.88 | 2,401,965.25 |
| Thailand | 301,954.00 | 344,185.69 | 382,171.66 | 405,008.06 | 476,076.00 |
| Vietnam | 104,051.21 | 163,281.58 | 188,601.28 | 249,800.55 | 305,786.44 |

Source: EXIM Data Bank, Department of Commerce, Ministry of Commerce, Government of India.

three agreements were concluded there: the Framework Agreement for Comprehensive Economic Cooperation, the accession document to the ASEAN Treaty of Amity and Cooperation, and the Joint Declaration on Cooperation in Combating International Terrorism.[2]

At the 3rd ASEAN-India Summit—this was held in Vientianne, Laos, in November 2004—there was discussion regarding the specific concessions made by Indian Prime Minister Manmohan Singh for lesser developed ASEAN members: Cambodia, Myanmar, Laos and Vietnam. The 4th India-ASEAN Summit was held in Kuala Lumpur, Malaysia, in December 2005 just before the 1st East Asian Summit (EAS) that included India. The India-ASEAN FTA was discussed at the 5th ASEAN-India Summit meeting in Cebu, Philippines, in January 2007 (ASEAN Chairman's Statement, 14 January 2007). India's inclusion into the EAS by lobbying various ASEAN members such as Singapore also indicated ASEAN's acceptance of India as a key player in the region. Table 2.1 illustrates the volume of Indian exports to ASEAN from early 2001 to 2006.

A report by consulting firm McKinsey projected that trade between India and ASEAN (ASEAN 10) could increase from around US$9 billion in 2000 to as much as US$24–30 billion by the end of 2007. Table 2.2 shows the volume of Indian imports from ASEAN countries

---

[2] ASEAN-India relations, ASEAN website, July 2005.

Table 2.2: India's Imports from ASEAN Countries in Rs lakh (100,000)

| Countries | 2001–02 | 2002–03 | 2003–04 | 2004–05 | 2005–06 |
|---|---|---|---|---|---|
| Brunei Darussalam | 169.6 | 156.29 | 154.97 | 242.27 | 389.35 |
| Cambodia | 532.35 | 294.46 | 126.77 | 108.27 | 343.61 |
| Indonesia | 494,475.78 | 668,276.06 | 975,121.13 | 1176,190.13 | 1,331,795.50 |
| Laos | 17.90 | 71.96 | 58.91 | 23.24 | 46.34 |
| Malaysia | 540,604.81 | 709,192.50 | 940,423.25 | 1,032,979.50 | 1,069,473.50 |
| Myanmar | 178,572.38 | 162,628.86 | 187,946.66 | 182,383.00 | 232,862.78 |
| Philippines | 45,232.53 | 59,898.34 | 56,111.23 | 84,199.37 | 104,260.26 |
| Singapore | 621,944.94 | 694,381.38 | 958,260.19 | 1,191,311.75 | 1,484,833.38 |
| Thailand | 201,779.47 | 183,418.67 | 279,868.84 | 389,050.75 | 536,409.94 |
| Vietnam | 9,019.16 | 14,123.01 | 17,560.23 | 38,865.36 | 58,169.04 |

Source: EXIM Data Bank, Department of Commerce, Ministry of Commerce, Government of India.

from early 2001 to 2006. Bilateral trade between India and Thailand has steadily expanded. In 2000–01, total bilateral trade amounted to US$843 million; this increased to US$1,060 million in 2002 and US$1,693 million by 2004 (Mehta & Narayanan, August 2006). In November 2001, during the state visit of the-then Thai Prime Minister Thaksin Shinawatra to India, both countries agreed to explore the possibility of establishing a bilateral FTA. A study undertaken by a Joint Working Group at the government level concluded that there was great potential for enhancing economic cooperation.

A Draft Framework Agreement towards an FTA was signed in 2003 and an Early Harvest Scheme at HS six-digit level was implemented on 1 September 2004 (Mehta & Narayanan, August 2006). In the Early Harvest Scheme, 82 items are listed and the customs duty on these items will be reduced to 50% of current levels. The 82 items include apples, mangoes, durum, wheat, air-conditioners, household refrigerators, cordless telephones and electrical fans. Import duties on these goods were 10%–100% in India and 10%–60% in Thailand (*Business Line*, 31 July 2004). The customs duty on the 82 items would steadily fall to 25% after September 2005 and have been duty-free since September 2006 (*Business Line*, 11 July 2004). The first phase of the agreement considers items such as machinery, precious stones and jewellery. Thailand ranked as India's 18th-largest trading partner and third among the ASEAN members in terms of investment approvals from 1991 to 2002. In 2000, Thai investments approved in India were around US$0.1 million; this rose to US$0.3 million a year later. The cumulative inflow of FDI from Thailand was around US$66.2 million at the end of 2001. In 2001, there were some 26 joint ventures between India and Thailand. Indian companies that had established a presence in Thailand included the Aditya Birla Group, Ballarpur Industries, Baroda Rayon Group, Usha Martin Industries and Ranbaxy Laboratories.

However, the Indo-Thai FTA has run into problems of implementation and has been criticised by several Indian economic institutions like the National Council of Applied Economic Research (NCAER). In 2004, the NCAER questioned the need for India to conclude an FTA with Thailand since it accounted for only 1.4% of India's total merchandise exports and 0.7% of India's total merchandise imports. The NCAER also questioned the compatability of the Early Harvest Scheme with WTO stipulations under the GATT, the 82 six-digit items under the Harmonised System of 5,000-plus six-digit items did not pass the criteria liberalising trade between the two economies. The delay in signing the Indo-Thai Framework Agreement on FTA was mainly due to a lack of consensus on rules of origin. India insisted on having both a general set of rules entailing change in tariff heading at Harmonised System (HS) codes and a 40% local content norm with product specific derogation wherever necessary. In contrast, Thailand remained firm on having just 40% value addition norms representing substantial transformation (Mehta & Narayanan, August 2006). The NCAER concluded that the Indian government did not seem to have done a sufficient enough degree of homework before entering into the agreement, and political considerations appeared to influence the outcome.

Another apprehension that India had over its trade agreement with Thailand was the latter's FTAs with China and Australia. These latter countries could use Thailand as a trade conduit to find easier access to the Indian market (*Business Line*, 31 July 2004). Both countries failed to settle their differences by the March 2005 deadline for a final agreement and negotiations remained stalled over the sensitive list of trade items. India named over 1,000 items on this list but Thailand presented only 100 items, and Thailand requested that this anomaly be rectified before talks progressed any further (*Asia Times*, 14 June 2005). However, the Federation of Indian Chambers of Commerce and Industry (FICCI) raised the alarm that cheaper imports from Thailand would flood the Indian market if the agreement were concluded. Among the 82 EHS items imported from Thailand into India in April–December 2005, the value was US$104.84 million. This is compared with the same basket of commodities valued at US$84.44 million in 2003–04 (Mehta & Narayanan, August 2006). In contrast, exports from India to Thailand on the EHS has shown a reverse trend. Indian exports on the list were valued at US$64.22 million in 2003–04 but fell to US$24.54 million from April 2004 to December 2005 (Mehta & Narayanan, August 2006). In a survey among 35 Indian companies whose products are featured in the list of 82 items, India's cost disadvantages are severely eroding the competitiveness of its companies compared to Thai companies. For example, the tariffs for electricity in Thailand are lower than in India and Thailand does not impose duty imports for main components such as glass parts and chemicals for manufacturing unlike in India. Coupled with the fact that India has other FTAs with different countries with ensuing access, Indian companies will be tempted to relocate their manufacturing bases in Thailand and this could lead to a flight of jobs from India. There were some 640 Indian-owned companies in Thailand in mid-2004 (*Business Line*, 11 July 2004).

### *India-Malaysia FTA?*

The process of enhancing economic linkages between India and the ASEAN region is also manifested in bilateral ties between India and Malaysia. In December 2004, Prime Minister Abdullah Badawi of Malaysia visited India and set about strengthening historical ties between both nations (*New Straits Times*, 26 January 2005). According to RL Narayanan, the former Indian High Commissioner to Malaysia, 'Abdullah's visit was a catalyst as it demonstrated at the highest level the commitment of Malaysia to improving and increasing economic contract and interaction with India' (*New Straits Times*, 26 January 2005). India's Minister of State for External Affairs, E Ahamed had met with Malaysia's Foreign Minister Syed Hamid Albar in Malaysia in September 2005 to discuss the progress of the Indo-Malaysia Joint Study Group's (JSG) report on the feasibility of a Comprehensive Economic Cooperation Agreement (CECA), between India and Malaysia. India's Minister of Commerce and Industry Kamal Nath had said that the JSG had carried out the feasibility study in the area of trade in goods and services. The JSG studied sectors like Information and Communications Technology (ICT), engineering, medical, healthcare and diagnostic services. Other services included education, biotechnology, advertising, finance, travel, transport, architecture as well as other services. Kamal Nath commented that both countries had agreed to develop a Framework Agreement for consideration. Malaysian trade with India was dominated by a few primary products such as palm oil and Malaysia is the largest exporter of palm oil to India. India and Malaysia have agreed to restart negotiations for a bilateral FTA by January 2008 (*Business Line*, 15 August 2007).

### *Batam Model: Johor-Singapore-Riau (SIJORI)*

Key aspects for closer economic collaboration between Singapore and India could hinge on using the 'Batam Model' that resulted in gains for Singapore and Indonesia. Batam is the most developed island in the Riau Archipelago of Indonesia. The island has a land area of 416 square kilometres and is strategically located 20 kilometres off Singapore, a 25-minute ferry ride away. Strategically, Batam benefited from its geographical position at the crossroads of international shipping routes between the Indian and Pacific Oceans. However, the island's rapid development did not begin until the mid-1970s[3] and is a result of strategic economic planning by both Indonesia and Singapore. The master plan to develop Batam into a base for oil and gas exploration was reviewed in 1977 because of the decline in oil and related activities globally. The development strategy was altered to embrace a wider vision of growth for Batam. The revised master plan took into consideration Batam's proximity to, and relation with, Singapore. In particular, it focused on Singapore's limitation for further growth. The abundance of natural resources would be Batam's comparative advantage to lure investors from Singapore to relocate in Batam. Although some Singapore-based manufacturers began to set up factories in Batam in the late-1970s, the real impetus for development did not occur until 1989. In that year, investment guarantee and joint economic cooperation agreements were signed between Indonesia and Singapore to create a conducive environment for foreign investors in Batam and other parts of Riau (Murray & Perera, 1996).

---

[3] The first master plan for Batam was prepared by Nissho Iwai, a Japanese consultancy firm, and Bechtel of the US. The study was commissioned by the Indonesian state-owned oil company Pertamina. Caroline Yeoh, Lau Geok Theng, Mark Goh and Julie Richardson (eds), *Strategic Business Opportunities in the Growth Triangle*, 1992, p. 14.

There were initially some doubts in the private sector about the Growth Triangle Model but these quickly dissipated after the foreign MNCs realised that the Singapore Economic Development Board (EDB) and government-linked companies (GLCs) were actively involved in developing and managing many of the industrial parks and resorts in Batam and another major Riau island, Bintan (Yeoh, Lau et al, 1992). The involvement of the EDB and GLCs assured foreign investors that their money was safe because of the proven track record of GLCs and their ability to deal with higher authorities in Indonesia (Yeoh, Lau et al., 1992). The ability of the GLCs to provide the key interface between foreign investors and the Indonesian bureaucracy was a determining factor that pulled investments into Batam. This was a critical factor because the 'red tape' and 'bottlenecks' in dealing with Indonesian bureaucrats were now transferred to a third party, that is, the GLCs which had a reputable track record in dealing with difficult business environments. Therefore, investors felt they were insulated from the maze of regulations and procedures in the Indonesian administrative system (Murray & Perera, 1996).

The centrepiece of the Batam project was the large-scale 500-hectare Batam Industrial Park (BIP). The purpose of the BIP was to encourage Singapore manufacturers and MNCs to relocate some of their operations to Batam (Murray & Perera, 1996). It is also important to examine the priority given by the Indonesian government to Batam's economic development. The Indonesian government set up three special agencies to oversee the island's development and this privilege was not extended to any of the other 13,700 or more islands throughout Indonesia. The three special agencies that facilitated foreign investment in Batam were the Supervisory Body of the Batam Island Industrial Zone, the Batam Corporation (PT Persero Batam) and the Batam Industrial Development Authority (BIDA). Furthermore, the Supervisory Body has political influence since it comprised government ministers and other senior officials and was directly responsible to the President of Indonesia (Murray & Perera, 1996).

Using the Batam Model as a case study, Singapore officials were able to derive lessons and pointers on how to collaborate in building a 'virtual Singapore' in India. However, the creation of special organisations to facilitate and accelerate economic development in various Indian states was not possible because of the doctrine of balanced regional economic development. In India, no state must be seen to be favoured by the central government. This is to prevent protests from other states, which could increase political instability.[4] Although conditions in India are different from those in Batam or Johor Bahru, there are similarities that link India to the Southeast Asian region and Singapore. However, conceptualising ASEAN, India and Singapore as part of an emerging Growth Triangle could not be explained fully by using the conventional Growth Triangle Model because the national boundaries of Singapore and India are not contiguous to one another. A common pattern of Growth Triangles in Asia is that they are linked to the openess of the NIEs (Pomfret, 1996). In the context of open regionalism, proponents of openness have argued for the inclusion of a wider range of issues other than border trade in goods and services and foreign investment flows. Open regionalism also covers methods to promote a greater degree of economic integration (Bora & Findlay, 1996). The promotion of economic integration invariably depends on the national trade policies of countries within the Growth Triangle.

## *CECA*

In discussions and studies that were undertaken in the lead-up to Singapore and India signing a free trade agreement, it was noted that both economies have significant areas of complementarity. The economic imports that India would be interested in from Singapore would include chemicals, electronic products, plastics and related products. In this regard, Singapore has made petrochemical processing and chemical exports one of its main export niches; it is also competitive in a wide range of plastics products and electronic goods (Mohanty, April 2003). Using the Batam Model, India could also plan to develop an exclusive production corridor for joint ventures with Singapore in India (Mohanty, April 2003). Singapore is greatly interested in the development of special economic zones in India.

India and Singapore signed an FTA called the Comprehensive Economic Cooperation Agreement (CECA) on 30 June 2005. This agreement covers a range of goods such as information technology, banking and the movement of professionals (BBC World, 8 April 2002). Bilateral trade between India and Singapore increased from US$1.5 billion in 1993 to over US$12 billion at the start of 2005. Singapore has become

[4] Interview with Dr Pranab Sen, Planning Commission, India, New Delhi, 12 October 1995.

the third-largest investor in India after the US and Mauritius. Total cumulative Singapore investments are around US$1.5 billion in India. What are the complementary links between India and Singapore? From the view of former Indian Prime Minister Atal Bihari Vajpayee, Singapore was encouraged to invest in India, especially in infrastructure, and India's human resources could strengthen the Singapore economy in its development plans (Channel News Asia, 9 April 2002). Before the CECA was concluded, Singapore had become India's fastest-growing export market with a 79% increase of Indian exports by the end of 2004. As a result, Singapore has become India's fourth-largest export market, contributing a 4.79% share of India's total exports (*The Straits Times*, 25 July 2005). Bilateral trade between India and Singapore increased by 50% to reach S$12 billion at the end of 2004 (*The Straits Times*, 29 March 2005). To strengthen bilateral ties further, an advisory panel—this consists of 10 members and comprises India's leading industrialists from companies such as Reliance Industries, Sanmar Group and Hindustan Lever—has been formed to promote stronger collaboration between both economies (*The Straits Times*, 4 February 2005).

The CECA was structured as an integrated package of several agreements that comprised trade in goods, services, investments and economic cooperation in areas like education, science and technology, air services and intellectual property. In order to implement tariff concessions, goods in India have been categorised into four lists. The phased elimination list includes 2,202 products in which the basic customs duty would be decreased to zero in a phased manner by 1 April 2009. In this context, the same timeframe has been established for 2,407 products in the phased reduction list for which Singapore would be offered a margin of preference of 50% to be calculated on the applicable customs duty on the date of the grant of concession. The negative list contains as many as 6,551 products. In turn, Singapore, which has existing zero customs tariff on all products except six, has agreed to bind all its tariff lines at zero customs duty, including beer.

A problematic area that was negotiated successfully was the rules of origin (ROO) requirement in product content. Singapore has a large number of products that are re-exported from the region but India has managed to convince Singapore to have more stringent ROO in place to prevent third-country exports, especially from China, from entering India on concessional terms. Under the revised ROO between both countries, 534 products (mostly chemicals, machinery and precision instruments) have been agreed upon from the general ROO list. In the services sector, India made commitments in nine sectors including professional services, computer and related services, real estate, rental and leasing, telecommunications, engineering, distribution, audio-visual, financial services and tourism. In return, Singapore made commitments in 12 sectors that corresponded to those in India either partially or fully. In addition, Singapore made additional commitments in areas like market research, retail trading and franchising, education, environment and health. This would entail the easing of restrictions from Indian professionals like teachers, accountants, doctors, IT workers and engineers. There is also mutual recognition of 129 education degrees given by recognised universities.

Under chapter nine of CECA, the movement of natural persons has been agreed based on the salary benchmark as a criterion for granting a visa for Singapore. A list of 127 professional categories was identified for the granting of a visa to Singapore. In the area of investments, India has agreed for the first time to grant pre-establishment national treatment on a positive list basis. This means that Singapore companies in India would be treated as local Indian companies. India has made commitments in 22 divisions including the manufacturing of food products, textiles, fashion apparel, chewing gum, bubble gum, dental chewing gum, cigarettes and matches. Singapore, in return, has taken commitments on a negative list. All manufacturing sectors are included except beer, stout, cigars, drawn-steel products, chewing gum, bubble gum, dental chewing gum, cigarettes and matches.

With its investor-friendly climate, Singapore seems an ideal place for Indian companies to expand into the region and unleash their vast human resource potential onto the global economy. While China is emerging as a strong hub for manufacturing because of its low wages, India is also emerging as a relatively lower-cost services hub for the world's MNCs. Some of China's advantages, which include lower wages, passive unions and high implementation rate, are a magnet for foreign investments but software services function on a different plane to manufactured goods. This is because software development in Indian IT Parks were written not only in first world environment but Indian software programmers are moving into value-added programming. This aspect of creative human capital is difficult to nurture and not easily replicated because, as discussed by Richard Florida, it is dependent on technology, talent and tolerance. Working under a chaotic but an actively lively democratic society, Indian software engineers and IT workers have been able to design new software and improve existing software programs for the 7,000 MNCs in Singapore. The software services that Indian foreign talent could provide will be of immense value to maintaining, expanding and developing new software programs for these MNCs. As Singapore strives to be a knowledge-based economy, there is potential for synergy between the two economies. Singapore also could be in an ideal place to carve a niche for itself to facilitate trade and linkages between the two Asian economic giants of China and India.

From the perspective of India, the CECA was a positive indication to other ASEAN members that India is serious about developing its role as a potential economic partner (Suryanarayana, July 2005). India's willingness and ability to deal with and manage the intricacies of dealing with a complex agreement has raised its profile in a region that has often viewed India as a lackadaisical player in the tough international economic arena (Suryanarayana, July 2005). Countries in the ASEAN region had viewed India as a vibrant democracy, although it did not put into practice the principles of a free market economy. Other CECA benefits included Singapore's credentials as a free market-savvy state would not have concluded an FTA without due diligence. In signing the CECA, Singapore is seen to be reasonably satisfied that the agreement will be implemented in the specific context of the Indian economic system (Suryanarayana, July 2005). By signing the agreement, India will be seen from the ASEAN perspective as having conducted its own due diligence and being satisfied that it would mutually benefit from the agreement.

The bulk of India's trade with the Southeast Asian region has traditionally been routed through Singapore. Singapore was one of India's largest trading partners in Southeast Asia[5] and bilateral economic ties looked set to improve. For example, tourists from India regarded Singapore as a family holiday destination and a large component of Indian tourists are from the 'Visit Friends and Relatives' category. The Singapore Tourism Board (STB) also noted that while Indians form only the ninth-largest group of foreign tourists to Singapore, they also tend to spend the most in terms of buying goods and for purposes of entertainment. In this regard, the STB and Singapore companies in the

---

[5] *Friends and Neighbours, India & ASEAN, Dialogue Partnership*, Indian Ministry of External Affairs, Paper presented at ASEAN Ministerial Meeting in Kuala Lumpur, Malaysia, July 1997, p. 8.

Table 2.3: Bilateral Trade between Singapore and India, 1999–2003

| Year | Singapore's exports to India | | Of which re-exports | | Singapore's imports from India | | Total trade | |
|---|---|---|---|---|---|---|---|---|
| | (S$ bn) | (US$ bn) | (S$ bn) | (US$ bn) | (S$ bn) | (US$ bn) | (S$ bn) | (US$ bn) |
| 1999 | 4.24 | 2.50 | 2.28 | 1.35 | 1.25 | 0.74 | 5.49 | 3.23 |
| 2000 | 4.80 | 2.74 | 2.71 | 1.54 | 1.86 | 1.06 | 6.66 | 3.81 |
| 2001 | 4.87 | 2.76 | 2.87 | 1.63 | 2.00 | 1.13 | 6.87 | 3.90 |
| 2002 | 4.71 | 2.67 | 2.79 | 1.58 | 2.08 | 1.18 | 6.79 | 3.85 |
| 2003 | 5.38 | 3.16 | 2.89 | 1.70 | 2.51 | 1.48 | 7.89 | 4.64 |

Source: FICCI website.

Table 2.4: India and Singapore Balance of Trade, 1999–2003 (US$ bn)

| Year | 1999–2000 | 2000–01 | 2001–02 | 2002–03 |
|---|---|---|---|---|
| India's exports | 1.86 | 2.00 | 2.07 | 2.51 |
| India's imports | 4.80 | 4.84 | 4.72 | 5.38 |
| Balance of trade | −2.99 | −2.94 | −2.84 | −2.87 |

Source: FICCI website.

tourism industry have become interested in investing in India, especially in developing infrastructure and its service industries.[6]

Singapore's exports and imports to India have seen an increasing trend since 1999 after the Asian Financial Crisis of 1997–98 (Table 2.3). Most of Singapore's exports to India (more than 50%) are re-exports. The balance of trade from 1999 to 2003 has been in Singapore's favour (Table 2.4). Total bilateral trade in 2003 was S$7.9 billion and this rose by 49% to S$11.8 billion at the end of 2004.[7]

In economic terms, complementarity between India and Singapore is based on the fact that Singapore has the capital, expertise and a matching regional outlook.[8] In the historical sense India views its integration into the Asia-Pacific region as something innate. During his Singapore lecture in September 1994, the-then Prime Minister Narasimha Rao said, 'We cannot ignore the fact that our civilisations are organically

[6] Ibid.
[7] Singapore Ministry of Foreign Affairs website.
[8] Ibid.

Table 2.5: Singapore Investments in India, 1995–2003

| Year | Annual (US$m) | Cumulative (US$m) |
|---|---|---|
| 1991 | 0.6 | 0.6 |
| 1992 | 23.0 | 23.6 |
| 1993 | 21.8 | 45.4 |
| 1994 | 84.6 | 130.0 |
| 1995 | 315.6 | 445.6 |
| 1996 | 93.0 | 538.6 |
| 1997 | 240.3 | 778.9 |
| 1998 | 194.3 | 973.2 |
| 1999 | 196.6 | 1,169.8 |
| 2000 | 71.2 | 1,241.0 |
| 2001 | 84.4 | 1,325.4 |
| 2002 | 77.5 | 1,402.9 |
| 2003 | 47.1 | 1,450.0 |

Source: Federation of Indian Chambers of Commerce & Industry (FICCI).

linked to those which have founded so many of the nation-states of East and Southeast Asia' (*The Straits Times*, 9 September 1994).

By the end of 2004, Singapore was the ninth-largest investor in India in terms of FDI. In 2004, Singapore's investment in India was S$62.07 million.[9] By the end of 2005, Singapore's total cumulative investment in India was S$2–3 billion. Singapore's investments in India are mainly in finance, ICT, infrastructure, property development and logistics. In comparison, India was not placed among Singapore's top 10 investment destinations. Singapore's top investment destinations were China and Malaysia followed by Hong Kong SAR, the US and Indonesia.[10]

### *Public Sector Perspective*

How does the Indian public sector view Singapore's ties with India? The Indian public sector sees great potential in India's economic cooperation with Singapore. India's Commerce Secretary Tajendra Khanna viewed Singapore as playing a significant role in developing India's infrastructure. Tajendra Khanna explained that India was keen

[9] Singapore Ministry of Foreign Affairs website.
[10] Singapore Department of Statistics website.

to tap into Singapore's experience to upgrade its ports and airports, to develop its residential townships and information networking. In terms of information networking, Tajendra Khanna said, 'Singapore Network Services has done an excellent job through its Electronic Data Exchange system. We are now in the process of transferring the know-how to India'.[11] With India's renewed emphasis on the second phase of its 'Look East' Policy, a trilateral agreement has been achieved with ASEAN member countries (with Myanmar and Thailand) for a road to connect the three countries and beyond from the north-east border of India. In addition, the decision to hold the ASEAN-India summit in November 2002 in Cambodia enabled the parallel ASEAN-Business Summit also in Cambodia to benefit from the presence of political leaders and their influence to enhance economic interaction. Together with Cambodia, Singapore was one of India's strongest supporters to be included in the inaugural East Asian Summit that was hosted by Malaysia in December 2005.

Besides trade, could Singapore assume another role to enhance links with India? Another role that Singapore is trying to develop for itself is as a catalyst or as a 'staging point' for Indian business ventures into China, and vice versa. Prime Minister Goh Chok Tong made the following statement at the Singapore-India Business Forum in April 2002, 'Within a seven-hour flying radius of Singapore lives half the world's population, including India and China. With the end of the Cold War, there is a strong desire among them to enter the global economy, for the development and prosperity such participation can bring' (Goh, 8 April 2002). In terms of Singapore's own efforts at regionalisation, CII Mentor Tajendra Khanna argued that emphasis should be on 'tapping new areas where investments are likely to be at a lower end, like Central America, Asia and Africa'. This, according to Tajendra Khanna, should be mutually beneficial to India and Singapore. On the issue of third-country investment, he argued that India and Singapore could function as gateways to one another for investment in third countries. The potential synergy between India and Singapore in terms of tapping into the growing middle-class markets, not only in India but also in markets like China, was emphasised by Prime Minister Goh Chok Tong. PM Goh noted that Singapore's investments in India expanded by five times between 1995 and 2000. Singapore investments as of

[11] Ibid.

end-2000 were approximately S$2 billion in India and bilateral trade reached S$12 billion by end-2004.

In creating a niche for itself between the two giant Asian economies, Singapore hopes to prosper in this regard as well as to bring benefit to China and India. In 1991, total trade between China and India was US$265 million. In relation to the Bangalore IT Park, GLCs like Ascendas Land, which is a subsidiary of Singapore's Jurong Town Corporation, is already playing a role by facilitating the entry of Chinese companies into India and Indian companies into China. In this context, Ascendas was able to develop its knowledge and expertise about India's business and economic environment through its involvement in the Bangalore IT Park, Singapore's flagship investment project.

India's software exports to Southeast Asia, despite the Financial Crisis of 1997–98 and the downturn in global demand for IT services, was still relatively strong in 2003. This is because the relatively more developed ASEAN members such as Malaysia, the Philippines, Singapore and Thailand continued to provide strong demand for e-services in commerce, business solutions and telecommunications. Are there potential problems in the IT sector between India and the ASEAN countries? Indian software companies have faced some difficulties such as the arrest of Mr Arun Jain, the CEO of India's Polaris Software, and his Vice-President Rajiv Malhotra in Indonesia because of a contract dispute with Indonesia bank Artha Graha (*Jakarta Post*, 18 December 2002). The dispute was over a US$1.3 million contract for software designed for the central processing of transactions, disaster recovery and branch server-related work. Political leaders from both countries—Prime Minister Vajpayee and Indonesian President Megawati—were involved in resolving this dispute (*Economic Times*, 18 December 2002). The political intervention led to the release of the Indian executives and moved the dispute towards more commercial settings (BBC News, 20 December 2002). However, it is interesting to note that the provisions of the contractual agreement for the software contract had stipulated a mediation process for settlement of disputes in the arbitration centre in Singapore. Polaris Software has also launched a subsidiary in Singapore to back up its operations in India to ensure continuity of operations in the event of any unexpected eventualities such as conflicts between India and Pakistan (BBC News, 5 June and 7 August 2002).

The new markets that India is exploring include South Africa, Latin America and some countries in the Asia-Pacific region. However, the US continues to be India's largest software export market, importing almost

57% of India's total software exports. Moreover, the domestic software industry in India is just as vibrant as the export component. Domestic computer companies in India between 1995 and 1996 launched more than 104 new software products. During the same period, foreign computer companies located in the Indian market launched over 122 new software products. The software companies in India have become more focused on specific segments of software development that cater to particular clients' ends such as in banking, aviation or retail sectors. Nearly two-thirds of the software companies are engaged in developing end-user application products and services. Given that software is the 'sunrise' industry in India, the software component of the Bangalore IT Park was designed to be in greater proportion to the electronics component because of the general application of software technology and its potential in India and overseas. In software development India has to monitor the rise of China, given the latter country's ambitions in this sector.

### *India's LEP and the Private Sector*

The private sector in India is represented by three major industrial organisations that collectively look after business interests: the Confederation of Indian Industry (CII), the Federation of Indian Chambers of Commerce and Industry (FICCI), and the Associated Chambers of Commerce and Industry (ASSOCHAM). The views of these three industrial organisations are important for the growth of trade relations between India and Singapore in the long term because they represent all the industrial enterprises in the whole of India. The CII views Singapore as the hub of newly emerging markets in China, Myanmar and the Mekong Delta. Therefore, India would be able to use Singapore as a base for packaging, manufacturing and networking with third countries in the region (Datta, June–July 1996). Mutual benefits can be gained by working with Singapore and this is why the CII chose to build its first ASEAN office in Singapore at the Singapore Chinese Chamber of Commerce building. The CII has a strong working relationship with International Enterprises Singapore and the Singapore Indian Chamber of Commerce and Industry.

The former President of FICCI, Deepak Banker, argued that economic complementarity was the main factor that makes India a natural partner for Singapore. This is because India is able to ameliorate three of the most serious economic constraints in Singapore: scarcity of land, labour and raw materials. FICCI also advocates that India and Singapore should be used as gateways for economic interaction with the rest of Asia. Singapore is an ideal gateway because of its membership to ASEAN and APEC. Moreover, Singapore has significant economic access to regional markets like China.

Deepak Banker suggested that Indian trading houses could use Singapore's infrastructure and its ethnic connections with NRIs for regional and global trading. Moreover, India is a member of the South Asian Agreement for Regional Cooperation (SAARC) grouping and has close links with the South Asian region. Therefore, Singapore could use India as a gateway to enter the markets in the South Asian region as well as those of the Commonwealth of Independent States countries, given India's longstanding relations with the latter. The FICCI is in favour of foreign investments in India and the priority sector in India for economic development is infrastructure where foreign investments and technology are required in large amounts. For example, in the power-generating sector, the modernisation and renovation of existing plants require substantial investments because of the need to construct roads, bridges, airports and port facilities. In this regard, the President of FICCI has always encouraged India to learn from the Singapore experience, particularly in the management of its airport and port facilities. The President of India's Associated Chambers of Commerce (ASSOCHAM) SM Datta also believes that there is great economic complementarity in terms of Singapore investing in India's infrastructure sector. A partnership with Singapore would help India to gain access to the ASEAN market and APEC region. Furthermore Datta also said that the Indian Diaspora is very important to India's trade relations with Singapore in terms of maintaining cultural affinity between the two countries.

## CHAPTER THREE

# COMPETITION AND REGIONALISATION

### *Global Competition*

By the end of 2005, India's FDI increased to US$4.4 billion and this rose again to US$11.1 billion at the end of 2006.[1] Some analysts had predicted the emergence of a bi-polar Asia due to the economic strategies of China and India (*The Hindu*, 10 July 2004). However, there will also be growing competition between China and India to be the leading Asian economy in terms of growth (*The Straits Times*, 2 April 2004). If India sustains a 6% growth rate for 50 years as predicted by some financial analysts, it will equal or overtake China in that time (Foreign Affairs, July/August 2004). Increasing competition has compelled Singapore companies to venture overseas and explore emerging markets like China and India. Regional competition is increasing—other ASEAN economies like Thailand signed a bilateral Free Trade Agreement (FTA) with India in October 2003 (Kyodo New International, Inc., 9 October 2003). Singapore also concluded an FTA with India in June 2005.

As a maturing economy, during the Asian Financial Crisis of 1997–98, the Singapore Ministry of Finance noticed that the private savings rate among Singapore citizens had declined and expected this would continue to fall because of the nation's 'greying' population. More healthcare costs will strain government expenditures and a greying population will mean a narrower tax base and declining revenues for the government. Hence, the government has to build a buffer and ensure a continuous revenue stream from its overseas investments through the process of regionalisation. Emerging markets such as India provide business opportunities for Singapore, and reduce the risks of investing overseas as Singapore spreads its investments across several countries to insulate itself against external shocks. In exploring business and investment opportunities overseas, a facet of state capitalism has seen the Singapore government implementing its economic regionalisation

---

[1] Fact Sheet on Foreign Direct Investment, Department of Industrial Policy and Promotion, Ministry of Commerce and Industry, Government of India.

Table 3.1: Venturing Abroad—Key Proposals

1. Government loan financing for large consortiums in big projects
2. A new government venture capital
3. A mechanism to second public-sector officers to private-sector joint ventures
4. Enlisting local companies in public sector projects
5. A Confederation of Singapore Industries as a platform for business dialogue
6. Greater recognition of local companies' achievements
7. Forming country investors' clubs overseas
8. Setting up an international business institute to train entrepreneurs and local managers
9. A Singapore International Foundation one-stop information centre for Singaporeans going abroad
10. Help for children's schooling arrangements by the Ministry of Education
11. Review of Mindef reservist procedures to minimise inconvenience to those working abroad
12. A more broad-based education curriculum to foster creativity and an entrepreneurial spirit
13. More publicity for tax incentives
14. Review of government rules and regulations
15. Developing indicators to monitor growth of the external economy
16. Private sector to lead the drive overseas
17. Regional Business Forum to monitor progress of regionalisation efforts
18. MTI to coordinate with MFA, EDB and TDB to support overseas investments

Source: Report of the Committee to Promote Enterprise Overseas, cited from Anna Teo, 'Govt may finance consortiums working on big projects', *Business Times*, 25 August 1993.

policy. In 1993, the Singapore government formed a Committee to Promote Enterprises Overseas in order to encourage private companies to venture abroad. The Committee was appointed by Prime Minister Goh Chok Tong and headed by the-then Minister of State for Finance and Communications, Teo Chee Hean (*Business Times*, 25 August 1993). The Committee examined various proposals as shown in Table 3.1. The sub-committee on Foreign Investment looked into several areas that are connected to promote enterprise overseas. The six areas are tax incentives, financing support, the government's role as a partner and facilitator in overseas ventures, rules and regulations, personal and family support and developing an entrepreneurial spirit among Singaporeans (*Business Times*, 18 May 1993).

The Committee made several specific recommendations to enhance the regionalisation efforts of the government. In terms of existing government agencies to spearhead the regionalisation drive, the Committee decided that the Economic and Development Board, Trade and Development Board (now International Enterprises Singapore (IE)) and the Ministry of Foreign Affairs are adequate for this role, but that they should expand their roles to assist Singapore investors to venture abroad (*Business Times*, 18 May 1993). Furthermore, the Committee recommended that the Ministry of Trade and Industry (MTI) should monitor and coordinate the work of the three agencies. In order to strengthen government-business linkages for its regionalisation drive, the government intends to create a regional business forum chaired by Minister Teo Chee Hean to monitor its regionalisation efforts. The secretariat of the forum will be established at MTI. Furthermore, MTI will also coordinate the government's overall support for overseas investments (*Business Times*, 25 August 1993).

In the context of financing the promotion of private business to invest overseas, the Committee recommended closer government support of such enterprises and a 'go-regional' fund.[2] The fund was targeted to reach US$150 million, with the government providing more than US$100 million and the rest of the funds to be sought from the private sector. The Committee recommended that the government should give credit lines to local and foreign financial institutions to lend to Singapore consortiums in large overseas projects. This was implemented when one of the Singapore consortium members investing in the Bangalore IT Park, L&M Corporation, received financial support for its ventures abroad. Moreover, the government could also share the risks—the GLCs and statutory boards could have a stake in overseas ventures by Singapore consortiums (*Business Times*, 18 May 1993). The Singapore consortium developing the Bangalore IT Park was a mixture of GLCs

---

[2] The fund is worth some US$150 million which will provide low-cost seed money for companies with potential, existing entrepreneurs and those who want to become one. The bulk of the money will come from the government and the rest from the private sector. A fund manager will be appointed to manage the fund. The purpose of the fund is to help companies: (1) Investments will be made in firms that are doing business regionally or have the potential to do so. (2) The focus will be on small to medium growth companies. (3) Priority will be given to those with a base in Singapore or with direct links to it. (4) Greater weight will be given to companies whose projects benefit the Singapore economy, such as resulting in higher value-added activities. Han Fook Kwang, '$150m fund to help firms go abroad', *The Straits Times*, 26 January 1994.

and private companies. For smaller companies venturing abroad, the government liberalised the approvals necessary from the Monetary Authority of Singapore (*Business Times*, 18 May 1993).

The two economic statutory boards in Singapore—the Economic Development Board (EDB) and the International Enterprises Singapore (IE Singapore)—were actively involved in the government's regionalisation drive. In its Trade and Investment Strategy for India, the Singapore Regional Discussion Panel for India recommended three broad strategies for India. These are building relationships to facilitate projects, business networking to ensure a wide base of corporate contacts, and institutional linkages to pursue Singapore's objectives in India (Singh, 1995). The EDB will focus on facilitating investments both inwards and outwards from Singapore, while the TDB will facilitate trade and exports. Furthermore, the Ministry of Finance will explore the possibility of transferring public sector officers to assist in private sector projects. The public sector officers will have expertise in areas such as infrastructure development or industrial estate management and town planning. Therefore, the public sector officers could be seconded to private organisations for a few years to assist those private sector firms (Singh, 1995). Moreover, to facilitate the private sectors' understanding of the Indian business environment, an India Business Group was established by the Singapore government.

### *India Business Group*

In January 1994, following Prime Minister Goh Chok Tong's visit to India, the political commitment of the Singapore government concerning trade relations with India received a further boost with the establishment of the India Business Group (IBG). Upon PM Goh's return to Singapore in January 1994, the Singapore political leaders felt that the formation of an informal grouping for Singapore-based companies interested in doing business in India would be useful in the long term (TRADESPUR, June–July 1996). The rationale for the establishment of the IBG was based on the premise that its members could share their views and experiences, thus raising the opportunity for cooperation in business ventures due to their common interest in the Indian market. The IBG has four aims and they are: (1) to monitor India's reform policies and business environment; (2) to provide feedback to the Singapore government on bilateral policy initiatives and the directions to be taken to strengthen India-Singapore business relations; (3) to raise issues of bilateral relations and concern with appropriate bodies in India; and (4) to identify emerging opportunities and recommend appropriate strategies for business development (TRADESPUR, June–July 1996).

The IBG was headed by a steering committee that identified relevant bilateral issues for further government-to-government discussions. The committee members are prominent captains of industry with considerable experience in regionalisation. The IBG as of 1996 had more than 200 members and the TDB provides the secretariat support for the IBG. The IBG is an integral part of the Singapore government's strategy to promote regionalisation into the Indian market. The Chairman of the IBG was, Davinder Singh, then a Member of Parliament and is himself of ethnic Indian origin. One task the IBG faces is to familiarise itself with the economic and political environment in India. The IBG seeks to achieve this through dialogue and policy debates with visiting Indian officials and businessmen to Singapore and through TDB trade missions to India (TRADESPUR, June–July 1996). According to Davinder Singh, the idea of organising trade missions to India is to expose local businessmen to India: 'Once they have that foundation, once they have understood India and the Indian psyche, they can take off from there themselves' (TRADESPUR, June–July 1996).

The aim of the IBG is to condition and increase the awareness of Singaporean businesses for the unfamiliar and unexpected in India. Furthermore, the IBG could also equip Singapore companies on how to handle problems that will emerge during the process of establishing a business enterprise in India. Davinder Singh commented: 'In every project there will be a teething phase, whether it is getting approvals, financing or investment delays' (TRADESPUR, June–July 1996). In order to solve these problems, it is important that Singapore businesses understand how politicians, bureaucrats and businessmen think in India and how they respond to events. Davinder Singh further added: 'They don't do it the way Singaporeans do. Only if the Singapore businessman understands this and adapts to the situation will he be successful'. Another phase of the IBG's task is to integrate the bilateral economic relationship with India into Singapore's regionalisation programme in a manner that is mutually beneficial to both. One of the advantages of this exercise is the establishment of close links with Indian politicians, bureaucrats and businessmen at the federal and state levels. This will assist the IBG with its other priority initiative of increasing interaction with organisations representing Indian industry and business

(TRADESPUR, June–July 1996). Another initiative to foster trade links between Singapore and India is the creation of Network India administered by IE Singapore.

### *Network India*

Network India was launched in October 2002 by the-then Singapore Minister for Trade and Industry, George Yeo. Network India essentially provides a platform to develop business linkages between companies that have an interest in the Indian market. The cultivation of a fraternity of Singapore-based companies and entrepreneurs with an interest in the Indian market will assist in the process of information dissemination, opinions and experiences. Network India also provides an invaluable feedback channel to Indian and Singapore policymakers on the actual implementation of their policies. Challenges faced by Singapore and Indian companies could also be aired through Network India, and these inputs could be used by the two governments when formulating new initiatives.[3] The chairman of the steering committee of Network India is Mr Sat Pal Khattar, while the committee members comprise CEOs of prominent companies involved in the Indian market, the Singapore Business Federation and IE Singapore itself.

At one level, Network India plans to leverage on Singapore's location in the Southeast Asian region to become a hub for the distribution of Indian products into the region (*Business Times*, 19 October 2002). The presence of 7,000 MNCs in Singapore will also enable Indian companies to make contact with these companies. It is envisaged that Singapore could facilitate the growing trade between India and China. Ashok Soota, the president of the Confederation of Indian Industry (CII), emphasised that Indian companies viewed Singapore as a means to increase their business ties not only with ASEAN but with China, Japan and South Korea as well (*Business Times*, 19 October 2002). For example, the Regional Director of Tata Consultancy Services (TCS) said that TCS has used Singapore as a base to launch and manage its subsidiary in China. Singapore also hopes to attract Indian companies interested in establishing disaster recovery centres for the businesses.

---

[3] IE Singapore Network India website.

To further deepen economic linkages between India and Singapore, a think-tank called the India Business Forum, comprising 25 Indian companies and based in Singapore, has been launched. The Indian Business Forum will become the corporate voice of India in Singapore. Indian companies numbering 26,000 form one of the largest contingents of foreign firms in Singapore. The number of Indian firms has more than doubled from 1,100 in 2001 (*Today News*, 21 June 2007). Trade between India and Singapore increased to US$13 billion in 2006 and Singapore has become India's second-largest source of foreign direct investment (*The Straits Times*, 20 June 2007). A new Joint Ministerial Committee (JMC), which is the highest level official body between India and Singapore, has also been established (*The Straits Times*, 21 June 2007).

### *Regionalisation Strategy*

The concept of regionalisation as used by the Singapore government is not a new economic strategy of the 1990s. What were the origins of the concept? The origins date back to 1986 when the Economic Committee of the Singapore government argued that: 'Singapore must seek opportunities wherever they can be found. The more widely and keenly we can spot opportunities overseas, the more secure and broadly based will be our well being' (*The Straits Times*, 30 May 1993). This report by the Economic Committee was part of the recovery plan to bring the Singapore economy out of the recession in 1985–86 (*The Straits Times*, 30 May 1993). In response to this, the Economic and Development Board commissioned several organisations, for example, the Institute of Policy Studies, the Entrepreneurship Development Centre and the Ministry of Finance to survey and implement group discussions on regionalisation issues (*The Straits Times*, 30 May 1993). The aim of the exercise was to gain consensus and feedback on the rationale for Singapore to expand its regionalisation drive.

Why does Singapore need to regionalise for further economic growth and development? There are several reasons as to why the Singapore government chose to emphasise regionalisation as a long-term economic strategy to ensure expanded growth and development (*The Straits Times*, 22 May 1993). However, as a nation that favours international trade, it is peculiar that Singapore would prefer regionalisation as opposed to globalisation. The-then Singapore's Deputy Prime Minister Lee Hsien

Loong gave the reason for emphasising regionalisation instead of globalisation: 'In general, it will be harder to break into the European or American markets than for us to make an impact in the Asian market. It's more competitive and complex (Europe and America) we understand it less and the chances of making mistakes are greater' (*The Straits Times*, 29 October 1992). Hence the Singapore government's focus on finding a role and creating a niche for its economy with other emerging Asian economies. The emphasis on regionalisation by the Singapore government came at a time when the government decided to adopt a more systematic approach to tap into the Asian region's emerging potential. Thus far, Singapore's private and public sector economic initiatives in the region were not planned as an overall strategy, as explained by Deputy PM Lee: 'We have been around the region, but I think we have not done it quite as systematically as we could. So we had to focus a little bit more attention on this, particularly by making use of our capabilities in our statutory and government-linked companies' (*Business Times*, 29 October 1992). With the assistance of the statutory boards and GLCs, the Singapore government is focusing on establishing strategic linkages with other Asian economies.

Singapore statutory boards have acquired the expertise and experience that the government deemed valuable enough to market to the region. Deputy PM Lee said, 'For example, take our Housing Board and Port of Singapore Authority...we run a good port, we have a successful housing programme and maybe some of these skills will be useful to other people' (*The Straits Times*, 29 October 1992). In refocusing onto the Asian region, the Singapore government has tried to blunt its globalisation drive, which has become synonymous with expanding its trade links with the developed western countries (*Business Times*, 25 September 1992). This shift in long-term economic strategy is not out of sync with the outlook of Singapore companies. This is because even without the strategic shift towards regionalisation, Singapore companies have for decades invested in Malaysia and some have even invested in Hong Kong and China (*Business Times*, 25 September 1992). The regionalisation strategy[4] was also implemented to ensure that based on economic growth and development, Singapore could maintain its industrial and technological lead over its competitors (Sharma, 1993).

[4] Creating an 'external wing' to its domestic economy by investing in the surrounding region.

Singapore's political leaders emphasised that Singapore would be left behind when other more outward-looking NIEs surged forward and would eventually reach the level of Singapore's economic achievement (*The Straits Times*, 16 November 1992). The former Senior Minister of Singapore, Lee Kuan Yew, commented: 'We are in danger of becoming an economy that nearly made it but had stalled halfway and got left behind' (*The Straits Times*, 16 November 1992). Referring to Taiwan, Hong Kong and South Korea, Senior Minister Lee said, 'With a domestic and an external economy, the other three NIEs had two wings with which to take flight. Singapore, however, had one wing built from the domestic economy. With only one wing we will stay on the ground and not get airborne' (*The Straits Times*, 16 November 1992). The need to ensure future economic expansion forced the Singapore government to practise its brand of state capitalism by propelling its investments and entrepreneurs overseas into the region.

To overcome the impediment of limited land and human resource, the Singapore government has to look beyond its shores to invest in new emerging economies like China, Vietnam and India.[5] The-then Prime Minister Goh said, 'There is so much we can do in the region. Our problem is that our manpower resources are limited' (*The Straits Times*, 22 May 1993). PM Goh explained that by establishing economic and investment linkages with other countries, Singapore could overcome its manpower and resource constraints (*The Straits Times*, 22 May 1993). Therefore, Singapore was interested in India as an emerging market with good potential not only for economic growth but also for its complementary economic strengths. In turn, Prime Minister Rao replied: 'India looked towards Singapore as a vibrant and responsive partner which would be able to complement India's economy' (*The Straits Times*, 26 January 1994). India has an abundance of skilled and professional manpower resources that Singapore could tap into (*Fortune*, 14 December 1992). India's other resources like land, minerals and basic industry have the potential to complement Singapore's own strengths in investment, management and high-technology industries.[6] Hence, both economies would benefit from economic complementarity.

[5] Interview with Trade Officer, Trade and Development Board, Singapore, 30 June 1997.

[6] Basic industry in this case means heavy industry such as, steel industry, mineral extraction, power generation and others.

The Singapore government also decided to emphasise the importance of India as an emerging market because it wanted to balance its investment projects in the region and to correct a misperception that Singapore favoured business links exclusively with China. While Chinese business networks between China and Singapore have been in place for decades, Singapore is situated between much larger countries that are predominantly Islamic in faith—Malaysia to the north and Indonesia to the south—and it would damage Singapore's image as a multicultural, multiracial and multilingual society if it were to maintain its preference to invest in China. PM Goh mentioned: 'We should not look just at China... now that would not be the right impression' (*The Straits Times*, 10 May 1993). He explained that other new markets are emerging in the Asian region and Singapore companies should invest in them: 'Although China beckons, there are also opportunities elsewhere. India and Vietnam will become attractive as they open up and welcome foreign investments. We should be among the first to get through the door' (*The Straits Times*, 10 May 1993). In addition, PM Goh urged Singapore companies to diversify their investments around the region because this 'makes good economic sense' (*Business Times*, 22–23 May 1993) should there be economic problems in a particular country or countries. PM Goh's emphasis in urging Singapore companies to invest in India also comes with the realisation by the Singapore government that, to some extent, Singapore seized the opportunity rather late to realise China's investment potential (*Asian Business*, May 1993). This was because the Singapore government was aware that it was behind the 'investment curve' when the Chinese government opened up its economy to foreign investors in 1979. The Singapore government does not intend to repeat the same mistake with India (*Asian Business*, February 1994).

Singapore's bilateral trade between China and India was steadily increasing from 1999–2001 (Table 3.2). As of 2001, Singapore exported

Table 3.2: Singapore Bilateral Trade with China and India, 1999–2001 (S$ bn)

| | 1999 | | 2000 | | 2001 | | Total trade | | |
|---|---|---|---|---|---|---|---|---|---|
| | Exports | Imports | Exports | Imports | Exports | Imports | 1999 | 2000 | 2001 |
| China | 6.6 | 9.6 | 9.3 | 12.3 | 9.5 | 12.9 | 16.3 | 21.6 | 22.4 |
| India | 4.07 | 1.2 | 4.8 | 1.9 | 4.9 | 1.9 | 5.5 | 6.7 | 6.9 |

Source: IE Singapore.

three times more to China compared with India. In this context, the Singapore government has tried to address the imbalance by trying to create renewed interest to explore opportunities in India. Does Singapore's regionalisation strategy have a convergence with India's own 'Look East' Policy? Under the broad framework of its regionalisation strategy, the Singapore government planned to encourage official links between India and Singapore. A major component of the regionalisation strategy is to co-invest and co-manage the development of large-scale industrial parks in partnership with the national or regional government authorities in the respective countries. These industrial park developments not only promote FDI by Singapore firms, but also enable the Singapore government to play the role of a 'one-stop' partner in Asia to attract MNCs. Leveraging on these projects, the Singapore government could afford investors from outside the region the same efficiency of infrastructure and transparency of various regulations as found in Singapore.

The emergence of the India-Singapore economic alliance was possibly initiated when Singapore's PM Goh met India's PM Rao for informal talks on the fringes of the Non-Aligned Movement (NAM) meeting in Malaysia in 1992. Thereafter, bilateral ties between India and Singapore strengthened when PM Goh visited India at PM Rao's invitation in January 1994. PM Goh was also accorded the status of Chief Guest at India's Independence Day celebrations (*The Straits Times*, 27 January 1994). The significance of PM Goh being made India's Chief Guest indicated that India was seeking to forge closer links with Singapore. This gesture to strengthen ties with Singapore was not an easy one for India to make because it was reported that Czech President Vaclav Havel had wanted to be invited as India's Chief Guest; however, PM Rao chose to extend that honour to PM Goh (*The Straits Times*, 27 January 1994). PM Rao viewed India's relations with Singapore as a means to expand his country's trade ties with the Southeast Asian region. He said, 'Now that we are a sectoral dialogue partner of ASEAN, we are looking forward to a further expansion and a deepening of our relations with the region as a whole' (*The Straits Times*, 26 January 1994).

Such a move by India—to choose Singapore above a former socialist ally, the Czech Republic—would have seemed unthinkable during the Cold War. This is in view of the fact that India favoured close ties with the Soviet Union and was anti-Western in its political posture before the collapse of the Soviet Bloc in 1989. However, in facing increasing uncertainty in a post-Cold War environment, India has chosen to expand its regional relations based more on economic than political considerations. PM Rao, in reference to constructing linkages with Singapore, commented: 'in a changing global economy where unpredictable forces sometimes operate, such constructive and stabilising linkages are welcome' (*The Straits Times*, 26 January 1994). Despite Singapore's small physical size relative to India, PM Rao believed Singapore's economic strengths complemented its own. Why did India choose to court Singapore? India chose to expand its relations with Singapore based on economic complementarity that would bring mutual benefits to both countries. PM Rao remarked: 'Singapore's resources of capital, technology and expertise can find excellent networking with India's agricultural and mineral wealth, our skilled manpower and our markets' (*The Straits Times*, 26 January 1994). The long-term economic aim of the Indian government in fostering close relations with Singapore is to lift the performance of the Indian economy towards expanded growth. PM Rao said, 'Our hope is that the range of Singapore-India contacts will be consolidated in the years to come and will register notable growth' (*The Straits Times*, 26 January 1994). This indicated that the Singapore-India nexus would encompass more than just economic issues.

Will the engagement of India with ASEAN increase regional stability? The Singapore government believed the inclusion of India as a major Asian power would counter and balance the growing economic and military might of China. But PM Rao was uncertain that India would be readily accepted in the region because of its past alignment with the Soviet Union. During a visit to Singapore in September 1994, PM Goh informed PM Rao that: 'Singapore would welcome India's eventual membership in these two forums (ARF and APEC) as India was a major player in Asia' (*The Straits Times*, 27 January 1994). However, when the APEC Summit of 1993 in Seattle closed, Indian pride was hurt when a decision was taken to freeze new membership for three years and the moratorium on new membership was extended to 2007. Referring to this decision, PM Rao commented that he 'does not want to knock on closed doors' (*The Straits Times*, 18 September 1994), to which PM Goh replied, 'The door is not locked. It may not be open, but it is not locked, India is waiting for the right opportunity to come in' (*The Straits Times*, 18 September 1994). PM Goh's response indicated the Singapore government's support of India in its long-term vision to join APEC. The convergence of national interests between

India and Singapore was supported by political commitment. PM Goh commented that 'Our stars are in confluence' (*Business Times*, 26 January 1991) and called for a 'long-lasting strategic alliance between India's and Singapore's private sectors' (*Business Times*, 26 January 1991). This established the political legitimacy to enable Singapore's officials to forge new and enhance existing linkages with their Indian counterparts.

There is an investment component to Singapore's strategic relations with India that involves examining India's potential on a regional and sectoral basis.[7] Singapore's regionalisation strategy took into consideration India's large size and focused on individual states for investment purposes instead of diluting its investments across the country (Singh, 1995). This is similar to Kenichi Ohmae's Zebra strategy which argues that for countries with immense territory, the real choice would be to choose the region in which to invest (Ohmae, 1995). Different regions require specific strategies to expand economic development. The choice of specific regional states in India for Singapore investment is dependent upon the economic sectors that Singapore investors are interested in and they would have to complement Singapore's own economic strengths, which include management, marketing, urban planning, design, export of franchises in education, fast food, retail and financial services (Singh, 1995). In India, the central and provincial state governments have been actively trying to attract foreign investment. The four southern Indian states of Andhra Pradesh, Karnataka, Kerala and Tamil Nadu are approximately a four-hour flight from Singapore. States such as Karnataka meet the skilled manpower needs for Singapore and have land area for construction purposes.

In this regard, Singapore has implemented a southern state strategy to focus on the dynamic Indian states, especially for IT. The attractions of the Indian states in the south include close proximity to the Madras[8] and Cochin[9] Export Processing Zones (EPZs). This has led to growing competition between these four states as they vie with one another to woo Singapore investors (*The Hindu*, 2 January 2000).

---

[7] Interview with the Regional Director South Asia, Economic and Development Board, 20 May 1997.

[8] The Madras EPZ consisted of units situated in Madras Export Processing Zone and approved 100% EOUs situated in Tamil Nadu, Andaman and Nicobar Islands.

[9] The Cochin EPZ consist of units situated in Cochin Export Processing Zone and 100% EOUs situated in Kerala, Karnataka and Lakshadweep.

*Principles and Approaches*

The process of regionalisation has the explicit aim of staying ahead of the other NIEs and the fast-growing Southeast Asian economies (Speeches, May–June 1993, Vol. 17, No. 3). Prime Minister Goh explained that the objective of regionalisation is to expand the national economy by building stronger private companies and establishing some of them as multinationals (Speeches, May–June 1993, Vol. 17, No. 3). One of the principles for regionalisation included the need for Singapore to diversify its investments and not put all its 'eggs in one basket'. According to P.M. Goh, this not only makes sound economic and political sense but also capitalises on the region's size and opportunities (Speeches, May–June 1993, Vol. 17, No. 3). There is an imperative need to venture into new markets to form a steady and durable relationship—not for quick exploitative profits (Speeches, May–June 1993, Vol. 17, No. 3). Nonetheless, the next stage comes with consolidating and building Singapore's strengths in traditional investment destinations such as Malaysia and Indonesia. Why the need to strengthen links with Singapore's traditional trading partners? This is crucial because Singapore's ventures into new regions must not weaken its historical link with its traditional partners (Speeches, May–June 1993, Vol. 17, No. 3).

Singapore's size and generally good reputation as a foreign investment partner assisted in the process of economic complementarity with India because Singapore was not seen as a threat to local Indian businesses. Nonetheless, Singapore investment must be seen to benefit the host country in terms of technology transfer and manpower training (Speeches, May–June 1993, Vol. 17, No. 3). This complemented India's objective of obtaining advanced technology and expertise through joint ventures with foreign partners. The Singapore companies venturing abroad are duly advised to invest in community projects to enrich the lives of the host countries' citizens (*The Straits Times*, 22 May 1993). When conceptualising the regionalisation strategy, the Singapore government realised that in large emerging markets such as India, the economic reforms implemented by the central government would fall short of desired objectives if the provincial state governments were not involved in the process of economic reform. PM Goh said, 'Commitment to reform from the central government alone will not be enough, state governments play a critical role because they can facilitate the implementation of projects or stymie it with innumerable hurdles' (Speeches, January–February 1995, Vol. 19, No. 1).

The Singapore government, through its knowledge of investing and trading with China, has adapted this experience for establishing economic links with India. Realising that certain states in India have the potential to expand their growth faster than others, by focusing on these more dynamic states, the Singapore government anticipated that the competitive drive of the other states would be unleashed. P.M. Goh said of the Chinese experience: 'China offers a useful lesson. Decentralisation has led to intense competition between its provinces for investments. Provincial and local officials see it in their interest to grant quick approvals. The result is sharply differing growth rates between the more dynamic provinces and the rest... But rapid income growth in the more dynamic areas eventually spurs the lagging provinces' (Speeches, January–February 1995, Vol. 19, No. 1).

Similarly, competition between Indian states for foreign investment and collaboration will spur economic growth. Therefore, the process of economic decentralisation in India, with the central government devolving more economic autonomy to individual states, was of great interest to the Singapore government because of the potential for rapid growth. How would the Singapore government meet the challenges of the Indian market? In response to the 'opening up' of new markets in the region, the Singapore government has outlined three approaches to assist its companies investing overseas (Speeches, May–June 1993, Vol. 17, No. 3). Initially, the government will provide business enterprises the freedom to invest in their preferred sectors. The government will then encourage, assist and facilitate the businesses' efforts by supporting them through various agencies such as the Economic Development Board and the Trade Development Board (*The Straits Times*, 22 May 1993). Alternatively, the Singapore government or a Singapore consortium will identify a few major projects in selected cities, regions or countries. These projects will utilise the capabilities and expertise available in Singapore, according to an organised Singapore Incorporated basis (*The Straits Times*, 22 May 1993). Furthermore, these projects would have economic linkages and 'spin-offs' for a wide range of Singapore businesses (*The Straits Times*, 23 May 1993). Through such projects, Singapore can transfer its expertise in master planning, development and operational management to the host country (*The Straits Times*, 22 May 1993).[10] The careful implementation of such projects will be highly

[10] Interview with Regional Director South Asia, Economic Development Board, 20 May 1997.

visible and can become the flagship of economic cooperation between Singapore and the countries that it has chosen to invest in.

Alternatively, Singapore could choose a suitable state whose leaders are eager to tap into Singapore's experience and expertise in drawing up and executing their economic development plans. This would help to establish broad and deep relationships with provincial state leaders that will be of benefit to Singapore businessmen (Speeches, May–June 1993, Vol. 17, No. 3, pp. 20–21). This approach—of focusing on a particular state—is important because Singapore investors have a vague knowledge of India and see it as a whole entity instead of a diversity of states with their own potential strengths and weaknesses. In evaluating the various methods that Indian states had adopted to market themselves, the Singapore Indian Chamber of Commerce (SICCI) commented that they have to demonstrate their advantages over other foreign rivals. For example, India should learn marketing techniques and each state could market a labour force that is skilled in a particular area, or a port with the best time-table between Singapore and India, or an airport with so many flights a week for products that need air-freighting (*The Straits Times*, 22 September 1993). By not marketing themselves adequately, these Indian states were at a disadvantage when competing with other emerging economies to attract foreign investments.

Realising that despite its domestic problems India has potential for economic expansion, the Singapore government in collaboration with SICCI, had initially concentrated its economic activities in India's southern states of Karnataka and Tamil Nadu. This was to foster greater understanding between Singapore officials and Indian state leaders, and to prevent Singapore's investments from being dispersed throughout India and producing negligible returns. To implement the regionalisation strategy, the Singapore government has established a regional business forum to monitor its regionalisation efforts. The secretariat of the forum is located within the Ministry of Trade and Industry (MTI). MTI was also tasked with coordinating government support for overseas investments (*Business Times*, 25 August 1993). Furthermore, the Economic and Development Board was responsible for facilitating investment abroad, while IE Singapore handled trade facilitation and exports (*Business Times*, 25 August 1993). As an added measure, the Ministry of Finance looked into the possibility of seconding public sector officers to private sector projects. This would enable public sector officers working in specialised areas like infrastructure, industrial estate development and town planning to share their expertise with private sector companies (*Business Times*, 25 August 1993).

### *Mechanics of Regionalisation*

How did the Economic and Development Board (EDB) facilitate Singapore investments into India? The answer: corporate networking. There are various forms of corporate networking and some have been expressed in the symbiotic relationship between labour, management and the government (*Business Times*, 27–28 February 1993). 'Corporate networking' also involves a network of financial assistance schemes supported by both the public and private sectors. The Singapore government intends to extend its strategic corporate networking into new directions in India. Corporate networking in India will involve the process of fusion, diaspora networks and a flexible consortium approach. The fusion concept is a process whereby local enterprises are encouraged to form a coalition of strategic partners that will develop, produce and market products that individual members are not capable of changing on their own (*Business Times*, 27–28 February 1993). Under the fusion concept, individual companies with complementary capabilities will forge strategic partnerships for specific joint projects. This would entail the government implementing the fusion concept under a Singapore incorporated basis, whereby a combination of public and private sector resources will be used to venture into emerging markets overseas (*Business Times*, 25 August 1993).

Moving into a cultural dimension, the diaspora networks of overseas communities like the Chinese and Indians provide cultural links for Singapore companies investing overseas (*Business Times*, 25 August 1993). The government could also exploit ethnic connections by the diaspora networks for mutual benefit. This connects with the Singapore government's emphasis of choosing a state or province in an emerging market and cultivating ties with its leaders to enable Singapore companies to secure some development projects. Prime Minister Goh said, 'This approach will enable us to build a broad and deep relationship with provincial leaders which in turn can be used to help our businessmen in securing some of their development projects' (*The Straits Times*, 22 May 1993). The Singapore government has acknowledged that India is devolving more power to metropolitan areas like Bombay,

Bangalore and Madras (*The Straits Times*, 5 June 1993). Minister George Yeo commented: 'Each metropolitan area is like a city-state, with its own set of local problems and opportunities, which Delhi is not able to influence in detail. Each metropolitan area must solve its own problems of attracting investments and creating industrial parks' (*The Straits Times*, 5 June 1993).

The Singapore government did not intend to disperse its investments on a large scale and was keen to focus on its key strengths of constructing specific projects, administration and marketing.[11] In response, the Indian government during the visit of former Indian Minister of Human Resources, Arjun Singh, to Singapore in July 1994, identified its two largest southern cities of Bangalore[12] and Madras[13] as key areas where Singapore investments could be channelled (*The Straits Times Weekly Edition*, 16 July 1994). Arjun Singh said, 'We are looking at specific areas in India where there can be investments from here [Singapore]. Two areas have been identified as possessing good potential, they are Bangalore and Madras' (*The Straits Times Weekly Edition*, 16 July 1994). However, Arjun Singh also explained that the earmarking of the two cities did not preclude Singapore investments from going elsewhere. This would adhere to the Indian government's continuing economic doctrine of having a balanced regional development at the provincial level.

In the process of establishing regional development, corporate networking is crucial as it involves the creation of a flexible consortium to be vertically or horizontally integrated (*Business Times*, 27–28 February 1993). Vertical integration comprises a combination of supplies and retailers under a firm in a specific sector of industry. Horizontal integration comprises a combination of different companies from different industries. The benefits of a consortium concept are economies of scale, transfer of knowledge, quality control, reliability of service and developing long-term relationships (*Business Times*, 27–28 February 1993). In using a flexible consortium concept, Singapore companies could get together and enhance their capabilities before investing overseas. The EDB has also instituted the International Direct Investment Programme

[11] Interview with Singapore Indian Chamber of Commerce and Industry (SICCI) official, Singapore, 2 September 1997.

[12] Bangalore is the capital of Karnataka state.

[13] Madras is the capital of Tamil Nadu state, is southern India's busiest port and aviation hub, and has deep cultural linkages with Singapore's mostly Tamil Indian population: Ravi Vellor, 'India identifies two southern cities for Singapore investments', *The Straits Times Weekly Edition*, 16 July 1994.

that encourages companies to invest overseas (Tan CH, 1995). This invariably means that GLCs such as Singapore Airlines, Singapore Technologies Group, Sembawang Group, NatSteel and Keppel Group are taking the lead to invest in several neighbouring countries.[14] The bias of promoting regionalisation through GLCs was deliberate.

According to former Singapore Trade and Industry Minister, S. Dhanabalan, the primary duty of the government was to assist the growth of the economy. Dhanabalan explained that: 'only those overseas efforts which have clear, direct and positive link to the home economy and helped to strengthen it deserved the active government encouragement incentives and assistance' (*The Straits Times*, 23 May 1993). He added that to implement a regionalisation plan that will have benefits for Singapore, a closer partnership between the private and public sectors is required (*The Straits Times*, 27 August 1997). Dhanabalan has since moved on to assume the chairmanship of Temasek Holdings, the Singapore government's investment arm. On the continued importance of the GLCs in the government's efforts to regionalise, Dhanabalan said in reference to the GLCs and their position in the Singapore economy, they 'cannot grow any more here...the size of Singapore's economy is limited—any Singapore company, whether part of Temasek or not, must face up to that' (*The Straits Times*, 4 July 2002). Dhanabalan explained that the developmental role that Temasek has played continues to be relevant but that its focus may be refined. Part of Temasek's continued role will be the nurturing of domestic companies from its current crop of GLCs and other local companies to be global or regional players (*The Straits Times*, 22 May 1993).

The issue of economic linkages and direct benefit to the Singapore economy while pursuing the regionalisation strategy needs to be addressed in more detail. The Singapore government has to ensure that its regionalisation efforts would result in direct benefit for the Singapore economy. One way would be to have GLCs involved in the flexible consortium when investing in regional countries. Another approach would be for Singapore to evolve into a 'region state', a concept used by Kenichi Ohmae to define a borderless natural economic zone, thereby linking Singapore to other economic regions. However, the implementation of a regionalisation strategy to create an external

[14] Interview with Ms Chong Siak Ching, MD, Arcasia Land Pte Ltd., 12 August 1997.

economy has the negative potential to create a 'hollowing out'[15] effect for the Singapore manufacturing industry with the loss of considerable jobs in the domestic economy. To prevent this, the Singapore government has adopted a 'troika' approach when engaging regional economies. The troika approach as developed by IE Singapore consists of three components: Singapore as the gateway for India to Southeast Asia, joint investments in third countries, and Singapore investments in India (*The Straits Times*, 9 September 1994).

In terms of enhancing economic complementarity between India and Singapore, the role of the Trade and Development Board (TDB) in Singapore was important because it was the leading organisation to develop business links between India and Singapore. A Trade Officer explained that TDB's role is that of facilitator between Indian and Singapore businesses. Indian companies are encouraged to use TDB's regional offices in Indian capitals to source out investment opportunities in Singapore. In return, Singapore companies were encouraged to use IE Singapore's information centre in Singapore to learn more about India.[16] Furthermore, IE Singapore also forms a major component of the Singapore government's strategy of monitoring and gathering economic information on India. According to Chua Taik Him (Former TDB Director of International Business Development), the aim behind Singapore's regionalisation drive is to focus on quality projects that could generate links with its domestic economy and lead to spin-off benefits over the long term (*Sunday Times*, 13 April 1997). At the end of 1996, Singapore had 278 such regional projects (*Sunday Times*, 13 April 1997).

### *EDB Strategy in Bangalore*

Singapore's regionalisation strategy is overseen by the Economic and Development Board (EDB). It is also the main coordinating agency and body that oversees investments in new markets that have opened up in the region, including China, Vietnam, and the Riau province in Indonesia and India (Tan CH, 1995). While the managers of foreign

---

[15] 'Hollowing out' means that with the relocation of domestic industries from Singapore into the surrounding region, the loss of manufacturing jobs will increase unemployment and have a negative social impact in Singapore.

[16] Interview with Ms Chong Siak Ching, MD, Arcasia Pte Ltd., 12 August 1997.

MNCs in Singapore and local investors are enthusiastic about the potential of new markets, they are wary of investing in these new markets because of poor infrastructure, red tape and unfamiliar management practices (Tan CH, 1995). The risks seem too great to entice investors into these new markets. Therefore, the Singapore government devised a strategy of creating a conducive and suitable environment for Singapore companies and MNCs to operate in new markets.

Figure 3.1 illustrates the strategic platform as conceptualised by the EDB for Singapore entrepreneurs in the Bangalore IT Park. The-then Singapore's Minister of Trade and Industry, S. Dhanabalan said 'they... are used to stability, continuity and consistency' when referring to potential investors in Singapore (*The Straits Times*, 16 April 1993). Therefore, the EDB has assumed the role of creating a familiar and comfortable platform whereby Singapore investors and MNCs can operate in a new and different environment.[17] Hence, through this strategic platform, the India-Singapore nexus is also expected to enhance trade and investment ties between the two countries.

### *Political Commitment*

Political commitment in support of economic collaboration between Singapore and India is an important factor to ensure the viability of the Bangalore IT Park. The political commitment from the Singapore and Indian governments towards ensuring strong bilateral trade linkages can be illustrated at two levels. The first level is demonstrated through the exchange of high-level official visits between Indian and Singapore leaders (Singh, 1995). The second refers to particular policies or initiatives undertaken by the Indian and Singapore governments that had facilitated business linkages (Singh, 1995). Table 3.3 shows the exchange of high-level official visits between India and Singapore between 1992 and 2005. There have been regular ministerial visits between India and Singapore to strengthen official ties and economic linkages. In the mid-1990s, the Singapore consortium was monitoring the dispute between Enron Power Corporation of the US and the Maharashtra state government in the construction of a thermal power station. Unlike the problematic relationship between Enron Corporation

[17] Interview with EDB official, 20 May 1997.

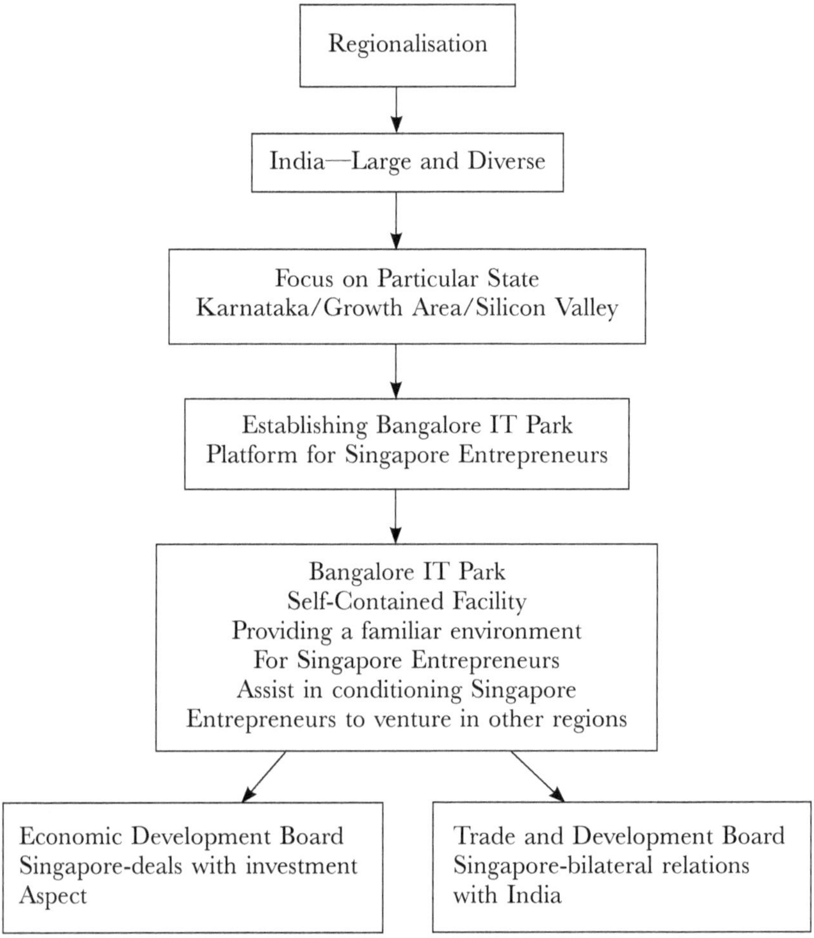


Figure 3.1: Singapore Strategy in India

and the Maharashtra state government, the Karnataka state government managed to remain on good terms with the federal government. According to a staff member of the Singapore consortium, 'We were glad that Deve Gowda was the Chief Minister during the critical phase of implementation and construction of the Bangalore IT Park. We were worried about the IT Park because of what happened to Enron Corporation. It also helped a great deal that Deve Gowda went on to become the Prime Minister'.[18] The relationship between the Singapore

[18] Interview with Singapore consortium official, 18 July 1997.

government, the Indian federal government and the Karnataka state government was moving towards greater complementarity, as indicated by the exchange of official visits. The exchange of visits[19] by the political leaders of both countries enables their views and ideas to be expressed during these meetings to resolve problems. The exchange of high-level official visits (Table 3.3) has been used towards building rapport between India and Singapore.

Table 3.3: Exchange of Major Official Visits between Singapore and India, 1992–2005

| Date | Official Visit |
|---|---|
| February 1992 | Singapore's Minister of Information and the Arts and the-then Second Minister for Foreign Affairs, George Yeo, visits India and the state of Tamil Nadu to examine 'Madras Corridor' concept and the proposed site. |
| March 1992 | Singapore's Minister of Trade and Industry, Lee Hsien Loong, to hold talks on trade and investment including talks on 'Madras Corridor'. |
| January 1994 | Singapore PM Goh Chok Tong, official guest to India's Independence Day celebrations, signs bilateral agreements on taxation, maritime transport and tourism cooperation. |
| July 1994 | Indian Human Resource Minister, Arjun Singh, visits Singapore and identifies Bangalore and Madras as key areas in which to channel Singapore investments. |
| September 1994 | Indian PM Narasimha Rao visits Singapore, deals worth US$800 million between Indian-Singapore companies concluded. |
| June 1996 | Indian Finance Minister, Palaniappan Chidambaram, visits Singapore as PM Gowda's representative at 1st Global Indian Conference. |
| January 1997 | Singapore Minister for Trade and Industry Goh Chee Wee visits Indian states of Karnataka and Tamil Nadu. |
| January 2000 | Singapore Prime Minister Goh Chok Tong visits India and inaugurates the opening of the Bangalore IT Park. |
| Nov.–Dec. 2000 | Singapore Minister for Trade and Industry George Yeo visits India. |
| March 2001 | Singapore Minister for Communications and Information Technology, Yeo Cheow Tong, visits India. |

[19] Singapore Prime Minister Goh Chok Tong visited India twice (in January 1994 and January 1995), former Indian Prime Minister Narasimha Rao visited Singapore in September 1994, and the Chief Minister of Karnataka visited Singapore in February 1996. Furthermore, other Cabinet Ministers from India and Singapore have also exchanged visits.

Table 3.3 (*cont.*)

| Date | Official Visit |
|---|---|
| December 2001 | Singapore Senior Minister of State-Ministry of Transport and Ministry Information, Communications and the Arts, Khaw Boon Hwan, visits India. |
| January 2002 | Indian Minister of Shipping, Vedprakash P Goyal, visits Singapore. |
| April 2002 | Indian Prime Minister Atal Bihari Vajpayee visited Singapore—India week. |
| October 2002 | Singapore Minister of State for National Development, Dr Vivian Balakrishnan, visits India. |
| January 2003 | Singapore President SR Nathan and First Lady visit India. |
| January 2003 | Singapore Minister of State for Foreign Affairs and Trade and Industry, Raymond Lim, visits India. |
| January 2004 | Singapore DPM and Minister for Finance, Lee Hsien Loong, visits India. |
| February 2004 | Singapore Minister for Foreign Affairs, George Yeo, visits India. |
| July 2004 | Indian Minister for External Affairs, K Natwar Singh, visits Singapore. |
| July 2004 | Singapore PM Goh Chok Tong visits India. |
| August 2004 | Singapore Minister for Transport, Yeo Cheow Tong, visits India. |
| September 2004 | Indian Minister for Overseas Indian Affairs, Jagdish Tytler, visits Singapore. |
| October 2004 | Singapore Minister for Trade and Industry, Lim Hng Khiang, visits India. |
| October 2004 | Singapore DPM and Coordinating Minister for Security and Defence, Tony Tan, visits India. |
| October 2004 | Indian Minister of Information, Broadcasting and Culture, S Jaipal Reddy, visits Singapore. |
| November 2004 | Singapore Minister for Home Affairs, Wong Kan Seng, visits India. |
| November 2004 | Indian Minister of Commerce and Industry, Kamal Nath, visits Singapore. |
| January 2005 | Singapore Minister for Education, Tharman Shanmugaratnam, visits India. |
| March 2005 | Singapore Minister for Trade and Industry, Lim Hng Khiang, visits India. |
| June 2005 | Singapore Prime Minister Lee Hsien Loong visits India. |
| July 2005 | Singapore Senior Minister Goh Chok Tong visits India. |

Source: *The Straits Times* (Singapore), Ministry of Foreign Affairs Singapore website.

The political commitment by the Singapore government towards economic cooperation with the Indian government is embodied in Singapore's wider policy orientation towards regionalisation. Which Singapore companies should spearhead trade and investment with India? Given the lack of knowledge and experience among Singapore companies in doing business with India, the government approached Singapore GLCs to undertake projects in India. Using the state capitalism approach, a consortium of Singapore companies was established to undertake Singapore flagship investment project in India.

CHAPTER FOUR

# STATE CAPITALISM AND REGIONALISATION

## *State Capitalism*

Like most developing countries, the Singapore government has taken an active role in establishing state-owned enterprises known as government-linked companies (GLCs) (Ramirez & Tan, July 2003). However, unlike most developing countries, the Singapore government has tried to transform these domestic firms into multinational companies (MNCs). The task of transforming GLCs into MNCs requires an adaptation to an external and multidimensional environment in the international market (Luo & Tan, 1998). Singapore's strategy of state capitalism has been quite successful and GLCs have evolved into important national institutions that are run on a commercial basis with a focus on bottomline performances (Ramirez & Tan, July 2003). This suggests that GLCs are not controlled by self-interested politicians or bureaucrats because of effective monitoring such as regular audits (Willner, 2001). Most of these GLCs were established in the 1960s and 1970s.[1] By the early 1990s, to further consolidate its national competitiveness and to enable the expansion of domestic capital, the government embarked on a regionalisation drive (Yeung, 2002). While overseas direct investments by local and private-owned firms have a longer historical lineage to the time Singapore was part of the Malayan federation, a concerted effort by the government to regionalise GLCs began only in the early 1990s. The view of the Singapore government was that in building an external economic wing through the process of regionalisation, Singapore would be able to exploit the opportunities of the regional economy and possibly insulate itself against a domestic economic crisis. Nonetheless, Singapore was not spared the adverse economic impact brought by the Asian Financial Crisis of 1997–98 because of its strong ties with the regional economies in Southeast Asia.

---

[1] 'Contribution of Government-Linked Companies To Gross Domestic Product', Singapore Department of Statistics, March 2001.

What type of state capitalism is practised in Singapore? The Singapore brand of state capitalism could be defined as state 'equity participation with private individuals or companies embarking on high-risk, high-reward ventures—or, misadventures in the event of failure'. The government has pointed out that the issue of ownership of state enterprises is not as pertinent as its profitability, which would add to Singapore's revenue. The first phase of state capitalism in Singapore has seen the rise of 'homegrown' companies such as the Development Bank of Singapore, Petrochemical Cooperation of Singapore, Singapore Airlines, Singapore Telecoms, Port of Singapore Authority and others. To continue their other main function as capital accumulators, the GLCs have gone on to the second phase of state capitalism, that is, to compete with other MNCs in the international market because the Singapore market is too small and has been liberalised to allow the entry of MNCs. In this regard, the GLCs do not compete directly with foreign MNCs but compete with local private entrepreneurs (Okposin, 1999). Therefore, as local private entrepreneurs venturing onto the international market, they will be competing less with local private companies. Venturing overseas is risky but Asian brand names such as Sony, Sanyo, Hitachi, Sumitomo Bank, Hyundai, Samsung and others have blazed the trail for other Asian companies. Through the regionalisation strategy, trade links between India and Singapore have been transformed into a strategic alliance that are of mutual benefit and should create more revenue than mere exploitation of individual resources (Urban, 1998). Singapore's economic interest in the Indian economy increased after India's 1991 economic reforms.

After the Asian Financial Crisis of 1997 and to meet the challenges of a rapidly globalising economy, the government of Singapore established the Economic Review Committee (ERC) to look into 'recreating' the Singapore economic model to enhance its international competitiveness. The ERC had a sub-committee on entrepreneurship and internationalisation that examined the role of GLCs in Singapore's economy (*The Straits Times*, 27 August 2002). The ERC's Entrepreneurship and Internationalisation Sub-Committee recommended that to nurture entrepreneurs and assist Singapore companies to venture overseas, the cluster approach should be employed (Channel News Asia, 13 September 2002). Citing the successful examples of the clustering approach used in developing business parks in Singapore, the ERC recommended that government agencies like International Enterprises (IE) Singapore (formerly the Trade and Development Board) should urge complementary firms to work together to explore overseas markets. Several academics have discussed developing India in specific areas. With regard to India's efforts to accelerate its economic development, Mark Holstrom and Philip Cadene (1998) have examined India's efforts at decentralising production in India, and have examined the development of Bangalore as an industrial district by the Indian government. India is too large to develop uniformly and needs to focus on particular states or regions which offer the best potential for economic growth and development.

### *Sectoral Focus Approach*

The new strategic plan for India, as conceptualised by IE Singapore, advocated that Singapore companies venturing overseas should focus on regional growth areas and specific sectors rather than concentrating in just one area or industrialised states (Tradespur, June–July 1996). The cause of this strategic shift was propelled by the decision made by IE Singapore to follow the lead of Singapore Indian businessmen. These growth areas include not only the major metro cities, but also secondary cities such as Pune, Gurgaon, Faridabad, Mysore, Vizag and Coimbatore (Tradespur, June–July 1996). From IE Singapore's perspective, non-resident Indians (NRIs) in Singapore have maintained strong economic links especially among the trading families with the private sector in India.[2] Singapore companies like Thakral Holdings and Melwani Private Limited have had a long presence in the Indian market and have more experience in dealing with businesses in India than the TDB because of their personal ties with India.[3] Given the existing links between Singapore and India, could India be considered a new market?

An IE Singapore officer pointed out that IE Singapore seriously focused on the Indian market only in 1989, when it decided to cooperate with the private sector and have local Indian companies show them the way into the Indian market.[4] The operational end of this strategy was that experienced Indian companies in Singapore with trade

[2] Interview with Trade Officer, Trade and Development Board Officer, 30 June 1997.

[3] Ibid.

[4] Ibid.

connections in India would have to comprise part of IE Singapore's annual trade delegation visits to India.[5] Furthermore, on IE Singapore's trade exploration visits to assess new opportunities in India, Indian business entrepreneurs from Singapore will normally head the private sector delegation. During one of the earlier official visits to India after the initiation of the 1991 economic reforms, Singapore's then Deputy Prime Minister Lee Hsien Loong headed the delegation. However, the deputy leader of the Singapore delegation was A Jumabhoy, a well-known and influential business leader of Indian origin and with strong business contacts in India (*The Straits Times*, 24 March 1992).

The exploratory visit by Deputy Prime Minister Lee Hsien Loong, who was then also the Trade and Industry Minister, was triggered by Singapore's growing interest in the changes sweeping the Indian economy and the potential to increase business ties between India and Singapore (*The Straits Times*, 24 March 1992). DPM Lee emphasised Singapore's growing interest in India's economic reforms by including influential business leaders in his delegation. The delegation comprised Alan Yeo, the-then chairman of the Trade and Development Board, senior officials of the Economic and Development Board, as well as businessmen with diverse interests. The deputy leader of the Singapore delegation, A Jumabhoy said, 'Singapore and India could enter a strategic partnership to manufacture items of interest to the region' (*The Straits Times*, 24 March 1992). According to Jumabhoy, Singapore had the potential to serve as a springboard for India to enter the ASEAN market. The discussion between the-then DPM Lee and Indian Commerce Minister P Chidambaram focused on joint ventures and exports to third countries (*The Straits Times*, 24 March 1992).

To better understand the Indian market, IE Singapore has opened offices in Madras and New Delhi to gather information and develop contacts for networking. In 1996, two trade missions were conducted to India, which were undertaken by the India Business Group (IBG) under the purview of IE Singapore. In order to create an external economic wing, the Singapore government has tasked the EDB and IE Singapore to facilitate the expansion of Singapore companies overseas. Singapore's regionalisation programme is driven by the private sector but the government supports the programme through two main approaches: (1) by broad-based mechanisms and (2) by specific measures. Broad-

[5] Ibid.

based mechanisms involve the use of flagship projects[6] and business councils.[7] Specific measures are co-investment[8] and investment support[9] from the Singapore government. There are many investment opportunities in the region but the Singapore government also stressed that local companies must consider a consortium approach to enhance their critical mass and complementary strengths (Tan CH, 1995). In this context, the EDB will assist local companies in such consortia arrangements and, where necessary, agencies such as the Jurong Town Corporation and the Port of Singapore Authority will provide the necessary equity participation in these consortia (Tan CH, 1995).

The Trade and Development Board (TDB) was restructured in 2002 to form International Enterprises (IE) Singapore, the aim of which is to internationalise Singapore companies and assist them to expand overseas.[10] It will continue to be the primary agency to implement Singapore's regionalisation strategy to create an external economic wing for the domestic economy. IE also promotes Singapore as a small and medium enterprises (SME) hub to attract enterprises from other countries to have a base in Singapore so they can collaborate with Singapore companies intending to venture into the region.

Two of the major markets that IE is encouraging companies to venture into are India and China (*Business Times*, 20 November 2001). IE facilitates local companies to explore investment opportunities in India by focusing on specific sectors and key states. Most of the

[6] Singapore is actively involved in the development of industrial parks in the region. These industrial parks are located in premier investment locations and they enjoy the full support and facilitation from both the Singapore and host governments. At present there are eight flagship projects developed as self-contained industrial parks. The industrial parks provide a stable and familiar working environment for MNCs and local companies. *Regionalisation*, Economic Development Board (EDB) Singapore, April 1997, p. 2.

[7] The Singapore government has established bilateral platforms for strategic collaboration with international and regional investment partners to open doors for investment opportunities in each other's countries. Although these business councils are led by the private sector, they are fully supported by the respective governments at the highest political level. Ibid.

[8] The EDB co-invests with companies in strategic projects with economic linkages to Singapore. The EDB builds and extends its relationship with leading companies through co-investment partnerships that reduce risks. A S$1 billion Cluster Development Fund was established in 1995 for the Singapore government to participate in risk-sharing projects with companies.

[9] The Singapore government also provides a comprehensive support framework for companies based in Singapore.

[10] IE website, Singapore, 25 October 2002.

prominent business corporations in India such as the Tatas and Birlas are located in the states of Andhra Pradesh, Gujarat, Karnataka, Tamil Nadu and Maharashtra (*Business Times*, 20 November 2001). Echoing the regionalisation principles laid down by Senior Minister Goh, IE's Regional Director for South Asia, Raheed Nargund, explained that 'the challenge for Singapore companies is to find the right partner, do your homework well and have a good value proposition. And don't take the one billion Indian consumers, particularly the increasingly sophisticated middle class for granted' (*Business Times*, 17 April 2002). Industry sources reported that Singapore has built a cache of funds to invest abroad and encourage its entrepreneurs to embark on a regionalisation and globalisation drive (*The Hindu*, 2 January 2000). The Singapore government also recommended specific regional states in India to Singapore companies. Most of these Indian states are in the south, with the exception of one or two that are in the north. For example, Mumbai in the state of Maharashtra is the financial centre of India, while the three southern states of Andhra Pradesh, Tamil Nadu and Karnataka, apart from having progressive governments and fairly good governance, are also in closer proximity to Singapore and have developed their human resource base in specific areas like IT, healthcare services and infrastructure development. In particular, Singapore could invest in the IT sector in India because Singapore has one of the strongest e-governance systems in the world. According to Raheed Nargund, Singapore could collaborate with the Indian IT companies and not only bring their research to market but also save them a gestation period of 10 years (*Business Times*, 17 April 2002).

The Economic and Development Board (EDB) of Singapore and the apex Indian business chamber, the Federation of Indian Chambers of Commerce and Industry (FICCI), signed a Memorandum of Understanding (MOU) during the visit of Indian Prime Minister Atal Bihari Vajpayee to Singapore in April 2002, in order to promote and facilitate investment by Indian technology companies in Singapore (*The Straits Times*, 9 April 2002). In this context, EDB Chairman Teo Ming Kian said that an India Centre has been established at JTC's technopreneur park in Singapore to accommodate more Indian technology start-ups. Significantly, Singapore was host to some 1,600 Indian companies in early 2006, up from less than 50 firms in 1997 (*Business Times*, 17 April 2002). As of 2004, about 150 Indian companies are establishing a presence in Singapore per year. By the end of 2005, there were approximately 1,700 Indian companies in Singapore and this figure increased to 2,600 a year later.

There are approximately 450 Indian IT companies in Singapore, including premier Indian IT companies like Tata Consultancy Services (TCS), Wipro, Satyam Computer Services and NIIT. TCS and Satyam have also established their Asia-Pacific headquarters in Singapore. While Singapore was encouraging these and potential Indian companies to globalise their business by using Singapore as their base, FICCI president Rajendra S was also encouraging Indian companies to source for venture capital on the Singapore Exchange and to use Singapore as a strategic location to establish business linkages in the Asia-Pacific region (*Business Times*, 17 April 2002). For example, Satyam Computer Services has invested S$500,000 in its Singapore office, employed 100 people and its clients in Singapore include Citibank, Sony and Alcatel (*The Straits Times*, 17 April 2001). While the Asia-Pacific region accounted for only 5% of its business, the bulk (75%) comes from North America. Satyam Chairman Ramalinga Raju believed that the IT sector in the Asia-Pacific region could grow by 10%–15% in the short term (*The Straits Times*, 17 April 2001). EDB highlighted Satyam's presence in Singapore as an example of the synergy that could be achieved by Indian and Singaporean firms collaborating with each other (*The Straits Times*, 17 April 2001).

Amid fears of terrorist attacks, many firms are eager to establish back-up sites to which they could move their personnel quickly to continue operations if disaster were to strike. Narayanan Murthy, the Chairman of Infosys which is one of India's leading software development firms, believes that Singapore is ideally positioned to house data back-up centres (*The Straits Times*, 23 October 2002). However, Singapore authorities and Infosys were initially reluctant to issue a block of 2,000 visas for Infosys software engineers. Consequently, competitors aiming to be data recovery centres (DRCs) like Mauritius stepped up their efforts to woo Indian business away from Singapore. Realising that it had to amend its regulations and practices to attract Indian IT companies to use Singapore as a DRC or business continuity centre, Singapore was successful in its negotiations with Satyam Computers to house their DRC in Singapore by issuing a block of 750 visas for the company's IT workers. Singapore has attracted other Indian software companies like Chennai-based Polaris Software Lab, which has invested S$3 million to open a business continuity centre in Singapore (*The Straits Times*,

23 October 2002). In turn, Singapore will focus on specific regional states in India to operationalise its Flagship Investment Strategy and approach to invest in the Indian market. While Mauritius may offer a lower-cost production centre, Mr Virender Aggarwal, Asia Pacific Vice-President at Satyam Computer Services, believed Singapore's economic vibrancy to be a better alternative to Mauritius and, hence, established its centre in Singapore in 2001.

IE Singapore has also facilitated the expansion of Singapore companies into the Indian market. Soundbuzz, a digital music provider, has credited IE for helping it to expand into the Indian market. The Chief Executive Officer of Soundbuzz, Sudhanshu Sarronwala, said that the Indian operation is on track and contributed 10%–15% of Soundbuzz's Asia-Pacific business (*Business Times*, 17 April 2002). The company started its Indian operations in Mumbai in 2000 because Mumbai happened to be India's film industry capital—Bollywood—and the music industry's nerve centre in India. According to Sarronwala, Soundbuzz joined IE's trade missions to various countries including India and benefited from the contacts and meetings that IE was able to arrange before the trade mission went to India. Soundbuzz's connection to the Singapore brand and the fact that the company was with an official IE delegation lent it added credibility (*Business Times*, 17 April 2002).

While parliamentarians may debate on the role of the GLCs in the domestic economy—whether their operations should be made more transparent and whether the government should reduce its stake in the GLCs—there was no disagreement on the continued relevance of the GLCs in expanding Singapore's economic interests overseas. The GLCs have the ability to partner other local companies to venture abroad and seek new business opportunities. A case in point is CapitaLand which was formed through the merger of Pidemco (a collection of government projects) and DBS Land. CapitaLand has engaged Singapore firms for its overseas projects and has bagged over S$50 million worth of projects in Shanghai (China) alone (*The Straits Times*, 18 July 2002).

### *Branding*

Singapore companies are relatively small compared with other MNCs and India is a huge market. How could Singapore companies compete against larger foreign MNCs in India? Moreover, how would Singapore

SMEs undertake projects in India given their larger scale economies and complexity? One strategy would be the ability of Singapore GLCs to pool together a diverse array of local companies with relevant expertise, knowledge and funding to compete for business opportunities in India. For example, CapitaLand's service apartment subsidiary, the Ascott Group, was able to band together a group of local companies such as KinderWorld Educare Centre to join forces to develop scale and a range of resources to establish an emerging multinational group of companies. KinderWorld, through its collaboration with the Ascott Group, had the opportunity to establish kindergartens overseas where the Ascott launched service apartments (*The Straits Times*, 18 July 2002). One of the main challenges facing GLCs will be to develop more internationally recognised Singapore brand companies. Ian Batey, an advertising guru who has developed one of Singapore's most profitable and recognisable brands—Singapore Airlines—said that the Singapore brand image is recognised overseas as being extremely efficient, competent and trustworthy, which is positive from the business and investment point of view (*The Straits Times*, 27 September 2002). According to the-then Singapore Senior Minister of State for Trade and Industry and Education, Tharman Shanmugaratnam, branding is crucial to Singapore's next phase of growth. While Singapore has some strong brands, more needs to be done as it was ranked only 23rd in terms of branding by the 2001 World Economic Forum Global Competitiveness Report on Micro-competitiveness (*The Straits Times*, 22 October 2002). In the Asia-Pacific brand survey of 2005, no Singapore brands were in the top five. Minister Mentor Lee Kuan Yew echoed the same sentiments when he said that Singapore should build on its brand name for having a reputation for high standards.

Building a brand name that is internationally recognisable will enable Singapore to cater to the expanding middle classes in China and India (*The Straits Times*, 16 October 2001). According to the Minister for Trade and Industry, Mr Khaw Boon Hwan, the Singapore brand is well regarded in India and China where tens of millions of consumers join the ranks of middle-income earners every year. These consumers will create a demand for better-quality service and Singapore is in a position to prepare its service industries to cater to this growing demand (*The Straits Times*, 17 September 2002). Coupled with the Singapore government's strategy to be a regional R&D hub, the services sector requires workers' skills to be improved while the government attracts foreign talent at the same time to create a knowledge-based economy.

In October 2001, the Singapore government established the Economic Review Committee (ERC) headed by the-then Deputy Prime Minister Lee Hsien Loong. The ERC was primarily tasked to examine ways to remake the economy (*Far Eastern Economic Review*, 11 July 2002). The ERC could be seen as an extension of the work carried out by the CSC. For example, the ERC established the Entrepreneurship and Internationalisation Sub-Committee (EISC) which recommended that the government adopt a more liberal system of issuing employment passes and immigration rules in order to attract foreign talent and entrepreneurs. The ERC also examined ideas submitted by Singaporeans overseas like those in Silicon Valley, California, US, who recommended that, in order to increase the competitiveness of Singaporeans, 10% of Singapore's best and brightest in government service should spend time in the private sector every year (*Business Times*, 8 April 2002).

The EISC has also suggested that GLCs should continue to expand into new businesses and collaborate with small and medium enterprises (SMEs). This is to enable them to exploit their respective strengths and operate in the international market. This has cast the spotlight on the role of GLCs, particularly on Temasek Holdings which maintains and manages the Singapore government's investments in various private companies. To encourage the expansion of Singapore's economy overseas, the government is using GLCs to acquire foreign assets (*Business Times*, 8 April 2002). The ERC also recommended that GLCs and multinationals that receive large government contracts should outsource part of their projects to SMEs to expand specialised niche industries in Singapore (*Business Times*, 8 April 2002).

### *Transforming GLCs into MNCs*

The restructuring of the Singapore economy is impeded by domestic constraints such as the shortage of both land and skilled workers. In order to overcome these challenges, the rationale seems to indicate towards transforming GLCs into globally or regionally integrated MNCs. The GLCs and the MNCs are two very different breeds, as Dunning argued: while GLCs treat foreign-based subsidiaries as autonomous revenue earnings, the globally or regionally integrated MNCs adopt a systemic and holistic approach towards its global operations (Dunning, 2000). This type of MNC treats its foreign affiliates as part of the overall network of interrelated activities that are designed to promote the interests of the MNC as a whole. Another important characteristic of this MNC is that it will take full advantage of natural and created assets that are geographically dispersed (Dunning, 2000). While John Dunning (2000) made the point that this type of MNC is able to exploit opportunities in liberalised markets through spatially agglomerative economies, the economies of India and Singapore are separated by 3,200 kilometres of ocean. To overcome the impediment of distance, the Singapore and Indian economies have neutralised this variable through technological advancement.

### *State Holding Companies*

Temasek Holdings manages about 80 large companies and many smaller companies, and has major stakes in 12 publicly listed companies and major private firms such as Port of Singapore Authority Corporation, Singapore Power and Singapore Technologies. These companies account for some 13% of Singapore's GDP.[11] In the next phase of Singapore's economic development in the knowledge economy, Temasek aims to build and nurture internationally competitive businesses that can leverage on Singapore's competitive strengths and enhance its economic resilience. The government's interest to upgrade and expand key economic sectors such as utilities, transportation, ports and telecommunications was necessary because in Singapore's early post-Independence era, the private sector was weak and infrastructure had to be developed. This has created a lingering effect and a historical tradition for Temasek to maintain control of utilities and infrastructure services (*The Straits Times*, 4 July 2002). While Temasek's critics have argued for its role to be more passive, Executive Director of Temasek, Ms Ho Ching, believes the company should play the role of catalyst to support the boards and managements of the various companies to steer their respective companies towards their objectives (*The Straits Times*, 27 and 28 June 2002).

Essentially, in Temasek's stable of companies, there are reportedly two groups of companies. Group A companies are those that the Singapore government needs to own and control, while Group B companies are

[11] Motion on Temasek Charter and EISC's Recommendations on Government in Business, Parliament of Singapore, Notice Paper No. 140 of 2002.

those that have the potential to regionalise and internationalise. In Group B, Temasek is open to these companies partnering other companies or shareholders. Temasek is also prepared to dilute its stake in the Group B companies to support their long-term success in the regional and international economies. Given that Singapore SMEs may have difficulty in raising the capital and forge business alliances, as required for regional and international forays, Temasek is likely to venture into new growth areas which entail high risks, large investments or long gestation periods to nurture new industrial clusters. Although conservative estimates of Singapore's external economy place a figure of around US$200 billion, the acquisition phase of the GLCs is far from over.[12] Temasek Holdings' portfolio is worth about S$90 billion. Despite the GLCs' reported exhaustion of their excess capital, they have forayed into the capital market to compete for sizeable amounts of investment capital. This would indicate that the building of Singapore's external economy is expected to continue until 2015. By this time, the factor income from the external economy is expected to constitute a large percentage of Singapore's gross national product.

### *Flagship Projects*

The process of regionalising local companies involves the creation of industrial parks through joint ventures in selected Asian countries like India. These industrial parks would utilise Singapore's expertise in management but establish joint ventures with other companies overseas to leverage on lower wages and property prices (*Financial Times*, 18 February 1997). The rationale for developing these industrial parks overseas was to extend the depth and scope of the domestic operations of Singapore companies. Another dimension to these industrial parks is the move towards attracting foreign MNCs with a presence in Singapore to consider investing in them as well. As Singapore is a base for some 7,000 MNCs, the development of such industrial parks would allow these firms to maintain their overseas headquarters in Singapore but move manufacturing to the cheaper but equally well-built and managed areas overseas. This scheme is coordinated by the EDB which will ensure

[12] Daniel Lian, Temasek Charter authorises external economy mission of GLC, Report by Morgan Stanley, 8 July 2002.

that the tenants of these industrial parks receive the same standards of infrastructure, facilities and management they have experienced in Singapore. Singapore companies will also benefit by having access to a wider market but cheaper sources of labour.

The industrial parks symbolise that Singapore's flagship projects are a long-term strategy to reposition the nation's companies in the heart of other Asian markets, and it is expected that it will be several years before the Singapore consortia see a return on their huge investments overseas (Tan CH, 1995). According to the chairman of the Bangalore IT Park's executive committee, the Bangalore IT Park was designed to be profitable by 1999 when the first stage of its development was fully taken up. The IT Park Bangalore (ITPB) was predicted to break even if it had an occupancy rate of slightly over 60% (*Financial Times*, 18 February 1997). According to the director of EDB's international business development division, the industrial parks as flagship projects allows Singapore-based companies to move into emerging economies in an organised and more confident manner because of the involvement of Singapore authorities such as the EDB (*Financial Times*, 18 February 1997). In addition, these industrial parks also carried the Singapore brand name and the expectations that went along with it.

The ITPB was developed by the Singapore consortium to create and maintain a positive business environment for MNCs needing to establish a presence in the Indian economy. Singapore's reputation for developing good infrastructure and managing high-technology parks were key factors to drawing in the MNCs. Refining the use of organisational ecology theory, local social conditions have a major impact on business development and growth (Knoke, 2001). MNCs that recognise the Singapore brand for transparency, consistency and reliability will be drawn to the ITPB in India if they are interested in the Indian market. In this way, India will benefit from the Singapore brand and its investments in the Indian market. Despite the chaotic scenes prevailing outside of the gates of the ITPB, MNCs residing in the ITPB are able to depend on developed world infrastructure and management to expand their business.

### *Focused Returns*

While some analysts believe that Singapore is still in an acquiring phase, other analysts opine that Singapore will resort to a focused return

Table 4.1: Singapore's Flagship Projects Overseas

| Country | Area (hectares) | Employment (no. of people) | Investment Co.: US$ m (as at Dec. 1996) |
|---|---|---|---|
| 1. China, S'pore Suzhou Industrial Park (divested majority stake in 2002) | 7,000 | 360,000 | 2,000 |
| 2. Wuxi-Singapore Industrial Park | 1,000 | 150,000 | 430 |
| 3. Batamindo Industrial Park | 320 | 54,246 | 725 |
| 4. Bintan Industrial Estate | 4,000 | 2,679 | 161.3 |
| 5. Bintan Beach International Resort | 23,000 | 1,352 | 128.6 |
| 6. Karimun Marine Industries Complex | 1,050 | 300 | 55 |
| **7. Information Technology Park, Bangalore** | **27** | **15,000** | **NA** |
| 8. Vietnam Singapore Industrial Park | 500 | 50,000 | 75 |

Source: *Regionalisation*, April 1997, Economic Development Board.

approach to ensure that they receive benefits from their regionalisation strategy. Singapore's drive to build an external wing for its domestic economy has focused on eight countries in the region (China, India, Indonesia, Malaysia, Myanmar, the Philippines, Thailand and Vietnam). Table 4.1 lists Singapore's overseas flagship investment projects. The eight flagship industrial parks in China, Indonesia, India and Vietnam help to facilitate Singapore companies to venture into the region (Tan CH, 1995). These industrial parks enjoy full political support and financial backing from Singapore and the host countries' governments.

Investment locations in the Asian region, specifically China, India and Indonesia were selected as regional sites for Singapore's flagship projects. Indonesia has four flagship projects, China has two and India one, this being the Bangalore IT Park. The flagship projects have been developed as self-contained industrial parks with business, commercial and residential facilities (Tan CH, 1995). More importantly, the industrial parks provide a set of stable and familiar working environments for MNCs and Singapore companies (Regionalisation Report, April 1997).

According to a Singapore government official, it was extremely difficult to entice Singapore investors overseas without providing for them a set of stable and familiar surroundings (Interview EDB Personnel, 20 May 1997). With the experience gained in developing industrial estates in Singapore and other Asian countries, GLCs, most notably the Jurong

Town Corporation and its subsidiaries, will develop industrial parks in new markets. Starting with Batam in Indonesia, Singapore companies have been contracted to build other industrial towns in China such as the Suzhou Township, Wuxi Industrial Park and Ningbo 2000 project (Tan CH, 1995). The same concept has been extended to industrial parks in Vietnam and the Bangalore IT Park in India (Tan CH, 1995). Therefore, the Singapore government minimises the risks for entrepreneurs in the new markets by eliminating the task of constructing facilities from scratch, and supports the industrial park with its reputation and experience in managing and maintaining such industrial parks.[13] In turn, the host government will benefit from Singapore's reputation and contacts with the foreign MNCs that have joined Singapore investors to invest in new markets.

With its internationally recognised legal system, wide use of the English language, and skilled and educated labour, India has provided the pull factors that attract foreign investments (Singh, 1995). Moreover, the drive towards regionalisation by the Singapore government and the move by the Indian federal government to continue with the 1991 economic reforms and liberalisation have created a convergence and economic complementarity. Karnataka and Tamil Nadu were more attractive than other regions of India because of their lower operating costs (*The Straits Times*, 27 February 1993), the presence of existing infrastructure,[14] a local pool of educated labour and a reasonable level of industrial progress.[15] The southern Indian states of Karnataka and Tamil Nadu have created basic industries to entice foreign investors. Tamil Nadu supports a diverse array of industries such as textiles, chemicals, fertilisers, automobiles and ancillaries, cement, iron and steel. These industries benefit from the skilled and educated pool of manpower from the 214 general colleges and 38 engineering colleges in the state. Corporate recruiters are often impressed with the graduates

[13] Interview with EDB official, Singapore, 20 May 1997.

[14] Bangalore has three domestic airports and 4,227 bank branches.

[15] In Bangalore there is a wide diversity of industries from textiles to aircraft. Furthermore, the state government has enhanced the scale of subsidy in thrust areas of the economy. Additional subsidies were given to special categories of entrepreneurs as incentives for installing equipment for utilisation of renewable sources of energy. Specified high-tech and non-polluting industries in tiny, small, medium and large-scale sectors permitted to be located within developed areas. Industrial investments in the tiny/SSI/medium and large-scale sectors would be provided with the option of either sales tax exemption or sales tax deferral. Special concessions for Export Oriented Industries including 100% EOU.

of Bangalore's technical colleges such as the Indian Institute of Science. In terms of college graduates, recruiters for MNCs realise that there is less of a difference in this category of labour than there is among day labourers and students in secondary schools.

While Karnataka has relatively better infrastructure compared to other states in India, the state of Tamil Nadu has better infrastructure. Karnataka has three airports, 4,227 bank branches and various types of industries. In addition, there is a wide selection of established industries in the state, including aircraft, rail, coaches, telephone instruments, electronic motors, glass, textiles, cement, fertilisers and others. Several incentives are given to industries that opt to invest in Bangalore. These incentives include the installation of equipment to utilise renewable sources of energy and proposed special concessions for 100% Export Oriented Units (EOUs). Furthermore, industrial investments in the small-scale industries sector will be provided with the option of either sales tax exemption or sales tax deferral and an additional subsidy will also be given to special categories of entrepreneurs (Bangalore State Website, 1995). The state government of Karnataka initiated its Industrial Policy Resolution in 1996 to facilitate the modernisation and expansion of its infrastructure to attract foreign investors.

In competition with Karnataka in bidding for the Information Technology Park, the state of Tamil Nadu also resorted to advertising its infrastructure facilities. Apart from its one international airport, Tamil Nadu has six domestic airports, two major seaports and six minor seaports. Tamil Nadu is also relatively well equipped with telecommunications[16] and financial facilities.[17] The state is connected to other parts of India with railway lines running between 690 stations. In total, Tamil Nadu has about 6,693 kilometres of railway lines and 170,499 kilometres of road network. The state has a natural affinity with Singapore because of the large minority of Tamils in Singapore. With its relatively better infrastructure, congenial industrial relations, traditional and existing links with Singapore, Tamil Nadu was an attractive destination but the state government was not able to exploit these advantages (*The Hindu*, 2 January 2000). For example, while the-then Tamil Nadu's Chief Minister M Karunanidhi made useful visits to Singapore in early

[16] Number of post offices: (1) doing postal business only—7,346; (2) doing postal and telegraph business—4,631. There are 5,632 telegraph offices and 1,244 telephone exchanges.

[17] There are 4,316 bank branches in Tamil Nadu.

1999, he was preoccupied with the next election and did not follow up on issues linked to development and industrialisation.

In contrast, Karnataka's Chief Minister, Mr SM Krishna, was able to convince Singapore that pending and delayed proposals for the Bangalore IT Park could be pushed through and new projects could be cleared to prevent bottlenecks (*The Hindu*, 2 January 2000). The Singapore government then decided to focus on Karnataka for economic complementarity and the political commitment shown by the state government.[18] In terms of economic complementarity, the Singapore government focused on the market potential for computer software and electronics in India. In looking at various industrial sectors in India, the Singapore government was keen on the electronics and the software sectors in India because of its enormous potential for future growth.

---

[18] Interviews with EDB Regional Director for South Asia, 20 May 1997 and Projects Manager L&M Corporation, 18 July 1997.

CHAPTER FIVE

# KNOWLEDGE-BASED ECONOMY

## *Introduction*

The emergence of the knowledge-based economy[1] has seen the importance of information, and research and development (R&D) as the source of wealth creation in society (Solvell & Burkinshaw, 2000). Singapore's political leaders have acknowledged that the new imperatives for wealth creation among nations are not traditional capital and labour, but knowledge and intellectual capital. Senior Minister Goh remarked that 'the new knowledge economy is to the advantage of a resource-poor country like Singapore' (*The Straits Times*, 13 October 1998). However, Singapore's small population of four million, of which one million are expatriates, and a declining birth rate will pose major challenges to developing a knowledge-based economy. Nonetheless, Singapore has been preparing itself in key strategic thrust areas to meet the challenges of the next growth wave in the globalised economy. Arguably, the need for foreign talent has sparked off a debate over future employment issues but Singapore's creative industries have contributed significantly to the economy. Minister Mentor (MM) Lee Kuan Yew has remarked that foreign talent could be contributing as much as 20% of Singapore's total GDP. Creative industries in general exhibit significant linkages with each other and they form an ecosystem of creative industries.[2]

---

[1] KBE embodies the ability to constantly innovate through accessing, processing, using and creating knowledge: Heng, Tang, Choo and Singapore MTI, 'Mapping Singapore's Knowledge-based Economy', Economic Survey of Singapore, Third Quarter 2002.

[2] Heng, Choo and MTI, 'Economic Contributions of Singapore's Creative Industries', Ministry of Trade and Industry, Singapore Ministry of Trade and Industry, First Quarter 2003.

*Creating a Base for KBE Clusters*

Firms working in the knowledge-based economies (KBEs) derive their competitiveness from firm specific competence that has been developed through a combination of tangible and intangible resources. The specific competence in a firm is defined as tacit or non-codified knowledge in the organisational context. Using their specific competitiveness, firms are able to undertake tasks to practise and develop the tacit part of knowledge that their competitors are not able to imitate or duplicate in the short term (Mehra & Dhawan, 2003). Where would it be best to locate firms for the KBE to enable them to thrive and expand?

Michael Porter has used the concept of clusters to explain how KBEs could use linked industries to create critical mass in order to expand economic activities (Porter, November/December 1998). According to Porter, clusters affect competition which increase a firm's competitive advantage and its overall impact on economic development.[3] Balasubramanyam has also used the cluster approach to account for the expansion of the IT sector in Bangalore (Balasubramanyam et al., 2000). John Streamlau has written on the transformation of Bangalore into India's Silicon City and how this will affect economic development throughout India, but points out that there are adverse impacts to Bangalore's expansion of its software industry (Streamlau, November 1996). India's low cost but large and skilled IT human resource pool is the main attraction for IT MNCs in Bangalore. In this context, AnnaLee Saxenian has written a number of papers on the 'brain drain and brain gain' aspect of the IT sector, with specific reference to the loss of software talent from developing countries such as India to Silicon Valley in the US. Saxenian has also examined whether Bangalore could be considered the Asian equivalent of Silicon Valley in the US (Saxenian, 2002). In a more recent article, Ambika Patni reported on the progress of Bangalore in specific areas such as software development (Patni, Fall 1999). In contrast, geographers such as Mark Holstrom (Holstrom, 1998) have used the spatial approach to examine Bangalore

[3] Clusters affect competition in three main ways. First, by increasing the productivity of companies located in a specific area. Second, by driving the direction and pace of innovation. Third, by stimulating the formation of new businesses within the cluster. Clusters within a certain geographic area benefit from greater flexibility, closer relationships, better information and powerful incentives. Porter, Michael E. 'Clusters and the New Economics of Competition,' *Harvard Business Review*, Nov./Dec. 1998, Vol. 76(6).

as an industrial district with specific reference to the engineering and electronic industries.

David Rosenberg examined six locations worldwide, including Silicon Valley and Bangalore, to examine the benefits of a technology cluster (Rosenberg, 1998). He outlined several key features of software technology parks such as geography, company culture, venture capital, stock market capitalisation, universities as talent pools and government policies to foster IT growth (Rosenberg, 1998). Rosenberg described the IT hub in Bangalore as a 'silicon island, Third World Sea.' The chairman of Infosys, Narayanan Murthy, made a similar observation when he commented that Indian IT workers in Bangalore have to make the mental adjustment from living in a third world to working in a first-world environment on a daily basis. Are IT clusters sustainable over the long term from an infrastructure and people point of view? Locational advantages of established companies are dependent on the fluctuations of wages, changes in local environmental regulations, transportation alternatives and commodity suppliers (Galbraity & De Noble, 1992). As a case study, the emergence of the IT clusters in Bangalore will be examined using the variables mentioned. Initial assumptions of this paper are that the sustainability of IT clusters in India has gone beyond Porter's definition of clusters to include infrastructure. Moreover, as these 'silicon islands' or 'IT hotspots' mushroom across Indian cities wherever IT talent remains untapped, increasing detachment will set in from society at large, increasing the digital divide.

In the Singapore context, the creation of science parks[4] in the mid-1980s was established for institutional purposes and economic geography. The former essentially viewed the science parks as an institution that provided assistance to its tenants in specific policy-based or mechanism-based ways. For example, does the functioning of incubators and the degree of spin-offs in science parks confer advantages to its tenant firms? The spin-offs could be job creation and the quality of employment, contribution to R&D investment and output, venture capital raised and the roles of tertiary institutions with the science parks. In contrast, using economic geography, science parks and their

[4] Science parks are defined as property-based initiatives with an organisational entity that was established to assist the growth of KBEs, that are present onsite and knowledge-intensive activities: Yuehua Zhang, 'Effecting Science Park Management for Economic Development: Tracing the 20-Year History of the Singapore Science Park for Experience and Lesson', University of Waikato, New Zealand.

surrounding regions could be viewed as an area of specialised firms that are evolving in terms of inter-firm linkages and the effects of agglomeration (Koh, Toh & Tschang, 21 April 2003). Starting from an institutional approach, the science parks in Singapore should evolve into the economic geography approach and expand through inter-firm linkages and university ties by the effects of agglomeration.

In October 1998, the Committee on Singapore's Competitiveness (CSC) emphasised four factors to enable Singapore to enhance its competitiveness. To be an effective knowledge-based economy, the CSC recommended that Singapore should strive to be a global services hub, establish a strategic partnership between local companies and MNCs, and establish a skilled workforce (*The Straits Times*, 13 October 1998). To remain competitive in the face of increasing competition, Singapore's political leaders believed that Singapore must remake its economy by changing the mindsets of Singaporeans (*Far Eastern Economic Review*, 11 July 2002). To transform Singapore into a global hub of knowledge-driven industries, knowledge workers have to fill two-thirds of manufacturing jobs and three-quarters of jobs in services. While many countries try to emulate the paradigms of the Singapore model that was successfully worked to expand economic growth and development, Singapore leaders feel that the nation can no longer remain competitive if it simply continues with past policies. It is imperative that Singapore develops core businesses that will be hard to duplicate by other economies. In Singapore's new paradigm the model of development will depend on talents to create wealth using knowledge and innovation (*Business Times*, 21 January 1999). The-then Deputy PM Lee Hsien Loong emphasised the need not only to attract foreign talent but to tap emerging opportunities and attract foreign investments.[5]

The Singapore government has invested heavily in its industrial training programmes and tertiary institutions. The emphasis has been on science and technology subjects, and Singapore has also been sending its graduates for training abroad (Mani, 2002). However, even with the in-migration of technically trained personnel from overseas on a selective basis, Singapore still faces a shortage of personnel in the R&D field. This will continue to have a dampening effect on the

[5] Speech by Deputy Prime Minister and Chairman of the Monetary Authority of Singapore, Lee Hsien Loong, at the Credit Suisse First Boston Seminar, Singapore, 26 October 1999.

creative industries that Singapore is fostering as it continues to lag behind the US and the UK in its innovative capacity.[6] To counter this disadvantage, the regionalisation of Singapore's expertise and management in terms of constructing and managing high-tech industrial parks is encouraged. Singapore companies like Ascendas have invested and constructed IT parks with Indian counterparts in various locations in India. This facet of the regionalisation strategy is aimed at increasing the revenue stream for the Singapore government and to tap the large human talent pool in India.

To augment its own limited talent pool, the Singapore government has depended on the global mobility of skilled and professional labour to recruit foreign talent. The creation of high-tech clusters would enhance the mobility of talented workers because the costs of a job search are lower (Patibalanda & Petersen, 2002). In the context of rapid technological changes where speed is of the essence to spot a growing trend or demand niche, firms in a cluster would also be motivated to hire workers with specialised skills and knowledge. Moreover, if the firms in a high-tech cluster are not competing for the small domestic market in Singapore but exporting for the international market, several advantages could occur in the cluster. Repeated interaction in a cluster between firms would create a synergy that could facilitate the contracting out of work between them depending on complementary skills (Patiblanda & Petersen, 2002). Singapore firms could also benefit from their interaction with MNCs should their skills complement each other because they could undertake joint ventures and collaborate in third countries.

In the Singapore context, what are the criteria that would be included in an analytical framework to assess growth and evolution of its high-tech clusters? Some of the criteria in an analytic framework could be growth mechanisms, technological capabilities, global role and market integration. Growth mechanisms refer to capabilities and variables that sustain a science park enabling it to grow. Technological capabilities refer to the development and strengthening of facilities in R&D. Ultimately this could lead to specific competitive advantages in select technology sectors. Other variables could include direct support from the government, an environment that encourages R&D, a committed

---

[6] Heng, Choo and Ho, 'Economic Contributions of Singapore's creative industries', Ministry of Trade and Industry, Singapore, 2003, p. 65.

management team, good infrastructure, competitive rentals and familiarity with the market.[7] Global role and market integration relate to the linkages between the region and the global or national economies, and the creation of the region's niche in the global system.[8] In the 1970s, the Singapore Science Park (SSP) was established to support the government's initiative of gearing economic development towards the exploitation of new technologies.[9]

Former Singapore Trade and Industry Minister George Yeo said, 'We have to be realistic. It would be marvelous to have lots of Singaporean start-ups. But our population base is three million Singaporeans plus one million foreigners, and we've got to do many things with that limited resource' (*International Asian Business*, 19 June 2000). Singapore is a latecomer in the high-tech industry and has to overwhelmingly locate and negotiate or procure access to resources that it is critically short of—like human capital. The process of seeking new contracts is also important for latecomer IT firms that are leveraging on their various comparative advantages. This is because not only does it replenish their cash flow but also exposes them to superior technological and organisational skills that they seek to acquire and adapt to suit their needs (Mathews, 2002).

Given Singapore's lack of land area, could the science park expand beyond the territorial confines of Singapore and leverage on the larger manpower base of the countries in the region? This has led to the development of sub-regional cooperation and linkages called 'growth triangles'.[10] Experimentation with the Singapore, Indonesian and Johor (Malaysia) (SIJORI) growth triangle was a move towards creating complementarity between Singapore and its neighbouring economies. The Batamindo Industrial Park on Batam Island (Indonesia) was developed so that Singapore companies in the manufacturing sector could move their operations offshore to reduce their manpower

---

[7] Yuehua Zhang, unpublished 'Effecting Science Park Management for Economic Development: Tracing the 20-Year History of the Singapore Science Park for Experience and Lesson', University of Waikato, New Zealand.

[8] Ibid.

[9] Ibid.

[10] 'A growth triangle is a transnational economic zone spread over well-defined, geographically proximate areas that usually parts of three countries', Min Tang, 'Growth triangles: a new approach to Asian economic co-operation', in Hafiz Mirza (ed.), *Global Competitive Strategies in the New World Economy*, Edward Elgar, UK, 1998, p. 187.

costs and at the same time provide employment opportunities for the neighbouring economies. The Batamindo Industrial Park was contiguous to Singapore's territory in that it is half an hour away by ferry and Singapore investors could monitor their investments easily. What about investing in neighbouring countries that are not contiguous to Singapore but are a four-hour flight away? Could the concept of spatial proximity be widened for investment offshore? In spatial proximity, an essential prerequisite is good information transmission and communication (Van Dijk & Rabelotti, 1997). Would distance be a problem in the process of communication and information transmission? The liberalisation of India's telecommunications sector through the New Telecommunications Policy of 1994 and 1999 (NTP 94 & 99) came at an opportune time to support the expansion of the IT industry.

The distance between Singapore and India is relatively short—a four-hour flight. However, the two countries share several other 'proximities'. Singapore and India share common cultural proximity as they have a common heritage of being British colonies, are English-speaking and there is a large minority of Indian Singaporeans (Bramanti & Ratti, 1997). Cultural, ethnic and religious networks are also important and a part of spatial proximity (Bramanti & Ratti, 1997). To facilitate and widen the network in creating trust as confidence-building measures, Singapore and India had frequent exchanges at the political level before memorandums of understanding were signed. Some of the main challenges Singapore companies face in India include the federal system of governance in India that could entail dealing with opposing political parties at the centre and state levels, the bureaucratic delays, the fragmented power structure in a democratic system, and the sheer diversity of the various regional states. India is literally many countries in one sub-continent. How could Singapore companies manage to deal with the different states in India?

The Singapore government has evaluated the potential of different regions in India and not India as a whole. Kenichi Ohmae called this process the 'Zebra Strategy' and in relation to India, no two regions are completely similar or different; hence an intimate understanding of the region is required before investments are undertaken (Ohmae, 1995). However, unlike Ohmae's 'zebra stripes' which depend on consumer preferences to vary the products being marketed and sold, in India, various states have different strengths and weaknesses that foreign investors can leverage on (Ohmae, 1995). Using the Zebra Strategy to evaluate India's strengths and weaknesses, the Singapore government has decided to focus on the software manufacturing sector in India.[11]

### *Software Industry*

How were the IT clusters able to thrive despite the infrastructure problems faced by Indian cities? Two schools of thought try to explain how the state, if at all, fostered the development of the IT sector. Some academics argued that the government had no idea how to intervene in the IT sector because it was growing too rapidly and was earning huge revenues. This policy of benign neglect was not accepted by some who insisted that the state did provide the foundations for the IT and BPO sectors to 'take off'. This school of thought argued that in 1986 the federal government announced a new software policy that included a Development Agency, export subsidies and tax holiday provisions (Contractor & Kundu, 2004). These measures were supplemented in 1988 with a Software Technology Parks (STP) scheme (Saxenian, 2002). The STP scheme was introduced by the Department of Electronic (DOE) to ensure that the infrastructure and administrative support for exporting IT services were available in India (Saxenian, 2002). Similar to an export-processing zone (EPZ), an STP provides export-oriented software firms in designated zones with five-year tax exemptions and guaranteed access to high-speed satellite links and reliable electricity. The DOE also provides basic infrastructure such as core computer facilities, reliable power supply, communication facilities including internet access, and ready-to-use office space. Firms in the STP scheme could also import all equipment without duty and import licences and have 100%-foreign ownership in exchange for a sizeable export obligation (Saxenian, 2002). In June 1991, the STP was registered as an autonomous agency, which was an indication that the DOE wanted to avoid direct government involvement but wished to facilitate the expansion of the IT sector.

After the liberalisation of the Indian economy in 1991, to facilitate the growth of the software sector, a satellite earth station was established in the southern city of Bangalore in Karnataka to enable high-speed communication services. Thereafter, India's first international gateway

[11] Interview with Singapore Consortium Official, 18 July 1999.

and network operations for IT were established at the Software Technology Parks of India (STPI) in Bangalore's Electronic City. The STPI is an autonomous society; it was established by the government under the Ministry of Information Technology for the purpose of promoting the export of computer software.[12] The STPI also facilitates links with leading international telecoms providers and has operations across more than 25 states. Besides Bangalore, other cities such as Hyderabad and Chennai have also developed their own STPs to lure both Indian and MNCs involved in the IT sector. However, Bangalore is considered to be India's leading IT hub for software exports. The Bangalore Technology Park has evolved since its inception in 1991. The original STP concept was a physical entity and companies have to hire space and export their software from these STPs. Rapidly changing technology and business conditions dictate that a virtual STP could react faster to changing business trends. In this regard, companies could acquire STP status in their chosen locations and, upon approval of their status, the STPI will grant them the STPI benefits.

A National Task Force on Information Technology and Software Development was convened to provide suggestions on how the government could facilitate the growth of the IT and software sectors. The task force suggested a number of recommendations: tax incentives, customs bonding, finance and venture capital, cyber laws, domestic market, manpower and infrastructure (Seshagiri, 1991). In 1999, India acceded to the WTO's Protocol on TRIPs (intellectual property rights) and laws were passed in India to enforce copyright (Contractor & Kundu, 2004). Following India's accession to the WTO, in October 1999, the-then Indian Prime Minister Vajpayee announced the formation of the Ministry of Information Technology (MIT) to transform India into a global IT superpower (*Asia Times*, 7 December 2000). MIT was tasked to be the nodal institutional mechanism to facilitate IT initiatives from various sources such as the central government, the state governments, academia and the private sector for the overall growth of the IT sector. MIT's main target was to implement a comprehensive plan to achieve a target of US$50 billion in software exports for India by 2008. In October 2000, India's Information Technology Act came into force,

[12] The STPI is also a licensed International Communications Service Provider and a Category A Internet Service Provider (ISP). The STPI has carrier relations with major telcos in the world including Concer, Worldcom, KDD, Teleglobe, C&W and others.

making India one of the few countries in the world and the second after Singapore to have an IT law. Regional governments in the various states also began to attract direct foreign investments in the IT industry. The various state governments took their cue from the federal government on IT matters and implemented their own IT strategies.

The attraction to the electronics and software sectors in India was due to the fact that India has the second-largest pool of English-speaking scientific manpower in the world, after the US.[13] One of the main criteria of clusters is to have a ready pool of English-speaking skilled and professional human talent which cater to the manpower needs of the cluster. The source of this manpower could originate from the universities and colleges in the state or other states in India (Preer, 1992). The public and private sector partnership is also important to ensure that the universities keep in touch with the needs of the private sector; the private sector in return assist the universities to produce high-tech workers who possess the required skills.[14] Interviews conducted with various IT companies in Bangalore and Hyderabad revealed that companies such as Texas Instruments, Infosys and Wipro provided funding and equipment to several universities in those states.[15] In addition, Indian IT companies also have exchange programmes with various universities to leverage on the R&D undertaken in various campuses.[16]

Table 5.1 illustrates that there has been a steady increase in demand for India's software exports. The Indian software development sector mainly caters to an international market and exports most of the software programs that it designs. India's trade with the global economy is also heavily dependent upon the US economy and India should diversify its economic links. After decades of neglect due to the Cold War, the thawing of India-US relations has the potential for positive spillovers, as well as for India's interaction with the Southeast Asian region (*Business Times*, 22 March 2000). The visit by US President Bill Clinton to India in March 2000—the first by an American President to India in 22 years—marked a significant realignment in India's geo-strategic and foreign economic relations (*The Hindu*, 20 March 2000). At the end of

[13] *National Conference on Software and Telecom Industries*, 11 January 1997, Windsor Manor Sheraton, Bangalore, India.

[14] Ibid.

[15] Interviews with Texas Instrument official in Bangalore, June 2004 and interview with Wipro official in Bangalore, India, June 2004.

[16] Interview with Infosys scientist, Bangalore, June 2004 and interview with Sierra Atlantic official in Hyderabad, September 2004.

Table 5.1: Indian Software Industry, 1995–2006 (US$ million)

| | 1996–97 | 1997–98 | 1998–99 | 1999–2000 | 2000–01 | 2001–02 | 2002–03 | 2003–04 | 2004–05 | 2005–06 |
|---|---|---|---|---|---|---|---|---|---|---|
| Domestic software market | 670 | 920 | 1,250 | 1,700 | 2,450 | 2,500 | 1,700 | 3,900 | 4,800 | 6,000 |
| Software exports | 1,085 | 1,750 | 2,650 | 4,000 | 6,300 | 7,800 | 9,500 | 12,800 | 17,200 | 22,500 |
| Indian software industry | 1,755 | 2,670 | 3,900 | 5,700 | 8,750 | 10,300 | 12,200 | 16,700 | 22,000 | 28,500 |

Source: NASSCOM, and High Commission of India and India Ministry of Communications and IT.

Table 5.2: Profile of Indian Software Export as Percentage, 1996–2002

| | 1996–97 | 1997–98 | 1999–2000 | 2000–01 | 2001–02 | 2002–03 |
|---|---|---|---|---|---|---|
| Percentage of export market | US 58%<br>Europe 21% | US 65%<br>Europe 20%<br>Japan 5% | US 61 %<br>Europe 24%<br>Japan 3.5% | US 63%<br>Europe 24% | US 67%<br>Europe 24% | US 69%<br>Europe 23%<br>Japan 3% |

Source: National Association of Computer Companies (NASSCOM) India.

2000, the US market accounted for 22%–25% of India's total exports to the value of about US$10 billion (*Business Line*, 14 June 2001). Significantly, of India's total exports to the US, software accounted for US$3.5 billion. India estimates that with a steady annual growth rate of 45%, India's IT services market should reach US$25 billion by 2004 and US$50 billion by 2008 (*Business Times*, 11 July 2000). However, as Table 5.1 shows, Indian software exports reached only US$17.2 billion in 2004 and US$22.5 billion in 2005.

Table 5.2 shows that the US has been India's main software export market, followed by Europe and much lower in third place is Japan. The export of Indian software at the end of 2003 was predominantly to the US with 69%, followed by Europe with 23% and Japan with 3%. The percentage share of IT exports to the US has steadily increased from 1999 to 2003. This leaves the Indian software sector highly vulnerable to the vagaries of the US economy and their European counterparts. To insulate and cushion the Indian IT industry, major IT companies have been discussing and implementing their own 'derisking' strategies. These derisking strategies include market penetration into alternative non-US IT markets, the creation of a competent and value-added Indian IT brand globally, moving into more lucrative but challenging contracts such as consultancy but maximising locational advantage for outsourcing work, and exploring niche markets when competing with global IT firms.

India exports software to about 181 countries. To facilitate more software exports to emerging markets, Nasscom signed several MOUs with countries like Israel, Singapore, Ireland, Mexico, Morocco and Myanmar in 2000. Nasscom is also exploring potential markets in South Korea, Japan, Malaysia and Australia (*Financial Express*, 2 August 2000). The CEO of Infosys in India, Nandan Nilekani, said that Indian software companies should open regional sales offices and collaborate with local partners and reconfigure their organisations to address segmented and differentiated regional markets (*Financial Express*, 2 August 2000). India's software companies and the Indian government have tried to diversify Indian software sales from the US towards Europe and or Japan. The UK is one of the largest markets for Indian IT in Europe. There are approximately 350 Indian firms in the UK, of which 275 are in the IT and software sectors (*Business Line*, 13 February 2003). To facilitate the movement of Indian employees to the UK, the British High Commission has opened several new visa application centres across India. Table 5.3 provides a brief background in terms of value of the main export markets for Indian software.

Apart from the UK market, India is seeking greater access for its software companies to other economies in Europe. Indian software exports to Germany increased from US$92 million in 1992 to US$148 million in 2000 (BBC News, 17 May 2000). Germany is also increasing its visa numbers to allow more Indian IT professionals to work in the country. Before the IT downturn in 2001, Germany had faced an acute shortage of IT professionals and had offered 20,000 work visas to compensate for the shortage (BBC News, 17 May 2000). In addition, German software companies are betting on the market potential

Table 5.3: Exports of Indian Software to Various Parts of the World (US$ billion)

| Year | North America | Europe | East Asia | Middle East |
|---|---|---|---|---|
| 2001–02 | 4.91 | 1.79 | 0.32 | |
| 2002–03 | 5.84 | 2.35 | 0.35 | 0.17 |

Source: Nasscom.

of IT in India. For example, a well-known German software company called SAP has established and expanded its development arm, SAP Labs India, by investing US$20 million in a new product development centre in Bangalore (BBC News, 11 February 2004).

Other European countries, like Belgium, are trying to position themselves as entry points for Indian companies into Europe (*Economic Times*, 25 August 2003). Some major Indian IT firms, for example, Tata Consultancy Services (TCS) are also developing offshore centres in Eastern Europe to have a greater foothold in the European market. For example, TCS has established its Budapest centre in Hungary which employs 100 people, of whom 80% are recruited locally to undertake work for one of its major clients, General Electric (*Economic Times*, 25 August 2003). TCS chose Budapest over Romania and the Czech Republic as an offshore development centre because it had comparatively better infrastructure and more computer-literate workers who spoke English (*Economic Times*, 25 August 2003). TCS's other European clients include telecoms companies Ericsson and Nokia, insurer AXA SunLife, Standard Chartered Bank and Deutsche Bank. To familiarise itself with Europe, TCS and other IT major companies like Infosys, Wipro and Satyam have developed their own European language-training programmes for their employees.[17] The trainees have to take these courses seriously because they will be examined and graded in terms of their language proficiency before they are dispatched to work overseas.

The Middle East is another emerging area for business opportunities among Indian IT companies. India has a long history of relations with the Middle East and Gulf States (Khan, 1999). The Sultanate of Oman, Bahrain, Kuwait and Iran are fast emerging as alternative markets for software produced in India (*Financial Express*, 2 August 2000). In 2003, India's Electronics and Computer Software Export Promotion Council (ESC) estimated that IT exports to the Middle East were approximately US$170 million (Indo-Asian News Service, 18 October 2002). The ESC sponsored an Indian IT pavilion at the IT Conference—called GITEX 2002—in Dubai and three Indian IT companies from the ESC delegation have confirmed their plans to establish offices at Dubai Internet City (DIC). In an interview with a middle-level Indian IT firm specialising in Global Information Systems (GIS) software in Bangalore, the company mentioned that Oman and

[17] Interview with Indian IT companies, Hyderabad, September 2004.

Qatar were its major clients. The clients from Oman and Qatar work closely with the Indian IT firm to design a security system that would track their vehicles 24 hours a day. The company official informed us that their Middle Eastern clients were comfortable in divulging sensitive information to them as specifications for the IT project because they were given permission to inspect the company unannounced at any time to gather report on the progress of the project.

When growth in the global IT market, especially in the US, plunged in 2001, India's larger IT companies such as Satyam looked elsewhere, especially to Europe, to take up the slack for growth (BBC News, 24 October 2001). The North American market is Satyam's biggest and accounted for 76.5% of its total US$271.8 million revenue in early 2000. The company has since established new centres in the UK, Singapore and the Middle East. Ideally Satyam aims to have at least 30% of its revenues coming from Europe. In 2002, it also established an office in Shanghai, the People's Republic of China (PRC, hereafter China) and developed a 10,000 sq ft software development centre at the Shanghai Pudong Software Park (*Business Times*, 3 March 2003). However, there are impediments to transacting business in China: the rising cost of software professionals, the language barrier, and the lack of clarity concerning regulatory frameworks and intellectual property (IP) protection. Nonetheless, a study by consultancy firm Gartner estimated that the Chinese software development is poised to grow from US$1.8 billion in 2002 to US$27.1 billion by 2006. In March 2002, Satyam increased its total revenue to US$378 million. Besides Satyam, India's largest IT company, Tata Consultancy Services (TCS), has also established operations in China. TCS has several offices in China: its headquarters are in Shanghai; the Beijing office will undertake marketing, legal and client relationship; and TCS will have its development centre in Hangzhou. TCS estimated that its Asia-Pacific market including China contributed about 10% of its revenue in 2003, which was over US$1 billion.

Other areas in the Asia-Pacific region like Japan and Southeast Asia are also being explored as alternative markets for Indian IT companies. For example, Satyam is looking into business possibilities in the Southeast Asian region. In general, this is consistent with India's 'Look East' Policy to engage with the Southeast Asian region (Sarma & Mehta, 2002). Though the software and outsourcing potential for the Southeast Asian region as a whole is still developing, there are countries like Singapore and Malaysia with substantial business opportunities.[18] In 2003, TCS established its Asia-Pacific headquarters in Singapore which will also cover Australia and New Zealand. The challenges faced by TCS in undertaking business in Southeast Asia are varied and are due to the diversity of corporate governance and systems in the region. In terms of transparency and regulatory framework, Singapore has an edge over Malaysia and Thailand. For example, once specifications and terms are agreed, Singapore clients generally take a 'hands off' approach in project development. In contrast, in Thailand, clients usually have their own IT professionals working alongside the Indian vendor team and this may impede the progress of the project. However, in terms of IT talent, Malaysia has a clear lead because of the large presence of Filipino IT professionals available in Malaysia's IT hub, the Multimedia Super Corridor (MSC). The downside to IT business in Malaysia is the need to acquire the MSC status that includes benefits such as tax breaks but could be costly for companies (interview with TCS official). However, establishing a presence in the region has helped TCS to expand its capabilities. For example, the company has acquired Aviation Software Development Consultancy India Limited (ASDC) from Singapore Airlines (SIA) for S$5.3 million. ASDC was a joint venture between SIA and TCS that provided SIA with the specialised skills to develop and maintain airline-related software. Apart from the ASDC acquisition, TCS has also entered into a partnership with NEC Singapore to collaborate in four key areas: security products and solutions, sale of NEC supercomputers, e-government solutions, and web integration and software development.

Japan is the third-largest IT market for Indian companies after the US and Europe but the challenges in undertaking business in Japan relate to language and cultural barriers. While Japan is a leader in the computer hardware sector, it lags behind in the development of software programs, which indicates the large opportunities available for Indian firms in Japan (*Express Computer*, 11 February 2002). It is estimated that the software sector and related services have contributed over 7.5% of the total GDP growth in India. A joint report by India's Nasscom and McKinsey predicted that by 2008, the IT sector in India could provide at least 2.2 million jobs and attract FDI of US$4–US$5 billion. The main

[18] Interview with Satyam, Singapore Executive.

component of exports refers to services rendered to other companies overseas. For example, an MNC may locate its headquarters in the US but, via satellite and telecommunications links, it is able to locate its financial and program design overseas (in India, for example) where the cost of manpower services are much lower. The offshore export component is expected to increase due to the formation of Software Technology Parks, liberalised economic policy, and visa restrictions by the US and some European countries.

When the Singapore government examined the growth of the software sector and market in India, it looked at the sector's export potential and decided that this was the sector in which it should invest its money. Bangalore has become India's equivalent of the Silicon Valley in the US, but is more aptly known as the 'Silicon Plateau', the hub of India's computer industry and software technology (*Express Computer*, 11 February 2002). Bangalore has traditionally been the hub of India's science and information technology capital.[19] The skilled and professional manpower of Bangalore comes from its 9 universities, 51 engineering colleges, 169 polytechnics and 35 Industrial Training Institutes.[20] In the computer field, Bangalore's reputation became popularly known only in the 1980s, when computer experts with Bangalore credentials began making a name for themselves overseas (*Fortune*, 14 December 1992). The state of Karnataka has an annual output of 30,000 skilled professionals of whom 8,000 are trained in IT and electronics.[21] This prompted foreign computer companies to take a closer look at the untapped potential and talent graduating from Bangalore's technological institutes. For example, Texas Instruments started a software programming operation in Bangalore in the mid-1980s. According to Richard Gall, Managing Director of Texas Instruments in India, 'We came because of the amount of talent that was available here... we couldn't hire enough software designers in Europe to meet demand and India was producing more than it could use' (*Fortune*, 14 December 1992).

---

[19] *Information Technology Park, Bangalore*, EDB Publication, 1997, p. 8.
[20] Ibid.
[21] Ibid.

### *Evolution of IT Industry in Bangalore*

In the early 1990s, Chief Minister Deve Gowde of Karnataka was supportive of the IT sector but went on to become the Prime Minister. In late 1999, SM Krishna took over as Chief Minister in Karnataka and continued the state's development as an IT hub (*Financial Times*, 1 December 1999). Krishna introduced several incentives to attract more investments like cyber parks, one-stop IT unit of approval, a convention centre built to international standards and fiscal measures. The fiscal measures included incentives such as exemption from stamp duty, 100% exemption from entry tax on computer hardware and other inputs which proved popular with MNCs. By the end of 2001, there were more than 100 MNCs in Karnataka and the cumulative investment in the software[22] industry amounted to some US$1.3 billion.

Table 5.4: Milestones in the Evolution of the IT Industry in Bangalore

| Years | Events |
|---|---|
| 1984 | Texas Instruments enters India for offshore development |
| 1986 | DOE announces software policy |
| 1991 | Software Technology Parks of India (STPI) is set up |
| 1992 | Exclusive satellite international gateway for export industry is set up |
| 1997 | Government of Karnataka announces its own state IT Policy |
| 1998 | Number of IT companies under STPI grows to 253, with total projects worth US$840 million |
| 1999 | Indian Institute of Information Technology, Bangalore (IIITB) and the KITVEN Fund are established |
| 2000 | Number of IT under STPI grows to 782, with total projects worth US$1.1 billion |
| 2001 | Number of IT companies under STPI grows to 928, with total projects worth US$1.58 billion |
| 2001 | Number of hardware companies under EHTP grows to 24, with hardware exports worth US$0.076 billion |
| 2002 | Number of IT (software) companies under STPI grows to 1,038, with total projects worth US$2.06 billion (as of May 2002) |
| 2002 | Number of hardware companies under EHTP grows to 27, with hardware exports worth US$0.17 billion (as of May 2002) |

Source: Bangalore IT website.

[22] 'Software' is a term used to refer to the instructions that direct the operation of computer equipment and information content that computers manipulate.

Following the arrival of Texas Instruments to Bangalore, other foreign MNCs such as Motorola and IBM have also established their own software-programing offices in the city (Table 5.4). Some companies like 3M have started to expand their operations in part due to the locally available managerial and technical talent (*Financial Times*, 1 December 1999). In this respect, the technical talent available in Bangalore has been able to attract foreign investors such as those from Singapore. Therefore, the Singapore government decided to base its flagship investment project, a S$670 million IT park in Bangalore (*The Straits Times*, 13 March 1996). The Bangalore IT Park, being Singapore's flagship project in India, was also a symbol, not only to advertise Singapore's capabilities to India, but to show other Singapore companies especially small and medium enterprises (SMEs) that it was possible to succeed in business opportunities in India.

### *Technology*

In the 1970s and 1980s, the Indian computer industry limped along because of its self-imposed isolation after removing International Business Machines (IBM) or Big Blue from the local market. However, this had unforeseen benefits because, free from old-legacy computer systems, India managed to leapfrog obsolete technology. For example, without IBM, there was no proprietary software base and everything became open as India turned into a Unix power. This period of technological isolation further compelled Indian companies to develop and procure indigenous technology. A number of established but unlikely firms went into the IT business. For example, companies such as Wipro, which is known more for being a producer of vegetable oil, toiletries and soaps, started to produce indigenous software products.[23] Post-1999, the returning MNCs discovered that India had homegrown expertise and talent in software development. For India to realise its ambition of being an IT superpower, it has to move up the value-added chain and be involved in strategic consulting, R&D and provide more web-based and e-commerce interactive services. Most of India's firms are engaged in generalised activities that compete mainly on the basis of costs and will have limited success in migrating to higher value-added

---

[23] Interview with Wipro Senior Manager at Wipro HQ in Bangalore, India, June 2004.

Picture 5.1: Texas Instruments, Bangalore

work. The dilemma is this—to dispense with low-end work could mean a reduction in profits and focusing on innovative and creative work will mean increasing expenditure on R&D.

Following the norm, technology-intensive firms in the early stages of their product lifecycle tend to locate around major research universities to leverage on technology transfer opportunities. However, as the firms mature, in-house capabilities and R&D will begin to rival and even exceed university-level research. In this instance, the firms will rely on other factors such as the local environment, land costs or regulations (Galbraith & De Noble, 1992). To ascertain how technology influences the development of the IT cluster in Bangalore some trends should be examined. These could include the type of capital equipment used that governs the level of sophistication of machinery or production processes. The end-product is also dependent on the level of R&D required at the design stage (Galbraith & De Noble, 1992). Indian spending on R&D has to increase. The Indian IT industry has to recognise the importance of innovation and creativity in order to create a position of strength and move up the value chain. Indian firms tend to classify miscellaneous spending under the category of R&D, thereby inflating the dismal figure of true R&D spending. Nonetheless, there are some Indian IT companies, such as Bangalore based-Silicon Automation Systems Limited (SAS), that have become well known in the system chip business. While Indian IT companies have been reluctant to spend on R&D, MNCs have no such qualms and are leveraging on Indian talent for innovation and creativity. For example, Indian engineers in MNCs have moved into the chip-designing niche. Multinationals such as Texas Instruments (TI), National Semiconductors and Intel are increasing their numbers of microchip designers in India. For example, TI has the largest chip-design centre in Bangalore and is expected to recruit up to 2,000 engineers in 2002–07. The company has close links with tertiary institutions in Bangalore and employs about 75 engineers in India every year. TI and other companies like DCM Data Systems and Philips are also working with educational institutions to help design the curriculum that will be most useful to them after the students graduate.

### *Technology Transfer—Indian IT Parks*

What could the Singapore consortium offer to Bangalore? On show to the world at the Bangalore IT Park are Singapore's capabilities in the designing, planning, constructing and managing of industrial and technology parks. Furthermore, Singapore companies will manage the Bangalore IT Park after its completion to ensure the necessary follow-up actions and to train locals to manage the IT Park.[24] The management personnel at Bangalore IT Park have all been trained by Ascendas and all are locally recruited except the Chief Executive who is from Singapore. There is a great deal riding on the potential and success of the Bangalore IT Park. This is because the Indian central government and Karnataka state government hope that the Bangalore IT Park will attract further foreign investments to the state and to other regions in

[24] Interview with Consortium Official 18 July 1997 and interview with CII Director for Southeast Asia, 10 June 1997.

India.[25] According to a former CEO of ITPL, the three key areas in which Singapore has extended assistance to its Indian partners are in the area of planning, method of construction and management.[26] It was estimated that the Indian construction industry and its expertise were 5–20 years behind the demands and expertise of modern construction.[27] The assistance extended by the Singapore consortium to its Indian partners in the planning stage involved imparting knowledge on the demands of a high-tech manufacturing facility. This included all aspects of manufacturing operations at the Bangalore IT Park such as loading and unloading of supplies, water and electricity supply, movement of goods within the facility, raised flooring and lighting requirement. The Singapore consortium extended assistance to its Indian partners in the area of construction methods by essentially mechanising the labour-intensive methods of Indian construction. Architects and engineers from Construction Industry Development Board (CIDB) and Jurong Town Corporation (JTC) in Singapore were flown to Bangalore to ensure that proper procedures were implemented during the construction of the Bangalore IT Park to maintain quality control. Particular attention was given to technical drawings of the Bangalore IT Park in order to prepare a programme of construction in proper stages so that building work progressed rapidly. The programme of construction was important because it gave an indication as to the type of equipment that should be installed in the proper sequence with the estimated time of completion for each stage. The management of construction stressed on two fundamental areas of quality and operational efficiency. For example, sub-contractors that were hired to install lighting fixtures were given a fixed date to start and finish their work in order to prevent them from damaging other fixtures already in place should they start or finish on a different date. Another example was the fire and laboratory safety factor of the Bangalore IT Park which required a higher-than-normal standard of construction.

Since there was a significant amount of technology transfer from Ascendas Land to Indian conglomerate Larsen & Toubro Limited (L&T), L&T gave its full cooperation to the Singapore consortium.[28] The level of technology transferred was sufficient to enable the Indian

---

[25] Interview with Senior Consortium Official 16 July 1997.
[26] Ibid.
[27] Ibid.
[28] Ibid.

builder L&T to start building other industrial parks on its own in India.[29] The transfer of technology to host countries was one of the key objectives of the Singapore government during its regionalisation drive, through which Singapore and the host countries would benefit. During the construction phase of the Bangalore IT Park, the level of government-to-government cooperation was crucial to the project. Ascendas Land assumed the apex role in the Singapore consortium once the Bangalore IT Park was under way.

Problems that the Singapore consortium has encountered include the Indian administrative and management system. For example, cash flow in India is very tight (unlike in Singapore) due to the relatively higher cost of borrowing in India.[30] Therefore, there were inadequate spare components available at short notice and this was a cause of some friction between the Singapore consortium and the Indian builders. In Singapore, there are usually reserve funds on short call that can be used to meet unexpected demands but this was not the case in India. In addition, Singapore builders are generally used to working on projects at a faster pace than Indian builders who seem more 'casual' about shortfalls and not meeting expected deadlines for completing different stages of the project. The Bangalore IT Park is a compact and integrated construction that has workshops and laboratories in high-rise flats. This construction is different from what the Indian builders were used to—Indian construction companies usually build low-rise structures and factories that sprawl over a large compound. Although differences over business and work ethics emerged, these were resolved, as can be seen in the building stage of the Bangalore IT Park in the next chapter.

The Bangalore IT Park is a unique type of industrial park as it is the first of its kind in India to consolidate and integrate IT operations that will tap into the 'Silicon Valley' potential of Karnataka.[31] The Bangalore IT Park is about 27.4 hectares in size and was financed as a joint-venture project by the private sectors from Singapore and India (*The Straits Times*, 26 November 1993). A consortium of six Singapore companies had a 40% stake in the Bangalore IT Park project. One of India's biggest industrial conglomerates, Tata Corporation, has 40%

---

[29] Interview with Senior Consortium member, 12 August 1997.
[30] Interview with Singapore Consortium official, 13 October 1997.
[31] Interview with Singapore Consortium official, 18 July 1997.

and the Karnataka state government owns the remaining 20%.[32] The Bangalore IT Park was developed in two stages over three years. The IT Park comprises office and high-tech production units, including two blocks reserved by American multinationals IBM and AT&T.[33] In addition, there is a residential section with 520 freehold condominium units, a clubhouse and variety of retail outlets. The mixture of tenants includes foreign MNCs, and Singaporean and Indian companies involved in high-technology and IT research activities.[34] Within a week of the Bangalore IT Park's launch, firm enquiries for 30% of its space were received (*The Straits Times*, 14 September 1995). The first phase of the Bangalore IT Park was completed before the Business Process Outsourcing phenomenon hit India in early 2000 after the scare of the Y2K event had passed. The process of mitigating the adverse impact of Y2K has also proven to the world that India has very skilled and competent IT workers who are paid much lower wages than their counterparts in the developed countries.

*IT Parks and Business Process Outsourcing*

While Singapore managed to build the Bangalore IT Park, the complementarity with the Indian economy in terms of India's large human resource base was justified with the Business Process Outsourcing[35] (BPO) phenomenon. The BPO boom in India has been significant because from hardly anything in 2000, employment in India's BPO sector reached nearly 1.3 million by 2005. By the end of 2005, India's software and BPO exports reached US$23 billion (*Business Times*, 11–12 February 2006) from US$11 billion in 2003 (*Times of India*, 3 December 2004). The BPO sector is on course to achieve annual outsourcing exports of US$60 billion by 2010 based on 33% growth per annum (*Business Times*, 11–12 February 2006). At the World Economic Forum in Davos, Switzerland, among the 102 countries listed, India was

---

[32] The consortium of five Singapore companies are: L&M Properties and RSP Architects, Technology Parks, Singapore Technologies Industrial Corporation, Sembawang Construction and Parameswara Holdings: ibid.

[33] Interview with Senior Singapore Consortium official, 12 August 1997.

[34] Ibid.

[35] 'Outsourcing' is defined as the delegation to another authority—the insourcer—of the authority for the provision of services that is done under a contract that incorporates service-level agreements: Dimitris N Chorafas, *Outsourcing, Insourcing and IT for Enterprise Management*, Palgrave, MacMillan, UK, 2003, p. 5.

ranked third in terms of the availability of engineers and scientists.[36] The BPO/IT-enabled Services (ITES) boom has hit India in a big way because manpower costs remain the last major component in MNCs which could be reduced by innovative measures.

In line with the thinking of MNCs across many countries, cities and time zones, the main preoccupation is driven by profits and companies could save on labour costs by exploiting the production possibilities of telecommunications and IT in India (Wilson, 1998). Bangalore has become the home of India IT, including BPO services for exports and at least one-quarter of all IT exports from India come from the city. A study by Nasscom and KPMG to evaluate the leading ITES-BPO clusters in India that included 10 states has ranked Karnataka first on the list. The criteria for the evaluation framework included the following: assessment of human resources which includes number of graduates, average salary for ITES and attrition among others; the prevailing infrastructure, such as the availability and cost of facilities and utilities and the quality of life; the profile of ITES services provided such as the number of companies, nature of ITES work, policy support and positioning; the presence of support groups like local industry associations; and lastly, the physical features of the cluster like geographic location which will denote the space available for expansion.[37]

India's IT and outsourcing industries have overcome several problems including the 9/11 terrorist attacks which has reduced the number of H1-B visas for Indian IT professionals going to the US, opposition to Indian IT firms bidding for projects from US MNCs because of security, and the IT meltdown in 2001–02 (*Economic Times*, 22 April 2003). Another problem to hit the Indian outsourcing industry was the backlash against the loss of jobs in the US and Europe. In 2003, a study by Forrester Research Inc predicted that by 2015, the US would have lost 3.3 million service sector jobs to other countries including India (*Omaha World Herald*, 11 August 2003). The politicisation of outsourcing was again responsible for complaints against the misuse of L-1 visas in the US. The L-1 visa is a category in which workers from low-wage countries are brought to the US through inter-company

[36] 'India's strength: Knowledge resources', rediff.com, 28 November 2005, URL: http://www.rediff.com/.

[37] Correspondent, 'Karnataka, top BPO destination in India', Rediff.com, 9 June 2004, URL: http://www.rediff.com/.

transfers and, it is alleged that some of them have been loaned out to other companies in the US (*Business Line*, 4 July 2003). The debate continues for outsourcing because while it causes job flight, the savings from outsourcing have breathed new life to struggling US MNCs (*Rocky Mountain News*, Denver, Colorado, 12 July 2003). However, other MNCs have outsourced jobs to India to lower their costs and increase profit margins. For example, UK insurance firm Royal & Sun Alliance has shifted 1,100 jobs from the UK to save more than US$18 million every year (BBC News, 11 October 2004).

As of 2004, more than 77 MNCs had established their R&D centres in Karnataka and the state is still ranked among the leading seven states in India for human development capabilities. Karnataka's institutions produce around 28% of India's IT professionals and more than 20,000 people are employed in the ITES-BPO sector. The state has also taken positive measures to encourage the ITES industry, for example, the Millennium IT policy that offers incentives such as tax exemptions for 10 years, entry tax exemption for computer hardware, computer peripherals and other capital goods. In addition, the entire state has been networked with fibre optic cables. Most of Bangalore's ITES industry is concerned with financial services, technical support and insurance claims processing. Given its potential for R&D work, many companies are leveraging on Bangalore for value-added work BPO activity that is termed 'knowledge process outsourcing' (KPO).

### *Knowledge Process Outsourcing*

In a study completed by the CII called 'India in the Knowledge Economy', KPO work has been projected to reach US$17 billion by 2010. Areas with significant potential for KPO include pharmaceuticals, biotechnology, ICT, legal support, intellectual property, R&D, and development for automotive and aerospace industries (*Deccan Herald*, 20 June 2005). Indian IT firms are moving up the value chain by offering more sophisticated services to customers in the US, Europe and Asia. For example, Indian accountants are preparing tax returns for Americans and financial analysts in Mumbai are preparing brokerage reports for Wall Street firms in the US (*USA Today*, 2 August 2004). There was a 45% growth in India's R&D investment during 2002–04, valued at US$6.8 billion. The government sector undertakes 85% of all R&D through its research laboratories and public sector units (PSUs). For example, the Council of Scientific and Industrial Research (CSIR) has some 38 laboratories and 80 polytechnology transfer centres (*Asia Times*, 9 September 2005). From 2000 to 2004, more than 230 MNCs had established R&D laboratories in India (*Asia Times*, 30 October 2004). These high-tech companies are coming to India to create innovative ideas by recruiting young graduates from India's universities and elite technological institutes (*New Scientist*, 19 February 2005).

Once undertaken in the US, laboratories in Bangalore are undertaking cutting-edge research for General Electric, Texas Instruments and Cummins (*USA Today*, 2 August 2004). General Electric Capital International Services (GE) started operations in India in 1997. Since 2000, GE has hired Indian scientific and engineering talent to work on R&D projects. These are in areas of electronic and electrical systems technology, ceramics and metallurgy, catalysis and advanced chemistry, polymer science and new synthetic materials and power electronics. Another MNC, Nortel, also decided to hire Indian scientific and technical power because India was producing competent engineering and programming graduates in the thousands who spoke English. While the motivation for Nortel was access to graduates with the best and brightest skills, the company managed to save on manpower costs. In comparison, Indian graduates receive about 30% of equivalent wages in relation to their US counterparts.

In addition, Indian expatriates are returning to India to help in this KPO revolution because they envisage better prospects for themselves in India than in the US or Europe. These returning members of Indian Diaspora have a large part to play in the returning brain drain that will impact positively for India. These people are a valuable resource pool because they have a variety of skills and expertise in product management, project management, marketing and other skills essential for product development (*Economic Times*, 2 November 2004). An Ireland-based market consultancy firm calling itself Research & Markets reported that innovation in India is being driven by the R&D budgets of major technology companies investing in their development centres in India. The top 10 infotech companies in the world that include Microsoft, Intel, Oracle and Texas Instruments have their second-largest development centres in India. According to Research & Markets, the R&D outsourcing market for IT in India will likely grow from US$1.3 billion in 2003 to over US$8 billion by 2010. The demand for chip engineers is growing at the same rate as for software engineers. Bangalore plays host to a number of these infotech firms—Intel, Texas Instruments and Oracle. Texas Instruments (TI) was the first to establish its R&D centre in Bangalore in 1985 and has over 200 patents to its credit. TI's Bangalore operations will employ at least 2,000 IT professionals by end-2007.[38] The company has the largest development centre in the chip design area and the bulk of its digital signal processing is done out of India (*Economic Times*, 30 September 2002).

Oracle has more than 6,400 people in its operations in Bangalore and Hyderabad, working on the company's database, development tools, application servers and e-business. The company filed 10 patents in 2002 but by 2004, it had more than 125 patents (*Asia Times*, 30 October 2004). Consumer giant Philips will invest more than US$500 million from 2004 to 2009 to expand its Philips Innovation Campus (PIC) in Bangalore. Philip's expansion will increase its employee numbers to 2,600 by 2007. Intel's largest development centre outside the US is in Bangalore, India, and employs 1,800 people (*Economic Times*, 13 April 2004). Its development centre in Bangalore was established in 1999 and is creating hardware designs for Intel microprocessors and chipsets, design and development of next-generation Ethernet switching silicon, network processors and enterprise software (*Asia Times*, 30 October 2004). The company is planning to expand its Bangalore development centre to work on more next-generation products. According to its Director, Sales and Marketing for South Asia, RK Amar Babu, Intel is on an expansion spree with the completion of its first building in the new campus in Bangalore that could accommodate 1,000 people and work has started on the second building (*Economic Times*, 13 April 2004).

AOL Time Warner Inc has also expanded its global operations by establishing a joint venture called iPlanet E-Commerce Solutions in Bangalore. The joint venture is between Sun Microsystems Inc, which is renowned for network computing, and AOL's portal and web-browser unit Netscape (*Washington Post*, 6 March 2001). AOL's set-up has hired scores of Indian engineers to develop e-commerce services and software targeted at corporate markets. Other smaller infotech firms, like the US company, 3Com Corporation, and German industrial giant, Siemens, have also established R&D set-ups in Bangalore. 3Com established its R&D centre in a partnership with start-up firm Mars Telecom. This new

[38] Interview with TI marketing executive, TI premises, Bangalore, June 2004.

centre will complement 3Com's R&D facilities in the US, the UK and Taiwan. Siemens also envisages conducting high-end futuristic research in medical, IT and security animation for its Bangalore centre (*Asia Times*, 30 October 2004). Another factor that will encourage India's rise as a KPO is the links that the returning Indian Diaspora has with Silicon Valley in the US. The professional and social networks that have been established in the US such as The Indus Entrepreneurs (TIE) have been encouraging its members to return to India to establish start-ups. Since 2000, hundreds of Indian entrepreneurs have returned to India from the US and have started their own business (*Businessweek*, 8 December 2003). The rise of India as a KPO hub is further evident as hundreds applied for positions with MNCs like Microsoft and Juniper Networks Inc for job openings in India (*Businessweek*, 8 December 2003). The rise of India as a KPO hub has been credited for saving infotech companies from bankruptcy during the IT meltdown. For example, web-hosting software firm Ensim Corp relied on its 100-strong engineer team in Bangalore to keep designing lower-cost new products right through the IT downturn (*Businessweek*, 8 December 2003).

The move away from low-cost but lucrative BPO work into more innovative but risky KPO work is a dilemma facing Indian IT companies, especially for the major players TCS, Wipro, Infosys and Satyam. Value-added KPO work involves R&D, huge amounts of investments, and the returns in terms of patents and innovation are not guaranteed. However, KPO work is more lucrative and prestigious and should be attained by India's major IT companies if they are to be taken seriously. For example, one of Europe's largest banks, ABN Amro, outsourced a US$2.2 billion project in 2004 as a means to save US$335 million and reduce its workforce (*Asia Times*, 8 September 2005). About 3,200 jobs will be shed and at least 2,000 jobs will be transferred to vendors in India. The US$2.2 billion outsourcing contract was awarded to IBM and two Indian companies—TCS and Infosys (*Asia Times*, 8 September 2005). However the biggest share of the project went to IBM at US$1.8 billion, while TCS was awarded US$260 million and Infosys received US$140 million. While this could be looked at as a positive development for the Indian outsourcing industry, the bottom line is it was IBM—not the two Indian vendors—that was entrusted to look after the entire IT infrastructure and network of the bank (*Asia Times*, 8 September 2005).

While Indian IT companies have managed to grow their outsourcing business by double digits compared with competitors like China, Russia, Singapore and the Philippines, there is room for improvement. President of Nasscom Kiran Karnik has said that Indian companies are focused on custom application development and application outsourcing, which accounted for only 10% of the global IT services market (*Business Line*, 13 February 2003). According to Karnik, Indian companies have negligible presence in service lines like network infrastructure management, IS outsourcing, IT training and education, hardware support and installation. With the mainstreaming of outsourcing activities, Indian companies have to penetrate new segments like systems integration (accounted for 22% of global IT services market). Other significant markets are in packaged software support and installation (accounted for 13% of the global market) and IT outsourcing (accounted for 18% of the world market) (*Business Line*, 13 February 2003).

Is it possible for Indian IT firms to ascend the technology food chain? An Indian IT company called Mind Tree Consulting located in Bangalore is viewed as a leading indicator of whether Indian companies have the ability to graduate into the more advanced and lucrative reaches of the technology industry (*New York Times*, 26 March 2001). Founder of Mind Tree is Ashok Soota, the former vice chairman of Wipro who helped India's drive in the early 1990s to become the back office of the computer business by writing software codes for big US companies. Mind Tree has won assignments from Lucent Technologies and BP Amoco, and was designing web-based reservations system for Avis, a unit of Cendant. It is also advising Harvard University on ways to promote sports events on the internet. Apart from e-commerce projects, Mind Tree also advises companies such as Cisco Systems, Alcatel and Fujitsu on network management issues (*New York Times*, 26 March 2001).

India's development as a serious KPO player is also dependent on the perceptions that potential customers have of Indian IT companies. In this regard, the branding of Indian IT will be significant in terms of marketing business value and competitive edge that Indian IT verticals are offering to global enterprises (*Express Computer*, 24 March 2003). While Nasscom has taken the lead to build an Indian brand that is synonymous with IT, other trade federations like the Confederation of Indian Industries (CII) have taken on the challenge to develop a larger

Indian brand. The CII has established a subsidiary company called the India Brand Equity Foundation (IBEF) to promote the Indian brand overseas.[39] Efforts made by IBEF to promote a new India was evident by its campaign called 'India Rising' as an emerging economic power at the WEF Davos Meeting in Switzerland in November 2005.

India has some 229 universities and 458 engineering colleges and some (such as the 7 Indian Institute of Technology (IITs)) are comparable to the Ivy League universities in the US. The IITs accept only 3,000 students of about 400,000 applicants; this is far fewer proportionately than the Ivy League acceptance ratio. Besides the IT sector, other occupations in India are steadily developing, such as management and business graduates. In this context, Singapore-based employers must be willing to pay competitive salaries because Indian professionals are in great demand across the world. IT professionals in the US can expect to earn a starting salary of S$45,000 and supervisors could earn as much as S$130,000. Moreover, with rising incomes in India, the competition for Indian IT professionals has become more acute with the fast-disappearing disparity between Indian and overseas salaries. To compete with India as a rising BPO hub, Singapore could emerge as a 'hub and spoke' model in the globalisation of services. Singapore has become a BPO offshoring hub that has extended its spokes to not only India but China and the Philippines. Singapore's Infocomm and Development Authority (IDA) is keen to prevent the country from outsourcing all its service sector jobs overseas and tries to encourage companies to retain complementary jobs in Singapore with those BPO jobs in India.[40]

How would Singapore and India complement each other in the BPO industry? India has depth and breadth of professional and technologically skilled labour, who are available at low cost and are fluent in English. Skills in the English language facilitate communications with the developed English-speaking countries like the US and the UK. While its general infrastructure needs improvement, India has made great strides in its telecommunications sector and the establishment of IT Parks across India. Singapore could be complementary to India in several ways, such as a free trade agreement with the US and a highly advanced transport and internet infrastructure. Singapore has competent and transparent markets and a judicial system with strong intellectual

[39] Interview with CII representative in Singapore, 12 February 2006.
[40] Interview with Singapore IDA official in Singapore, August 2004.

property rights. For example, Indian IT companies like Polaris Limited, when drafting contracts for software exports, will include clauses for the arbitration of disputes in Singapore. Singapore also has sophisticated managerial talent attuned to Western standards and provides a more attractive location to Western managers than India. Singapore could also provide services in the areas of regulatory compliance, auditing, data security and risk mitigation which support call centres and back-office work.

In 2000, according to Singapore's then Minister for Trade and Industry, George Yeo, with instantaneous communications, distance matters less. Sony, for example, is a company that has exploited the advantages of BPO. Sony India was established as a 100% export-oriented software development centre (SDC) in 1997 and provides support for Sony Systems Design International (SSDI) and other companies of the Sony Group worldwide (*The Straits Times*, 18 January 2000). On a typical project, 40% of the work time is spent on design and configuration, and 60% on decoding work. SSDI drives the project and takes care of the accounts and management activities. A development team is maintained in Singapore to design and work out customers' needs and these specifications are then sent to the India office. The India office starts programming and coding processes and first-level testing. Using this operational system, the SSDI has gained tangible benefits by leveraging on India's talented pool of IT engineers, achieving faster turnaround times for projects, and better project control while retaining system and software knowledge. As a result, SSDI was not able to assume higher valued-added activities. SSDI could now develop CD-ROM infotainment titles and upgrade its technologies. The self-contained and first world feature of the IT Park has benefited SSDI. SSDI's Director, Kee Eng Hock, explained that the office environment is better than the average in India with stable power supply, leased lines and upgrading facilities.

A Singapore company that has outsourced to India is Rotary Engineering Limited (REL), a Singapore mainboard listed ISO9001 that has established operations in Bangalore. REL is a turnkey company that provides specialist services for the oil, petroleum, chemical and petrochemical industries (*The Straits Times*, 18 January 2000). In 1997, REL established a 100%-owned subsidiary company in India called the Rotary MEC Engineering (India) Private Limited (REI). This company supports REL's engineering capabilities in Asia, including providing design and detailed engineering services for projects as well as the role as REL's India HQ-sales and coordination office. REL Chairman, Chia Kim Piow, said that the cost of maintaining an engineer at Bangalore was 30%–40% less than in Singapore. In this regard, to encourage Singapore companies to move into India to explore business opportunities and utilise Indian talent like in the IT sector, the Singapore government encouraged its GLCs to develop a flagship project in the IT sector.

# CHAPTER SIX

# INNOVATIVE IT CLUSTERS: THE BANGALORE CASE

## *Bangalore Cluster*

Why was Bangalore chosen as India's silicon plateau? Part of the answer lies in the historical decision to turn Bangalore into India's city of the future by the country's first Prime Minister Jawaharlal Nehru. In the 1950s and 1960s, large public sector enterprises like Bharat Electronics Limited (BEL) and Hindustan Aeronautics Limited (HAL) were established in Bangalore by the government. Together with national defence laboratories and the Indian Institute of Science, they formed the crux of Bangalore scientific foundations. In the 1970s, the Indian Space and Research Organisation (ISRO) and Bharat Heavy Electronics Limited (BHEL) were also established in Bangalore. In the 1980s because of the rising rent and land prices in Mumbai, an influx of industrialists relocated the high-technology parts of their businesses to Bangalore. Table 6.1 illustrates the main events that have transformed Bangalore into India's IT capital. With its strong base of government defence labs, such as those developing aeronautical technology and the presence of automotive and electronics companies, Bangalore was provided with a suitable environment for the take-off of the IT industry in the mid-1980s. This process of clustering high-tech companies and R&D set-ups provided the foundation for innovation. It could be argued that, for various reasons, the government had chosen Bangalore to stimulate technology innovations.

## *Infrastructure*

The lack of infrastructure and 'bottlenecks' had prevented the timely imports of materials and exports of components, causing computer MNCs such as Hewlett Packard to move its 400 million manufacturing unit from India to China (*Deutsche Presse Agentur*, 6 August 1997). Table 6.1 indicates the level of investments that India has to allocate for infrastructure development. India's Finance Minister has drawn up

Table 6.1: Investment Required in India's Infrastructure (US$ billion)

| | 1996–2000 | 2001–06 | 2006 |
|---|---|---|---|
| Investment required | 115 to 130 | 130 to 215 | 267 |

Source: MG Srinath, 'Infrastructure reforms holding India's economic progress', *Deutsche Presse Agentur*, 6 August 1997 and US$267 billion required in infrastructure by 2006, *Economic Times*, India, 17 May 2001.

Table 6.2: Infrastructure Costs Projection for India in Specific Sectors by 2006

| Infrastructure by 2006 | Costs of expansion | Projected increase |
|---|---|---|
| Electricity | US$178 billion | 1,11,500 MW |
| Telecoms lines | US$55 billion | 52 million connections |
| Roads | US$27 billion | |
| Ports | US$7.3 billion | |

Source: 'US$267 billion required in infrastructure by 2006', *Economic Times*, India, 17 May 2001.

an ambitious plan to develop four major sectors of India infrastructure: power, telecommunications, roads and ports.

Table 6.2 shows the projected costs and areas of infrastructure expansion. The Singapore government realised that infrastructure facilities in India, for example, electricity generation, road networks, railway lines and telecommunications, are inadequate to support a 'mega' project like the Bangalore IT Park (EDB, 1995).

Bangalore suffers from a power deficit and 'brown-outs' are quite common, prompting the need for businesses to have their own captive electricity generators, which increases the costs of their operations; but there is no alternative for the foreseeable future. The transportation networks in Bangalore could also be improved, especially its roads, which were not designed to accommodate the huge increase in the volume of motorised vehicles. Bangalore's image as an IT hub from the point of view of foreign investors also suffered when it was shown that the state government was poorly equipped to handle the massive floods which inundated the state in early June 2004. Table 6.3 illustrates the information and electricity-generating network in Karnataka.

Table 6.4 shows the transportation networks and export processing zones (EPZs) in Karnataka. Although Karnataka has some 134,000 kilometres of road networks, they need to be expanded and upgraded to attract more MNCs and foreign investment. Potholes along main roads,

Table 6.3: Information and Power Network in Karnataka, 2002

| Infrastructure | Unit of Measurement |
|---|---|
| Power deficit | 4,000 million Kwh |
| Plant load factor | 64.9% |
| Installed captive capacity | 15.5% |
| Projected power deficit | –20.8% |
| Tariff industrial | Rs 1.77/kwh |
| Number of phones | 560 733 |
| People per phone | 80.25 |
| Phone services | DOT, Hughes Ispat |
| Cellular services | Modi Communications |
| Radio paging | Arya, Hutchison Max |

Source: Government of Karnataka.

Table 6.4: Infrastructure Network in Karnataka, 2002

| Infrastructure | Unit of Measurement |
|---|---|
| Railway track length | 3,089km |
| Domestic airports | 6 |
| International airports | 1 |
| Cities linked | Ahmedabad, Calcutta, Delhi, Mumbai, Thiruvananthapuram |
| Road length | 133,987km |
| National Highway Length | 1,968km |
| Ports | 2 (New Mangalore, Port Karwar) |
| Industrial zones and parks | 23 |
| Export processing zones | 1 |
| State-identified priority sectors | Electronics, informatics, pharmaceuticals, telecoms, leather and leather products |

Source: Government of Karnataka.

crumbling pavements and badly maintained drains and storm-sewers seem to be a common sight in the city centre.

The long drawn-out tender and selection process to construct a new international airport in Bangalore is also reflective of the slow process of decision-making that discourages MNCs and foreign investment (*Business Times*, 17 July 1998). The congestion of Bangalore's main roads and the government's inability to plan for an increased volume of traffic adds to the lost manpower costs. This has resulted in the major IT companies consolidating their operations in self-contained campus-like facilities on the city's outskirts. Captive power-generating plants are also the norm in IT 'hotspots' such as the Bangalore International Technology Park Limited (ITPL) and Electronics City.

### *Self-contained IT Cluster*

The Singapore consortium, which included Jurong Town Corporation's subsidiary Ascendas Land, decided to develop a high-tech park of which JTC has particular expertise in. JTC pioneered the high-tech park concept (*Business Times*, 3 April 2000). Singapore was attracted to Bangalore because of its potential as India's 'Silicon Valley' but it had to overcome the lack of full infrastructure support for the Bangalore IT Park.[1] According to the CEO of the Bangalore IT Park, Jonathan Yap,[2] as time progressed, Ascendas through its subsidiary the International Tech Park Bangalore (ITPB) realised that it had to invest in its own power-generating plant to ensure a continuous supply of power and for the expansion of the IT Park. The ITPB has invested in a 12.5MW dedicated power plant (DPP) and the DPP operates in synchronisation with the Karnataka Power Transmission Corporate Limited to ensure high reliability. As the decision had been made to have the IT Park self-contained, it was built with its own water, electricity and telecommunications facilities (Picture 6.1). This would also satisfy the stringent requirements needed to placate the anxiety and concerns of MNCs wanting to occupy the IT Park but which fear the unreliability of infrastructure facilities in Bangalore. Furthermore, the various amenities would enhance the quality of life of the knowledge workers, and residential apartments were also built onsite. The quality of life is also a main criterion for the creation of a technopolis such as the IT cluster in Bangalore (Preer, 2002). However, this would increase considerably the costs of the construction project. Debating the advantages and disadvantages of the Bangalore IT Park, the Singapore government and consortium decided to proceed with its construction.[3] The profile of the Bangalore IT Park is shown in Picture 6.2. The mixture of buildings in the Bangalore IT Park can be categorised into three main groups.

---

[1] Interview with Singapore Consortium member, 18 July 1997.

[2] Presentation by Jonathan Yap, CEO, Ascendas India, 'The Ascendas IT Park Story', at Conference on 'Connecting India', Asia Pacific Business Summit, 12–13 April 2006, Singapore.

[3] Interview with EDB official, 20 May 1997.

Picture 6.1: Office Buildings at Bangalore IT Park

The four-storey factory and production area that were designed for light industrial use covers a total floor area of 57,000 square metres. In addition, there will be six 12-storey high-tech office blocks, four 8-storey mid-rise and eight 22-storey high-rise residential blocks.

The 12-storey high-tech office blocks house corporate management staff and software research, and have a total floor area of 112,000 square metres. The mid-rise and high-rise residential blocks were meant for engineers, management staff and expatriate staff on secondment. These blocks have a total floor area of 131,790 square metres comprising 764 units/flats with floor areas of about 150 square metres, and the units are to be sold only to the tenants and employees of the Bangalore IT Park. According to the former chief executive of Information Technology Park Limited (ITPL), Allan Yeo Hwee Tiong, 'The Park had been designed for technology-oriented Indian and foreign companies involved in electronics, information technology, telecommunications and related industries' (*The Straits Times*, 25 January 1997). This limited the options of the Bangalore IT Park and made it vulnerable to the changing business environment of the high-tech industry worldwide over which it has no control.

Bangalore IT Park was constructed over two to three years because the project was enlarged from a SGD$200 million to a SGD$670 million

Picture 6.2: Bangalore Information Technology Park

| | |
|---|---|
| Location: | Bangalore, capital of Karnataka state, 18km from Bangalore City, 12km (20 minutes) from Bangalore Airport. |
| Size: | 27.2ha (69 acres built up—room for expansion)<br>Five completed buildings, nearly 2 million sq ft of business space, 200-room Taj Palace Hotel under construction |
| Employment: | Projected employment 15,000 (As of 2005: 19,300) |
| Companies: | As of 2005: 126 companies |
| Industries: | High-tech facilities for software development, R&D work<br>Light clean manufacturing, eg electronics, telecommunications and related industries. Technical support centre, sales and marketing offices. |

project (*The Straits Times*, 8 September 1995). According to Allan Yeo Hwee Tiong (former CEO of ITPL), the initial project was expanded as a result of 'strong interest from MNCs, Singapore companies and also Indian companies' (*The Straits Times*, 25 January 1997). Taking into account the interest shown by Singapore and Indian companies, the original plans for the project had been modified to incorporate better designs, improved offices and additional facilities requested by potential investors (*The Straits Times*, 25 January 1997).

Table 6.5: First Phase of Bangalore IT Park

| Production | 318,250 sq ft | Opened December 1997 (Remarks) |
|---|---|---|
| Office | 651,410 sq ft | |
| Commercial | 200,000 sq ft | |
| Residential apartments | 150 units | |
| Clubhouse | 56,366 sq ft | |
| | | The Bangalore IT Park was officially opened in 2000, by the-then Singapore Prime Minister Goh Chok Tong. |

Source: Parameswara Holdings Ltd Shareholders Report, 10 July 1997.

The Bangalore IT Park was initially planned for completion in two stages. The first phase of the project costing SGD$230 million (*The Straits Times*, 4 April 1997) was completed by end-1995 and was ready for occupation at the same time (*The Straits Times*, 26 November 1993). However, the date of completion was extended to March 1997 and then to September 1997 (*The Straits Times*, 8 September 1995). There were essentially two causes for the delay. There were problems attributed to the acquisition of the land for the building of the Bangalore IT Park and bureaucratic impediments. The Bangalore IT Park was built on land that used to be mango and coconut farms. The state government was fully supportive of the Bangalore IT Park project and cleared legal obstacles that delayed its completion by several months (*The Straits Times*, 8 September 1995). Moreover, according to a director at Parameswara Holdings, the inability of the Indian partners to acquire more land when the project was enlarged meant that they had to build upwards to increase the amount of space for industrial and commercial use. The construction of multi-storey industrial and commercial complexes as a new form of technology in India increased the construction cost of the Bangalore IT Park.[4] The Singapore consortium faced more hurdles in terms of the approvals needed and the different management styles encountered in India during the construction of the Bangalore IT Park, which further delayed its completion.[5] According to a staff member

[4] Interview with Singapore consortium member, 20 July 1997.
[5] Interview with Singapore consortium member, 20 July 1997.

of the Singapore consortium, numerous accounts of 'red tape' were encountered during the construction phase of the Bangalore IT Park. This is because the central government still plays an important role in controlling the approval of permits for basic amenities like electricity, gas and water supplies.

Although fully supportive of the project, the state government had no authority to grant the approval of basic amenities for the Bangalore IT Park. Therefore, the requests had to be transmitted to New Delhi, which wasted time and effort. However, the Karnataka state authorities did support various other requests from the Singapore consortium and told them which bodies to approach to get the permits approved. Furthermore, there was no central coordinating agency in India that handled requests seeking governmental approvals. The bureaucratic obstacles became more confusing with the change in government at the federal level in the mid 1990s. With each change of government, there will be changes to the ministerial appointments. Opposition political parties will take turns to discredit newly appointed ministers and stall economic development. In India, politicians have to maintain their vote-banks, which are essentially their political support groups (Hardgrave & Kochanek, 1986). In order to keep the continued support for their vote-banks, politicians have opposed economic projects based on non-economic grounds. For example, a particularly powerful vote-bank were landlord farmers who, as in the case of the Bangalore IT Park, tried but failed to deter the completion of the IT Park.

During the construction of the Bangalore IT Park, the Singapore consortium had to confront and deal with many obstacles, leading them to the realisation that conditions in India are very different to those in Indonesia, as when they built the Batam Industrial Park.[6] In the high-tech electronics industry, a few months delay was a great deal and this potential problem was not adequately addressed when the initial project was enlarged. A staff member of the consortium complained that the initial project of SGD$200 million should have not been changed and the Bangalore IT Park should have been completed by the end of 1991 at the latest. The longer-than-expected completion of the project missed the growing trend in the property market in Bangalore and the upswing in the international electronics market. The property market in Bangalore is not as 'rosy' as it was in 1994–96. Moreover, the global

[6] Interview with Singapore consortium member, 18 July 1997.

electronics market has seen a downturn since the start of 1996 which lasted for two to three years.

### *Amenities*

The amenities at the Bangalore IT Park include the following:

- Banking and ATM facilities
- Book store
- Courier service
- Cyber parlour
- Food and beverage outlets
- Foreign exchange services
- Handphone service
- Insurance service
- Laundromat
- Legal service
- Lifestyle store
- Medical and dental clinics
- Music store
- Optician
- Photoshop
- Stationery store
- Supermarket
- Travel agent

Pictures 6.3 and 6.4 show the underground supermarket and shops at the IT Park. The business centre at the ITPB has an incubation centre for companies which would like to start operations immediately but which are waiting for a permanent office space.[7] The facilities available at the business centre comprise cabins, suites, discussion rooms and a conference room. Other services include secretarial support and video-teleconferencing facilities.[8] The health club at ITPB has a fully equipped gym, an aerobics studio and a steam room. The management support services of the IT Park include a computerised raised flooring system, landscaped surroundings, 24/7 security coverage with

[7] Interview with ITPB Official, Bangalore, June 2004.
[8] Interview with ITPB Official, 16 June 2004.

Picture 6.3: Underground Shopping Mall, Bangalore IT Park

Picture 6.4: Amenities at the Bangalore IT Park

TV monitors, satellite dish, utility supply, emergency generator and estate management.

### *Marketing*

The initial occupancy rate at the Bangalore IT Park was around 30%, whereas the projected figure was 50% (*The Straits Times*, 18 July 1997). In December 1998, this had improved to 50% despite the Asian Financial Crisis (*The Straits Times*, 14 December 1998). After the 'IT bubble' burst in the late 1990s, interest in ITPB increased because of the gradual recovery of the IT sector post-2000 and the 'Y2K' scare. While volatility in the global IT industry remained, events such as the Asian Financial Crisis and the recovery of affected economies indicated a new-found optimism in the IT industry tempered with realistic expectations. On the marketing of ITPB, members of the Singapore consortium were concerned that the investments they had ploughed into the Bangalore IT Park would not be repaid, especially if the IT bubble were to burst. At the time, companies that had committed themselves to occupancy at the Bangalore IT Park were: Siemens Components, Hitachi Asia, Singapore Medical Centre, Singapore Technologies, Singapore Software Centre, Rotary Engineering, RSP Architects, Times Bank, Canara Bank and Stallion Travel (*Parameswara Shareholders Report*, 10 July 1997). The initial composition of this group of companies indicated a strong representation of Singapore companies. The other companies were Indian-owned.[9] The lack of interest shown by foreign MNCs was disturbing given that the IT Park was originally enlarged based on strong demand by Singapore, Indian and foreign MNCs. However, this demand weakened because of the marketing strategy and the delayed completion of Bangalore IT Park.

According to a potential investor in the project, the concept of the Bangalore IT Park is economically and technically sound but the projected date of completion missed the growing trend in the electronics sector and dragged into a period of uncertainty for the IT industry. For example, Hewlett Packard had originally indicated interest in occupying one of the commercial blocks at the Bangalore IT Park but then

[9] Comment made by Mr M. Rajaram, Chairman of the Singapore Indian Chambers of Commerce and Industry (SICCI) at Connecting India, An Asia Pacific Business Summit, 12–13 April 2006, Singapore.

declined in June 1997 and decided to invest in China instead.[10] The company decided against siting a US$400 million inkjet printer factory for logistical reasons. The competitive advantages that Bangalore could offer were not adequate to override the problems of road and port 'bottlenecks'.[11] The question that is pertinent here is how Hewlett Packard (hp) was able to extricate itself from a commitment to the Bangalore IT Park near to its completion.

The problems indicated that the marketing of the Bangalore IT Park was responsible for allowing potential investors to renegade on their verbal promise to occupy the Bangalore IT Park. The marketing target for occupancy was set at 50% by the time the Park opened for operation in November 1997.[12] The marketing strategy was problematic because the Singapore consortium did not adopt the standard practice of marketing the Indian way. It is generally the norm in India that the construction of industrial projects requires downpayments at each stage of construction to ensure the commitment of investors to the project.[13] The marketing strategy adopted by the Singapore consortium was to build and complete the Bangalore IT Park without financial commitment from the companies interested in occupying the IT Park. Therefore, some companies (such as Hewlett Packard) chose to invest elsewhere because they were not financially committed to the Bangalore IT Park. MNCs have to meet their own planning and production schedules. Therefore, they cannot afford to wait for the completion of any project beyond a certain deadline and would have to resort to other alternatives. Moreover, MNCs from the US and Europe, as a business practice, do not purchase property as they prefer to lease property so they can shift their operations elsewhere when change becomes necessary.

---

[10] Interview with G. Srinivasan, General Manager, Soohans Group of Companies, 23 July 1997.

[11] Japanese electronic firms have also complained that the roads, ports and railway systems are so overburdened that freight remained undelivered for days: Dan Biers and Shiraz Sidhva, 'Life in the Slow Lane', *Far Eastern Economic Review*, 21 August, 1997, pp. 71–72.

[12] Interview with Singapore consortium official, 20 July 1997.

[13] Interview with Singapore consortium official, 20 July 1997.

Table 6.6: Bangalore IT Park/Land-Use Profile Residential, Commercial and Recreation Use

| Plot land use | Lot size (sq m) | Built-up area sq m | Site coverage (%) | Plot ratio | Building height (ft) | Car park provision |
|---|---|---|---|---|---|---|
| Residential | 73,224.17 | | 12 | 1.85 | | 700 |
| 8 blocks of high rise Condominiums Total 656 units @ 150m$^2$/unit | | 120,750.00 | | | 18,20,22 | |
| 4 blocks of mid-rise Condominiums @ 150m$^2$ per unit | | 11,040.00 | | | 8 | 64 |
| Amenities | | 3,953.70 | | | | |
| Subtotal | 73,224.17 | 135,743.70 | 12 | 1.85 | | 764 |
| Commercial Recreation club Serviced apartments | 23,746.16 | 23,000.00 | 23 | 0.97 | 4 & 8 | 225 |
| Subtotal | 23,746.16 | 23,000.00 | 23 | 0.97 | | 225 |
| Grand total | 96, 970.33 | 158,743.70 | 15 | 1.64 | | 989 |

Source: Bangalore, Bangalore Information Technology Park, L and M Investments Private Limited.

This strategy of being mobile and an aversion to tying up capital to reduce production costs was also overlooked in the marketing strategy of the Bangalore IT Park.[14] Table 6.6 indicates the plot land usage of the Bangalore IT Park. The slow take-up rate for the IT Park was also due to price—Indian entrepreneurs had voiced their concern that the Bangalore IT Park's services were more expensive compared with other locations in Bangalore.[15] While MNCs and foreign companies could afford the relatively higher prices quoted by the IT Park, many of the Indian companies were reluctant to buy space at high rates. Indian businessmen have informed the Singapore government that they can find cheaper alternatives to the services provided by the Bangalore IT Park and do not seem to be overly impressed with the high-tech outlook and character of the IT Park. For example, within Bangalore City

[14] Interview with Singapore consortium member, 23 July 1997.
[15] Interview with Singapore consortium member, 23 July 1997.

itself, office space could be found at Rs 15–20psf, whereas the Bangalore IT Park offered Rs 40psf (*The Straits Times*, 14 December 1998). The Singapore government and consortium replied that quality, reliability and efficiency of service would command a higher service and that cheaper alternatives would disadvantage Indian firms in the long run (*The Straits Times*, 14 December 1998). The self-contained facilities at the Bangalore IT Park surpasses those of its rivals such as those in the city of Hyderabad in Andhra Pradesh state. However, not all Indian firms require sophisticated technology, and using older technology would be more cost-effective for most firms. The high rates at Bangalore IT Park did not seem to reflect the general market rates in India and this was one main reason why Indian companies looked at alternative IT sites such as Cybercity in Hyderabad (*The Hindu*, 3 November 1998). While competition was a worry for the promoters, they agreed not to compromise on standards and concluded that if the Karnataka state government was able to provide the basic infrastructure facilities in the coming months, they were confident of a further 30% sale in spaces.

Acknowledging the marketing problem of the IT Park, the International Managing Director of Jurong Town Corporation (JTC) said, 'Initially we were targeting big-name MNCs. Then we started marketing on a much broader front after getting MNCs as anchor tenants' (*The Straits Times*, 14 December 1998). The effort to attract Indian companies was successful in persuading a giant software company Wipro[16] to lease 80,000 square feet. According to JTC, Wipro's arrival at Bangalore IT Park indicated that Indian companies believed they were obtaining value for money despite the higher lease prices (*The Straits Times*, 14 December 1998). The entry of Wipro signalled a change in fortune for Bangalore IT Park. Another Indian software giant, Infosys Technologies Limited,[17] also started showing interest in Bangalore. In fact, Infosys, India's largest software company with sales of US$181 million at end-1999 and a market capitalisation of almost US$21 billion, developed its own industrial park in Bangalore (*Business Times*, 21 January 2000).

[16] Wipro has over 20 years of experience in IT consulting, systems integration and engineering services. It has 30 offices worldwide, 13,000 IT professionals and services more than 300 companies worldwide, 50 of which are Fortune 500 companies. In 2001–02, Wipro's revenue was US$736 million, it was ranked 7th in terms of software services worldwide, and has a CMM Level 5 company status.

[17] Infosys has worldwide offices and employs 10,000 IT professionals. It is listed on the NASDAQ and had revenues of US$545 million at end-March 2002.

Wipro and Infosys are beneficiaries of the Indian Finance Ministry's hands-off policy, which abolished procedural requirements such as 'track record' scrutiny (this essentially means checking the level of profits made by companies). This enabled Indian companies to source for funds in foreign equity markets without obtaining prior government approval (*Business Times*, 21 January 2000).

The attractions of Bangalore—its trained workforce and 'Silicon Valley' potential—were too tempting for the Singapore government and consortium to ignore. However, constructing Bangalore IT Park as a self-sufficient project entailed several difficulties: obtaining the necessary approvals required to generate its own electricity supply, and having its own water-treatment plant and its own satellite dish for communication purposes. Unlike Singapore's earlier experiences in developing industrial and science parks in Indonesia, China and Vietnam, the Indian project was more complicated. Dewang Mehta (the late executive director of India's National Association of Software and Service companies (Nasscom)), with reference to the ITPB commented, 'If the take-up is lower than expected, it is not the fault of the Park management but because of Bangalore's own infrastructure constraints that are annoying investors' (*Business Times*, 21 January 2000). However, this was beyond the control of the Singapore consortium, which could only persuade the Karnataka state authorities to upgrade their existing facilities as quickly as possible.

### *Economic Crisis and Bangalore IT Park*

The marketing woes of the Singapore consortium were aggravated by the Asian economic crisis in 1998 that burdened the consortium and the Tata Group with punishing interest rate payments. To counter this problem, the Singapore consortium and the Tata Group decided to inject fresh equity of Rs 2.8 billion (S$117.6 million) into the project, over a period of two years; this would see the partners' share of equity rise from 40% to 46.5% each, while the Karnataka state government's share would be scaled back from 20% to 7%. However, the Karnataka state government retained its level of board membership and was given a seat on the executive committee of the Bangalore IT Park. Demonstrating its continued commitment to the project, the Karnataka government through the Karnataka Industrial Areas Development Board (KIADB) injected Rs 130 million into the IT Park.

While the promoters of the IT Park acknowledged that the Asian Financial Crisis had adversely impacted on investments from Southeast Asia, they believed there was still an investible pool of funds available in Singapore. They believed many Chinese entrepreneurs in Singapore were interested in taking a closer look at investment opportunities in India. However, India should go on a fast-forward mode and remain committed to the economic liberalisation drive. Comparisons have been made between China and India, and one of the key comparisons concerned the time needed to establish a company in India. The necessary approvals in India could take years because of a 'bottom-up' approach due to India's democratic style of governance. Consensus has to be sought from all parties in India before a project proposal can be approved and implemented. In comparison, China works on a 'top-down' approach that is similar to the governance style in Singapore. Approvals and permits can be obtained within a matter of weeks in China and a factory can start producing goods within a matter of months.

### *Information Technology Park Investment Private Limited (ITPI)*

The injection of capital was implemented through a separate holding company called Information Technology Park Investment Private Limited (ITPI).[18] ITPI consisted of the various Singapore consortium members that owned 40% of the Bangalore IT Park.[19] The rest of the Bangalore IT Park is owned by Tata Corporation (40%) and the government of Karnataka (20%) as shown in Table 6.7 (Parameswara Holdings Ltd, Shareholders Report, 10 July 1997). The CEO of ITPI was Ms Chong Siak Ching, who was concurrently the General Manager of Arcasia Land Private Limited, and was in charge of the marketing and maintenance of the Bangalore IT Park.

[18] Information Technology Park Investment Pte Ltd is a company incorporated in the Republic of Singapore and has its registered office at 4 Second Chin Bee Road, Singapore 2261, Joint Venture Agreement, 28 January 1994, p 1.

[19] These Singapore companies among them have considerable experience and expertise in the business of establishing, developing, operating and managing IT business parks in Singapore and the Southeast Asian region: ibid., p 2.

Table 6.7: Partners in Bangalore IT Park

| Company | Percentage of share owned |
|---|---|
| Tata Corporation | 40% |
| Government of Karnataka | 20% |
| Information Technology Park Investment Pte Ltd (ITPI)<br>Consisting of:<br>A: Technology Parks (Arcasia) Pte Ltd—40%<br>B: Sembawang Industrial Corporation—20%<br>C: L & M—14.9%<br>D: RSP Architects—15.1 %<br>E: PHL—10.0% | 40% |
| Total | 100% |

Source: Parameswara Holdings Limited, Shareholders Report, and Joint Venture Agreement, 28 January 1994.

### *Information Technology Park Limited*

To administer the daily functions of the IT Park, the Tata Corporation, ITPI and the Karnataka state government have formed a separate company called Information Technology Park Limited (ITPL). ITPL will oversee the project implementation, management and eventual marketing of the Bangalore IT Park. Figure 6.1 illustrates the linkages between Information Technology Park Limited (ITPL) and the three partners developing the Bangalore IT Park. ITPL was headed by a senior member of staff from the Singapore consortium and the deputy is a senior staff from Tata Industries. The CEO is Singaporean Kang Kok Hin who was the Deputy Chief Executive and took over the helm at ITPL from another Singaporean Cheang Kok Kheong (*The Straits Times*, 19 April 1996). Cheang Kok Kheong was the Chief Executive of ITPL from 1994 when he took over the helm from another Singaporean (Alan Yeo Hwee Tiong) until June 1997 (*The Straits Times*, 19 April 1996). The Singapore consortium was heading ITPL because of the new technology and expertise that the consortium was introducing into India. According to Cheang Kok Kheong, the main functions of ITPL were to maintain and improve the property management system at the Bangalore IT Park. In order to manage it efficiently, the senior engineers employed by ITPL were sent to Singapore for two weeks' attachment to various government bodies such as the CIDB and the JTC to learn preventive maintenance. ITPL also ensured that the Karnataka state government was involved in the management of the Bangalore IT Park (*The Straits Times*, 25 January 1996). The inclusion of the Karnataka state government by ITPL in its operations was important because the state government was able to resolve land use problems associated with the IT Park.[20]

As CEO of ITPL, Cheang Kok Kheong also had to select key staff members to handle the daily operations at the Bangalore IT Park. The completion of the IT Park required regular meetings to assess progress reports. Since the company board of ITPL was not able to meet on a regular basis, an executive committee was formed to monitor its progress. The executive committee comprises the representatives of the various companies of the Singapore consortium, Tata Industries and the Karnataka state government. According to a staff member from the Singapore consortium, the formation of an executive committee for projects undertaken by Singapore companies overseas is standard practice. The EDB is also represented at the executive committee meetings to monitor the progress of the Bangalore IT Park project. The executive committee meets once a month, alternately in Singapore and in Bangalore. The Chairman of the executive committee is Major-General (NS) Lim Neo Chian, a former senior military officer of the Singapore Armed Forces (*The Straits Times*, 24 January 1997).

### *Countering Negative Perceptions*

The problems encountered by Enron Corporation made the Singapore consortium realise that it was fortunate to have dealt with the Janata Dal Party of Prime Minister Deve Gowda in Karnataka.[21] In order to prevent future problems from arising with the management of the Bangalore IT Park, the Singapore consortium has established ITPL. However, the formation of the ITPL has not eradicated completely the negative perception that Singapore investors have in general about investing in India. Members of the Singapore consortium have expressed concern about the marketing aspect of the Bangalore IT Park. Furthermore, it

---

[20] Interview with Singapore consortium official, 18 May 1997.
[21] Interview with Singapore consortium member, 20 July 1997.

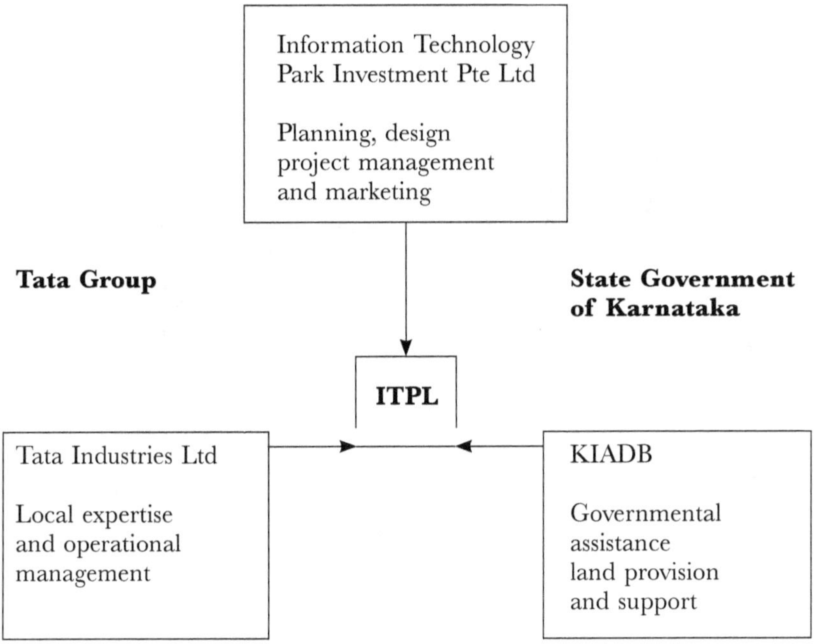


Source: Interviews with Singapore consortium staff and brochures on Bangalore IT Park.

Figure 6.1: Information Technology Park Investment Private Limited (ITPL) Singapore Consortium (ITPI)

has been difficult to convince Singapore investors to invest in India.[22] However, the Singapore consortium is fully supportive and committed to the Bangalore IT Park. It has already spent millions on its construction and does not want to abandon the project.[23] Phase Three of the ITPB is ongoing and, according to Jonathan Yap, a sixth building is being drawn into the expansion plans for the Park. Picture 6.5 shows Phase Three of the IT Park with the construction of the fifth building called Inventor; the other four buildings are Discoverer, Innovator, Creator and Explorer (*Ascendas Press Release*, 10 April 2007). As of April 2007, the ITPB had six buildings, with the latest named Navigator; it is the largest at 400,000 square feet bringing the total built-up area to 2.3 million square feet over 20.3 acres of land (*The Straits Times*, 12 April 2007).

[22] Interview with Singapore consortium official, 20 July 1997.
[23] Interview with Singapore consortium member, 20 July 1997.

Picture 6.5: Bangalore IT Park—Phase Three

The new building Navigator can accommodate up to 4,000 employees and had some 80% occupancy at its launch. Thus far, Ascendas has spent about S$330 million on the ITPB but it may develop another 3 million square feet of space at the ITPB over another 26 acres in the next phase at a cost of an additional S$270 million (*Ascendas Press Release*, 10 April 2007). A 200-room five-star business hotel located at the ITPB is expected to be operational in 2008. According to Minister Tharman, 'when it [ITPB] was launched, it was a very bold step. Today, the IT Park Ascendas is building in Dalian, China, is drawing lessons from Bangalore' (*The Straits Times*, 12 April 2007).

There is potential for the economic linkages between India and Singapore to expand further, but the ability of the two governments to generate excitement about investment prospects is constrained by the negative political images the media portrays of India. In the early stages of the ITPB's development, the frequent changes in the Indian government were particularly worrying for the Singapore investors, as they could just as easily invest in relatively more politically stable economies such as Malaysia, China and Vietnam.[24] The physical distance

[24] Interview with Singapore consortium official, 18 July 2007.

Picture 6.6: STD Booth, Bangalore

between India and Singapore is another problem because Bangalore is not as accessible from Singapore as Johor Bahru in Malaysia (a car ride) or Batam in Indonesia (a ferry ride) (interview with Singapore consortium official, 18 July 2007).

### *Indian Diaspora in Singapore*

The emerging trade relations and economic integration between India and Singapore is rooted in historical linkages. The founder of modern Singapore, Sir Stamford Raffles, established the administrative and legal systems both in Singapore and India. These systems were derived from British law and the British Civil Service (Speeches, Vol. 18, No. 4, July–August 1994). Furthermore, during the British Raj, many Indians mainly from the south of India migrated to Malaya, then consisting of Malaysia and Singapore.

The emerging Singapore-India trade relationship highlights the importance of the non-resident Indians (NRIs) as there are a number of prominent businessmen in Singapore of Indian origin. The Singapore government aims to build on informal relationships between private organisations into something more formal at the government-to-government level between India and Singapore. This is because formal contacts between India and Singapore are needed for the strategic purpose of enhancing economic complementarity (Chakravarthi, 1994). Formal contacts strengthen economic complementarity between India and Singapore by initiating and creating conditions that create more informal contacts. Formal contacts occur when the government identifies a need to establish a range of relationships with another country (Chakravarthi, 1994). For example, during the 1993 Indian Entrepreneur Conference in Singapore, cabinet ministers represented the Indian and Singapore governments. However, the conference provided a suitable environment for the 500 delegates to expand their personal contacts.

The-then Singapore Minister for Trade and Industry, BG George Yeo, said, 'India and Singapore can strengthen each other's international competitive position. We should build on the existing economic links between Bombay and Singapore and exploit established networks whether this be Marwari, Parsee, Sindhi, Khoja, Bhora or whatever' (Speeches, Vol. 17, No. 1, January–February 1993). Cultural links between India and Singapore were strengthened when BG George Yeo and the Indian Minister for Human Resources, Arjun Singh, signed a Memorandum of Understanding (MOU) in New Delhi in January 1993 (Chakravarthi, 1994). The signing of the MOU was followed up with rare Indian art exhibitions and the visits of Indian cultural groups to Singapore. For example, the National Museum of Singapore hosted the Alamkara Exhibition.[25] The exhibition brought to Singapore artefacts from the National Museum in New Delhi, including the casket containing the Buddha's relics (*The Straits Times*, 10 September 1994). The Alamkara Exhibition displayed more than 300 exhibits covering 5,000 years of Indian history (*The Straits Times Weekly Edition*, 16 July 1994).

India and Singapore have also institutionalised a greater strategy of increasing India awareness in Singapore. For example, the High Commission of India in Singapore organised a week-long event called 'Celebrating India' from 10–16 April 2006 to promote and showcase various aspects of India. These included fashion shows, fine arts performances, conferences and bazaars. Therefore, in addition to economic complementarity, there is also an element of cultural affinity. The ethnic factor is increasingly conspicuous in Singapore's business environment (*The Straits Times*, 30 May 1993). This is because there are various ethnic-based chambers of commerce in Singapore that maintain and

[25] 'Alamkara' is a Sanskrit word meaning to adorn or to decorate.

promote trade linkages with regional countries: the Singapore Chinese Chamber of Commerce, the Singapore Indian Chamber of Commerce, the Singapore Malay Chamber of Commerce and the Singapore International Chamber of Commerce. The Singapore government is returning to its 'roots' in an effort to expand its economy. This approach was previously used in Singapore's trade strategy with China. In its trade linkages with China, Singapore's mainly ethnic Chinese businessmen spearheaded the trade linkages between the two countries (*The Straits Times*, 30 May 1993).

Similarly, Singapore has a sizeable minority of Indians among its population. The Singapore government is keen to use this cultural approach to strengthen its trade linkages with India. The-then Singapore Minister for Information and the Arts, BG (NS) George Yeo, said, 'There is a lot of India in Singapore that makes Singapore very different from a city like Hong Kong. We want to enhance this Indian facet of Singapore' (*Speeches*, Vol. 17, No. 1, January–February 1993). According to Adit Jain (Managing Director, Economist Intelligence Unit in India), cultural affinity enhances the prospects of 'networking' which further changes the perceptions of India held by Singapore investors.[26] These, in turn, enhance the prospects for economic complementarity between Singapore and India. Singapore investors and businessmen are changing their perceptions of India as a result of cultural exchanges, seminars, conferences and official visits from India. Furthermore, economic complementarity provides the momentum for economic regionalisation as proposed by the Singapore government.

Joel Kotkins (1992) argued that the Indian Diaspora was an asset whose potential has not been fully realised by those in India. The Indian community in Singapore is approximately 200,000 strong and forms about 7% of the population (*The Straits Times*, 19 June 1996). They are mostly from the southern states of India and speak Tamil, which is one of the four official languages of Singapore. The most influential Indian family in Singapore are the Thakrals, who have offices in 23 countries—from Lagos to Sydney—and an annual turnover exceeding US$1.5 billion (*The Straits Times*, 19 June 1996). The Thakrals have established factories in China: they manufacture Panasonic video-cassette

[26] Adit Jain, Managing Director, Economist Intelligence Unit, New Delhi, 20 May 1997. According to Adit Jain, India is being increasingly seen as a viable market for foreign investment through the process of 'networking'.

recorders under licence from Matsushita in Shanghai and assemble 21-inch colour TV sets in Chengdu for the Chinese markets (*The Straits Times*, 6 January 1997).

According to the managing director of the Thakral Group, Inder Bethnal Singh, Thakral has a Direct Investment Division (DID), which identifies and invests in projects with strong earnings potential. The Thakral Corporation adds US$10–15 million annually to the DID to top up its funds. According to Inder Bethnal Singh, of the initial US$25 million in the DID, much was depleted in 1997 for investments made at the Gurgaon Technology Park in Haryana state in India and other projects in Australia. The presence of Singapore NRIs is another connection with India. Kenichi Ohmae (1995) has also commented on the importance of ethnic linkages between Singapore and India to deepen Singapore's ties with software-based, high-tech industries in India. However, Ohmae did not elaborate on the ethnic connection or 'people-advantage' between India and Singapore. The Singapore government has taken advantage of the ethnic ties between India and Singapore to ensure that its investments in India progress according to plan. The Singapore government ensured that it had at least one company that was run by an ethnic Indian among the Singapore consortium to understand the Indian business psyche.[27]

Parameswara Holdings, as part of the Singapore consortium developing the Bangalore IT Park, has an authorised capital of US$20 million and a proposed paid-up capital of US$10 million (*Business Times*, 15 April 1993). Moreover, the company is also positioning itself to initiate a capital venture capital fund to buy equities on India's stock exchanges (*The Straits Times*, 9 June 1993). Parameswara provides the cultural aspect of the Singapore consortium and not only functions as a 'spearhead' for Singapore investors in India, but more importantly functions as an intermediary to ensure smooth relations between Singapore investors and their Indian counterparts.[28] The company screened foreign investment proposals from Singapore investors and businessmen to ensure the viability of their projects. The main criterion used as part of the screening process was that potential Singapore investors have a local Indian partner because the latter would know the Indian market better. This criterion was part of the government principles for the regionalisation

[27] Interview with Singapore consortium official, 18 July 1997.
[28] Interview with Singapore consortium official, 8 May 1997.

strategy cited by the-then Prime Minister Goh Chok Tong (Interview with Singapore consortium official, 8 May 1997).

According to a staff member of the Singapore consortium, Parameswara's ability was not limited to opening doors for Singapore business. The company was also able to resolve problems given its well-placed connections with the Karnataka state and the Indian federal government. The Chairman of Parameswara Holdings, Mr S. Dhanabalan, and Vice-Chairman, Mr M. K. Chanrai, are equally well-received in both New Delhi and Bangalore. Apart from its networking abilities, Parameswara Holdings had also acquired financial capabilities to spearhead investments into India. Mr M. K. Chanrai said that the holding company was negotiating with several Indian banks to form a consortium to provide financing facilities for projects identified in India. This was part of the Singapore government's principles of regionalisation to provide financial credit to Singapore companies to venture overseas. The banks approached included the Indian Overseas Bank, Indian Bank and United Commercial Bank. Parameswara Holdings also has strong linkages to the Singapore government. In January 1994, S. Dhanabalan, the former Minister of Trade and Industry, replaced M. K. Chanrai as Parameswara's chairman. In response to questions fielded by reporters, Dhanabalan said that some Indian Singapore businessmen had asked him to take up the position as they 'needed someone to hold the different groups involved together' (*The Straits Times*, 7 April 1993).

Dhanabalan's appointment was seen to reflect another pro-government stance in the Singapore consortium.[29] According to a Parameswara director, Dhanabalan's appointment as the company's chairman was timely as he brought credibility to the holding company.[30] Although Dhanabalan is no longer a cabinet minister, his personal contacts and stature ensure that Parameswara Holdings is accorded accessibility at the highest official level in India (Interview with Singapore consortium official, 14 August 1997). One of Dhanabalan's first actions as chairman was to organise and lead a team visit to India in December 1994 (*The Straits Times*, 26 November 1994). Dhanabalan said that the visit 'would give me an opportunity to touch base and get the feel of the country'

[29] The induction of Dhanabalan was to give the SICC more status in the eyes of Indians in India. Dhanabalan's close relationship with the government is the main reason he was appointed to head SICCI in spite of having little trade experience on India.

[30] Interview with Singapore consortium official, 14 August 1997.

(*The Straits Times*, 26 November 1994). One of the key features of the visit was to evaluate investment projects in New Delhi, Bombay and Bangalore (*The Straits Times*, 24 November 1994). Dhanabalan and his team looked at projects that included the development of an industrial park in Noida, neighbouring New Delhi and the airport project in Karnataka (*The Straits Times*, 24 November 1994). While assessing the investment opportunities in India, Dhanabalan also emphasised that Parameswara's board of directors would team up with large companies with the relevant expertise and know-how in Singapore as well as in India for its ventures. Furthermore, Parameswara is implementing the fusion concept of the EDB and using corporate networking to link with other companies with complementary capabilities for specific joint projects. In looking for Indian partners that would complement its capabilities for joint ventures, Parameswara is lowering its risks by working with Indian companies that know the Indian market well. This seems to be a prudent move as Dhanabalan has identified a few areas of concern for investors such as the labour laws in India.[31] Dhanabalan commented that manufacturers could find it difficult to lay off workers because of Indian labour laws. Furthermore, potential investors from Singapore might find it difficult to evict errant tenants (*Business Times*, 26 November 1994).

### *Tata Group of Companies*

The problems in dealing with a newly emerging Indian market prompted the Singapore government to advice Singapore companies venturing into India to form joint ventures with Indian companies. The underlying rationale being that Indian companies would know the Indian market better and would be able to guide and advice their potential Singapore partners around the pitfalls and problems in investing in India. In this context, the Singapore consortium decided to cooperate with India's Tata Group of companies to develop the Bangalore IT Park. The partnership was crucial because Tata was the leading force

[31] Dhanabalan observed that while there are reasons to be optimistic about the investment scenario in India, manufacturers might find it difficult, if not impossible, to lay off workers because of labour laws: Gerry de Silva, 'Dhana: Parameswara not restricted to India', *Business Times*, 26 November 1994, p. 48.

in acquiring the necessary approvals for the Bangalore IT Park.[32] The Tata Group of companies had requested approval from the Foreign Investment Promotion Board (FIPB) of India by citing the complementary and compatability of the IT Park project with the long-term vision to expand Bangalore city's credentials as the 'Silicon Valley' of India. Moreover, in terms of resources and trained personnel, Bangalore offers cost advantages and a ready supply of trained workforce compared with other cities in India.

There are two main reasons why the Singapore government chose the Tata Group as its Indian partner to develop its first flagship project in India. Firstly, Tata is a large and well-known Indian corporation with assets of US$5 billion (*Business Times*, 17–18 September 1994). It comprises 100 companies and subsidiaries, including three of India's top 10 companies.[33] Included in the Tata Group of companies are consultancy firms that specialise in software development, engineering and infrastructure-related projects. Moreover, the Tata Group is well entrenched in the IT sector with successful joint ventures with IBM, Unisys and Honeywell. Furthermore, Tata Consultancy Services (TCS) is one of India's largest software export firms with annual revenues that totalled over US$4 billion at end-2006, up from US$100 million in 1994. There was a natural complementarity between the Tata Group and the Singapore consortium in building the Bangalore IT Park, through corporate networking and the fusion concept. Moreover, the Tata leaders knew the Singapore political and economic leaders well, and was one of the first firms to respond to Singapore's call for foreign investment in the early 1970s (*Business Times*, 17–18 September 1994). In the 1970s, Ratan Tata, Chairman of the Tata Group, established Tata Precision Industries in Singapore. This was followed by the establishment of a computer manufacturer, Tata Elxsi, and a biotechnology firm, Plantek, in the early 1980s (*Business Times*, 31 December 1991). Ratan Tata commented: 'I have always been a great admirer of the Singapore government and hence I maintained an informal relationship

[32] Letters from Tata Group of Companies to the Foreign Investment Promotion Board of the Government of India, seeking and receiving approval for the joint venture project, the Bangalore IT Park.

[33] *Proposal for the Development of an Information Technology Park in Bangalore in Association with Information Technology Park Investment Private Limited*, Singapore and Government of Karnataka, Tata Industries Limited, December 1993.

with officials at EDB and DBS for many years' (*Business Times*, 17–18 September 1994).

In 1992 the relationship between Ratan Tata and the EDB initiated the concept of the Bangalore IT Park project when Ratan Tata received a phone call from Philip Yeo, Chairman of EDB. Ratan Tata recounted: 'I have known Philip for a number of years. So when he told me that the Singapore government was interested in investing in an industrial park in India, I suggested he visit Bangalore' (*Business Times*, 17–18 September 1994). Ratan Tata and Philip Yeo visited Bangalore a few months later and met the chief executives of several companies in India. Ratan Tata commented: 'We quickly came to the conclusion that establishing an industrial park was not going to be feasible because the scale of operations was too small' (*Business Times*, 17–18 September 1994). The scale of operations required for an industrial park were far larger than that envisaged by the Singapore consortium because of problems in acquiring more land for the Bangalore IT Park. M Rajaram, a director of Parameswara Holdings, explained that a feasibility study was carried out to assess the potential of Bangalore which indicated that the level of prevailing infrastructure was inadequate to support industrial parks. However, according to Ratan Tata, 'But it was obvious that what would work in Bangalore was a white-collar driven high-technology park along the lines of Silicon Valley' (*Business Times*, 17–18 September 1994).

### *India's Silicon Valley*

Bangalore hosts the software technology centres of some of the world's largest IT firms.[34] Therefore, the EDB recommended to the Singapore government that instead of an industrial park, the project should be transformed into the construction of an IT Park to complement Karnataka's strengths in software technology (Interview with EDB Official, 18 June 1997). The involvement of the Tata Group was not planned when the EDB evaluated the Bangalore site for an IT Park.

---

[34] *Proposal for the Development of an Information Technology Park in Bangalore in Association with the Information Technology Park Investment Private Limited*, Singapore and Government of Karnataka, Tata Industries Limited, December 1993, p. 12, and Letter to the Foreign Investment Promotion Board from Ratan Tata.

While Ratan Tata did accompany Philip Yeo to Bangalore, the Tata Group did not intend to invest in the project (*Business Times*, 17–18 September 1994). However, according to Ratan Tata, 'when the offer came later from the Singapore government and we accepted, we knew that they were establishing a state-of-the-art facility for India which would attract multinational corporations from all over the world'. He said the main reason the Tata Group took a 40% equity position in the Bangalore IT Park was because of 'chemistry' (personal rapport) with the Singapore government. According to Ratan Tata, 'our relationship with the Singapore government is very good and we are really interested in teaming up with them for other projects'. Therefore, through personal and corporate networking, the Tata Group became involved in the development of the Bangalore IT Park project. The Chinese call the process of 'networking' *guanxi*. The process of *guanxi* entails the establishment of networks for trade in a formal or informal context among minority ethnic groups scattered around the world. This diaspora of ethnic communities can be a source of strength, not only for the diaspora itself, but also to the 'motherland' and adopted countries. At the very least, the presence of the Indian or Chinese diaspora establishes informal linkages between their adopted countries and the 'motherland'. The conveniences and ease of modern communication enhances the value of *guanxi* in today's context, yet this remains one resource that India has not exploited to the fullest.

The enhancement of cultural affinity between Singapore and India was also implemented through the creative use of immigration policies in Singapore. Sunanda Datta-Ray opined that Singapore is interested in fostering economic relations with India because of the political-cultural dimension—it would help to emphasise that Singapore is not a Chinese but a multiracial state (Asher, 24 November 1993). However, Singapore's interest in fostering economic relations with India was primarily driven by economics although there was a conscious attempt to maintain an ethnic composition that reflects Singapore's multiracial society. In this context, Singapore has attracted skilled and professional workers of Asian origin overseas to work in Singapore through several means. The government has offered places in its tertiary education institutions, namely, the various polytechnics and both universities, to students from ASEAN countries, China and, now, India. The reason for doing so goes beyond the transfer of knowledge, technology and skills. The scholarships provide a chance for overseas scholars to come and study in Singapore, create friendships with local students and get to know more about the country so this can be translated into possible partnerships or personal rapport for future use.

Singapore, through its High Commission in New Delhi, has also encouraged Indian foreign talent and businesses to take a closer look at the opportunities available in Singapore.[35] This is part of the Singapore government's strategy of recruiting foreign talent to remodel the Singapore economy based on knowledge and creativity (Heng & Low, 2001). Through the transfer of knowledge, skill, expertise and 'networking', it is hoped that these contacts could pave the way for greater economic cooperation and economic integration between Singapore and emerging markets. Cultural affinity is becoming a useful tool for countries wishing to develop and enhance their ties with India. An example of this was the increasing trend in New Delhi for foreign missions to post Foreign Service officers of ethnic Indian origin to India on the basis that they would be better able to develop personal links and rapport with Indian officials.[36] This perception was reinforced by a senior official from the Reserve Bank of India at the time, who commented that generally Indians do feel more at ease in talking with their own kind, or NRIs. Bangalore has evolved into the top 10 ranking as an IT hub, and this is directly linked to the approximately 30,000 software engineers who graduate from Karnataka's technical and tertiary institutes.

### *Like Hong Kong*

Singapore's position, sitting astride the trade routes between India and China, has not changed since it was a British colony. BG Yeo said this is a special position from which Singapore has benefited historically.[37] He added that in positioning itself, Singapore could be a Hong Kong to India. In encouraging Indian IT companies to use Singapore as a launching pad, PM Goh believed Singapore could be a good place for Indian companies to raise funds in both equity and loans, including venture capital (PM Goh, 8 April 2002). As Singapore is host to nearly 7000 MNCs from all over the world, it enables Indian companies based

[35] Interview with Singapore consortium official, 18 July 1997.

[36] Interview with Singapore consortium official, 18 July 1997.

[37] Extract of Transcript of Interview by BG George Yeo, Minister for Trade and Industry, with Arnaud Rodier of Le Figaro, 11 October 2001, Singapore Government Press Release, MITA.

there to have access to a large pool of partners for business expansion. To reflect Singapore's potential use to India, BG Yeo described Singapore as a modem for China and India to other parts of Southeast Asia, Central Asia and even the West.

IT firms (such as Satyam Computers)[38] believe that locating in Singapore would help their entry into the China market. PM Goh commented that Singapore should position itself for the rapid growth of the Chinese and Indian economies. As these economies grow, their expanding middle classes will want various consumer products and this will open new opportunities for the Singapore economy. The-then Singapore Senior Minister of State for Trade and Industry, Tharman Shanmugaratnam, explained that in a knowledge-based economy (KBE), clusters of enterprises and knowledge workers will enable cities and provinces or regional states to overtake the competition and form linkages across national boundaries.[39] The strategy is to position Singapore along the services supply chain between India, ASEAN and China. With thousands of MNCs and close to 30 foreign chambers and business associations, Singapore provides an ideal venue for the International Chambers of Commerce in which to base its Asia office. According to BG Yeo, 'Singapore is lucky to be well-situated between these two large growth areas' (China and India) (George Yeo, 9 January 2001).

### *Overcoming Challenges*

To meet the changing trends of the global IT industry, Ascendas having assumed the leading role in the Singapore consortium, implemented the next phase of its strategy which was to meet these changing market needs. Ascendas constructed customised buildings for companies and will consider establishing incubator centres for IT start-ups. According to Ascendas Deputy Chairman and CEO of JTC, Ko Kheng Hwa, the company had planned to make India a major focus and intended to

---

[38] Satyam Computers is exploring new markets as a strategy to diversify its exports away from the US which takes up more than 75% of its software exports. Satyam is looking into new investment ventures in Asia and has a presence in 35 countries. In 2000, Satyam had a customer base of 300 global companies of which 40 are on the Fortune 500 list. It has 7,000 employees and is the fourth-largest software company in India. In 2000, Satyam had revenues of US$271.8 million.

[39] Talking Points by Mr Tharman Shanmugaratnam, Singapore Senior Minister of State, Ministry of Trade and Industry and Ministry of Education, ASEAN Business Summit, New Delhi, 17 October 2002.

take advantage of the dotcom fever (*The Straits Times*, 24 January 2000). India, with its abundant pool of quality IT engineers, new awareness of the potential of the internet market, and responsive central and state governments, was sitting on an expansionary phase of the internet boom. In looking to develop IT start-ups, Ascendas would stop short of offering venture capital but may choose to provide novel rent-free agreements to promising start-ups in exchange for equity.

When the IT bubble burst towards the end of the 1990s, Asia also experienced the adverse impact of the Financial Crisis which affected the occupation rate of IT facilities the world over such as in the Bangalore IT Park (*Business Times*, 22 June 1998). The leasing rate at the initial phase of the Bangalore IT Park was 30% but was seen to be improving to reach 50% (*The Straits Times*, 24 January and 18 July 1997). Concerned about the Indian flagship investment project, Prime Minister Goh visited Bangalore in January 2000 to raise the profile of, and demand for, the Bangalore IT Park. By the time of his arrival in India, 75% of the office space at the Bangalore IT Park had been committed, the IT Park had gained ISO 9002 certification and was providing 2,500 skilled jobs for Bangalore. It is expected that when Bangalore IT Park is fully occupied, it will provide more than 5,000 jobs.[40] As a show of confidence, Singapore and the Karnataka state government signed an MOU aimed at cooperation and collaboration in the scientific and technological fields. This MOU will be used to promote bilateral programmes that would encourage entrepreneurship in high-tech fields as well as trade and investment through ties with high-tech companies (*The Straits Times*, 22 January 2000). Another MOU along similar lines had been signed between the NSTB, the Singapore TDB and Electronics Corporation of Tamil Nadu. According to the STDB International Operations Director Goh Oon Tong, 'Although the focus will be in IT, the applications will be broad-based' (*Economic Times*, 21 January 2000). With regard to Bangalore, Singapore as the 16th-largest investor in India looked upon itself as a catalyst to facilitate investments from various foreign investors (*Economic Times*, 21 January 2000).

[40] Speech by PM Goh Chok Tong at Official Opening of the International Tech Park Bangalore, 21 January 2000, Bangalore, India-MITA Press Release.

### *Government Support*

While Philip Yeo had made a huge difference to the dynamism of the Bangalore IT Park project, PM Goh had wanted to strengthen the overall bilateral trade between the two economies. PM Goh persuaded Indian companies to invest in Singapore as Singapore companies had invested in India, so that the regionalisation policy was not perceived to hollow out the Singapore economy and create job losses, which is a politically sensitive issue. The regionalisation strategy must derive benefits for Singapore investors and their host countries and, in this regard, the fragmentation of a company's structure across different geographic locations is the key that will benefit both India and Singapore through exploiting their comparative strengths. As geographical distance is no longer a concern with high-speed broadband connectivity, a company's operations will not be compromised if its components are not located in the same area and country.

While political support is crucial to the development of any enterprise, the personal endorsement of political leaders is likely to add greater importance and stature to a particular project. From the Indian perspective, PM Goh was known to be 'pragmatic and India-friendly' (*The Hindu*, 24 January 2000). During the marketing of the Bangalore IT Park in 1998, the Singapore consortium remained cautious about having an official launch for the IT Park. Reportedly, the consortium had been able to sell only 40%–50% of the space in Phase I of the IT Park, but had wanted to sell at least 80% before having an official launch. It was suggested that PM Goh could be invited to officially launch the IT Park some time in mid-1999. This suggestion came when a CII delegation visiting Singapore in late 1998, invited PM Goh to visit India in early 1999 to participate in their Annual Energy Summit or an equivalent annual event (*The Hindu*, 3 November 1998). While PM Goh was reportedly ready to launch the IT Park, the promoters from the Singapore consortium and the Tata Group were emphatic in their stand that the IT Park should be ready before an international launch (*The Hindu*, 3 November 1998). The promoters of the IT Park commented at the time, 'right now, even the roads have not been laid'.

PM Goh finally made the trip to India to inaugurate the Bangalore IT Park in January 2000. Apart from his personal endorsement of the IT Park, the momentum created thereafter also increased the occupancy rate. Reportedly, as PM Goh was inaugurating the Bangalore IT Park, his delegation comprising businessmen were scouting for investment opportunities. The business delegates accompanying PM Goh had a useful exchange with their Indian counterparts and raised their concerns with key Indian ministers, some of which included property ownership, frequent changes in India's trade tariff structure, and the difficulties of remitting money from India to Singapore (*Business Times*, 24 January 2000). PM Goh also suggested two other initiatives to enhance IT ties with India such as funding Indian entrepreneurs through start-ups by providing rent-free premises and allowances. In addition, he also mooted the idea of establishing technical training institutions in India such as a polytechnic (*Business Times*, 24 January 2000).

While PM Goh invited Indian businessmen to use Singapore as a launching pad into the Southeast Asian region, he also encouraged Singapore businessmen to tie up with Indian partners to tap into the Indian market. Top CII officials also praised PM Goh for his personal stamp and leadership in strengthening the partnership between India and Singapore (*The Straits Times*, 20 January 2000). The enthusiasm PM Goh has for India was reflected by CII when they mentioned that 'Mr Goh has always remained optimistic about India' (*The Hindu*, 24 January 2000). Despite the fact that the once-raging Indian Fever of 1994–95 had simmered down considerably, PM Goh's presence in inaugurating and the attention paid to the Bangalore IT Park had benefited its development. As the Bangalore IT Park flagship investment project became a symbol of bilateral cooperation between India and Singapore, the position taken by the Singapore authorities was that failure was not an option. The significance of the Bangalore IT Park went beyond the Park itself. PM Goh said, 'with the coming of the IT era, the strategic alliances of our two countries would bring great synergy' (*The Straits Times*, 22 January 2000). He believed that both countries have strengths that could be exploited for their mutual benefit. India has a pool of skilled IT specialists that complemented Singapore's experience in developing industrial and high-tech parks to world standards (*The Straits Times*, 22 January 2000). According to Ratan Tata, PM Goh 'is really the one who lit the fire' to propose greater linkages between India and Singapore. Ratan Tata added that the commitment, perseverance and long-term view of the Singapore investors and EDB and, in particular, its then chairman Philip Yeo, made a difference to the successful development of the IT Park (*The Straits Times*, 22 January 2000).

The Bangalore IT Park also fell within the overall strategy of Singapore's focus on the southern Indian states. Former Prime Minister Goh

Chok Tong, on his visit to India in January 2000 to promote ITPB, also covered the cities of Hyderabad and Chennai and met with the Chief Ministers of the southern states of Andhra Pradesh, Karnataka and Tamil Nadu.[41] The-then PM Goh referred to Bangalore as the Silicon Plateau of India and was impressed with the speed of its development and expansion since 1994. When he visited the Bangalore IT Park in January 2000, only 75% of the Bangalore IT Park had been committed and was the base for 59 companies (*The Straits Times*, 30 November 2000). Plans for the second phase of the IT Park were drawn up as PM Goh visited the Park. In June 2000, Jurong Town Corporation (JTC) decided that work would start on Phase II of the Bangalore IT Park (*The Straits Times*, 6 June 2000). While Phase I of the IT Park was far from being fully committed, the vibrancy and business expectations created by PM Goh's visit perhaps influenced 27 new clients to sign up at the IT Park and the state government of Karnataka, through the Institute of Biotechnology, had committed space for 15,000 square feet at the Park (*The Straits Times*, 6 June 2000).

Full occupancy at the Bangalore IT Park for Phase I was reached in November 2000 and the Park housed 91 companies, including famous brand names such as Hitachi, Sanyo, Glaxo, GE Plastics, Siemens and Sharp (*The Straits Times*, 30 November 2000). To mark the full occupancy of Phase 1 and the start of Phase II, another political figure from Singapore—the Minister for Trade and Industry, BG Yeo—attended the simple ceremony (*Business Times*, 30 November 2000). BG Yeo is also an influential and supportive figure in the process of expanding trade linkages between India and Singapore. He has been an ardent supporter of Singapore enhancing its trade and business linkages with India, and has said that cooperation between India and Singapore, especially in the fields of IT and biotechnology, was set for a 'flourishing period' (BBC Summary of World Broadcasts, 6 December 2000). According to him, investors should adopt a long-term view on India despite its fractious politics and entrenched bureaucracy. However, sounding a note of concern to the Indian government, BG Yeo said that while foreign investors should adopt a long-term strategy in India, they needed reasonable prospects for short-term and medium-term profit (*The Straits*

[41] Press Statement from the Prime Minister's Office: Official Visit of Prime Minister Goh Chok Tong to India, Ministry of Information and the Arts, Singapore, 17 January 2000.

*Times*, 8 March 1997). He added that India had a larger talent pool than Singapore and a lot of land, so India has the potential to perform much better (*Far Eastern Economic Review*, 25 January 2001). When the BJP political party assumed control of the central government in the late 1990s, it continued the reforms initiated by the previous Congress government (*The Hindu*, 18 December 2000).

With consistent economic policies, IT clusters in India such as Bangalore have evolved into the top 10 ranking as an IT hub across the whole country. Bangalore's status as an IT hub is also linked to the approximately 30,000 software engineers who graduate annually from Karnataka's technical and tertiary institutes. Singapore and India had also signed two agreements to promote the development of trade and investment through scientific and technical cooperation (*Economic Times*, 21 January 2000). The agreements in the form of MOUs were signed by the NSTB (now *ASTAR) and TDB (now IE Singapore) with Karnataka's Principal Secretary for Commerce, BS Patil. The other MOU was signed between the NSTB, IE Singapore and the Electronics Corporation of Tamil Nadu (*The Straits Times*, 22 January 2000). To strengthen India's and Singapore's linkages at the federal level, both countries established the Singapore-India ICT Task Force to promote bilateral cooperation between India and Singapore (*The Straits Times*, 22 January 2000).

### *Benefits to Regionalisation*

The underlying rationale for Singapore to launch its regionalisation plans to create an external economic wing is linked to its strategic plans to be a global hub for businesses, services and transportation. While in the past Singapore had succeeded in attracting foreign MNCs because of its low-cost but skilled labour, Singapore is now repositioning itself as a low-cost 'nerve centre' and staging area for regional and international business operations (Drodge, 1997). Another essential component to be a business hub and staging area is the availability of high bandwidth communications to induce foreign IT firms such as those in India to shift more knowledge-intensive activities to Singapore. The availability of high bandwidth communications, video-conferencing, email and electronic sharing of multimedia documents enables a company's staff in different areas such as marketing, engineering, programming and designing to collaborate and coordinate their work close to real time but thousands of kilometres apart. Technological advancements would also enable foreign MNCs in Singapore to outsource some of their operations to India while maintaining a presence in Singapore.

The availability of high-speed and bandwidth communications between India and Singapore was made possible with the completion and operation of an undersea fibre optic cable called 'aquanet', officially launched by PM Vajpayee and PM Goh Chok Tong in April 2002. The undersea cable stretches to 3,200 kilometres, and connects Chennai in southern India to Tuas in Singapore. This first phase of aquanet cost US$250 million and was undertaken through a joint venture company between Bharti Corporation of India and SingTel of Singapore. The undersea cable is 8.4 terabits in bandwidth and can handle 130 million telephone connections at the same time. The second phase is to connect Chennai to Mumbai, India's financial capital and in the northeast of India. In total, aquanet will be 11,800 kilometres in length and cost about US$650 million. SingTel had initially paid Bharti US$400 million for a stake in Bharti's telecom companies.

As Singapore's flagship investment in India, the ITPB has weathered several challenges that included the global IT downturn, the Y2K phenomenon and the Asian Financial Crisis. The resilience of ITPB as an iconic symbol of the potential for Singapore and India economic alliance remained for several reasons. Ascendas Pte Ltd has adopted a strategy of building up a portfolio of business space across India but has centred this strategy on the ITPB. The acquisition by Ascendas of the Tata Group's 47% share in ITPB was seen as the implementation of this strategy (*The Hindu*, 13 April 2005). Ascendas has become the majority shareholder, with 82% held by its joint venture company Information Technology Park Limited (ITPL) (*The Straits Times*, 13 April 2005). According to the-then Chief Operations Officer for Ascendas India, Goh Kok Huat, 'It is business as usual. Ascendas will continue to deliver the same high standards of management that it has been providing since day one in 1994, when the Park welcomed its first group of tenants, many of whom are still with us today. ITPB will embody the best of our practices in real estate across Asia' (*The Hindu*, 12 April 2005). From the Tata Group's perspective, the Managing Director for Tata Industries Ltd, KA Chaukar, said, 'We are happy to say that we have partnered in the creation of a pioneering and world-class facility. The International Tech Park Bangalore has catalysed creation of a vibrant IT industry in Bangalore and put India securely on the world IT map.' He further said that, 'Whilst the divestment of our stake is in line with the Group's strategy to exit non-core areas of interest, the Tata Group will continue its business relationships with ITPB as hitherto. We have had an excellent and fruitful 11-year-long relationship with Ascendas and wish them the best as they increase their ownership.'

Ascendas has announced a rebranding of ITPB to an Ascendas perpetual A Brand identity to reaffirm long-term commitment to Bangalore as an investment location. The rebranding is part of the company's intent to widen its scope beyond the Park and assume a city-wide strategic view to assume more projects and joint ventures (*Deccan Herald*, 10 June 2005). In March 2006, Jonathan Yap was appointed as the CEO of Ascendas, India, and assumed responsibilities for the development and management of IT Parks, Ascendas India IT Park Trust, as well as expansion plans for Ascendas (*The Hindu*, 4 March 2006). According to him, 'We hope to do more beyond ITPB. With the repositioning of the park, we are effectively moving away from ITPL approach to a city-wide approach to Bangalore. This opens up the possibility of doing more in Bangalore in addition to ITPB' (*News Today*, 10 June 2005). In June 2005, Ascendas Pte Ltd launched a S$350 million Ascendas India IT Parks Fund seeded by ITPB and Vanenburg IT Park. The private real estate fund has a term of seven years and is constituted in Singapore as a private trust (*Ascendas Press Release*, 16 June 2005). The Fund was privately placed to selected institutional investors around the world. Ascendas has a 30% stake as sponsor of the Fund, while the remaining 70% stake has been over-subscribed and taken up by international and Singapore-based investors. This private real estate fund is unique because it is focused on matured income-producing assets with development potential and fits into Singapore's overall IT strategy in India. The Fund has a term of seven years and is expected to reach S$800 million in size by 2012 (*The Hindu*, 18 June 2005). The ITPB as Singapore's flagship investment project has become a benchmark for what is considered 'world class' in India and it has also proved that such high-tech parks can be built in India (*The Straits Times*, 31 March 2007). Ascendas has moved on to developing other IT Parks across various states in India.

CHAPTER SEVEN

# BEYOND BANGALORE IT PARK

## *Beyond Bangalore*

The emergence of India as one of the main hubs for Business Process Outsourcing (BPO) of IT-enabled services (ITES) for the global economy has seen foreign companies establishing subsidiaries or engaging Indian partners to undertake their BPO work. The IT/ITES growth in BPO activities is fuelling a huge demand for suitable office spaces. The projected short-term demand for top-quality ITES sites in India will be some 20 million square feet. In comparison, the existing top-quality commercial space available in India's major cities at the end of 2003 was around 50 million square feet, indicating a growth of 40% by the end of 2004. This would indicate that other states besides Karnataka, such as Andhra Pradesh, could decide to tap into the demand and benefit from the 'spillover' IT effect from Bangalore.

Picture 7.1: HITEC City, Hyderabad

### *Andhra Pradesh—HITEC City*

The former chief minister of Andhra Pradesh, Chandrababu Naidu, was the main motivator behind HITEC City. While Naidu was part of the fragile United Front Party at the federal level, his own party in Andhra Pradesh—the Telegu Desam—controlled an overwhelming majority of 242 out of 292 seats (*The Straits Times*, 19 May 1997). The Naidu government had borrowed heavily to finance the development of HITEC City and improve infrastructure. From the mid- to late-1990s, Andhra Pradesh's debt and fiscal deficit had quadrupled. The first phase of HITEC City was not adequate to meet the growing demand of the IT sector (*Business Line*, 29 October 1999). The second phase of HITEC City was in a different location covering around 250 acres of land. The state government of Andhra Pradesh allocated about 158 acres of land for the first phase of its HITEC City. Picture 7.2 shows Cyber Gateway at HITEC City.

By examining the policies of other states, especially Karnataka, in attracting foreign investments in IT, the Andhra Pradesh (AP) state committee decided to include incentives in its own policies: exemptions

Picture 7.2: Cyber Gateway at HITEC City

from sales tax and additional power supply to attract foreign IT investments whether as joint ventures with Indian companies or as foreign direct investments. The AP state government established the Hyderabad Information Technology and Engineering Consultancy (HITEC) City in the state capital of Hyderabad to attract IT companies. Built at a cost of US$375 million in the late 1990s, 50% of the land area at HITEC City was set aside for constructing ready-to-occupy buildings, while the other 50% would be independent campuses built to custom specifications for individual IT companies. The ready-to-occupy buildings are Cyber Towers and Cyber Gateway. HITEC City has been co-promoted by Larsen and Toubro (L&T), an Indian conglomerate, and the Andhra Pradesh Industrial Corporation Ltd (APIIC) based on an equity participation of 89:11 in the joint venture (*Business Line*, 19 November 1998). In terms of infrastructure, HITEC City has uninterrupted electricity supply and is exempt from statutory power cuts. It also offers high-speed connection to the internet through fibre optic cables to communication links throughout the world. Other infrastructure developments include roads, hotels, shopping complexes, petrol kiosks, medical centres and housing for workers. The state government has also built a four-lane expressway from the airport to HITEC City, and there are plans for a new and bigger airport. The main marketing strategy used by the-then Chief Minister, Chandrababu Naidu, to attract IT companies to HITEC City were its lower office rentals, lower real estate prices and overall lower cost of living compared with its rival city, Bangalore (*Asia Today*, 15 April 1997).

The lure of Hyderabad for IT MNCs has been the availability of skilled IT talent, good infrastructure, a responsive and efficient state government, and relatively low rental space starting at Rs 24psf (per square feet) compared to Rs 25–40psf in other major towns like Bangalore and Mumbai. The HITEC City project was managed by L&T Infocity, a joint venture between L&T and the APIIC (*The Hindu*, 25 June 2001). HITEC City is located near Madhapur village, adjacent to the exclusive Jubilee Hills area in Hyderabad, and was built across 158 acres to provide 5 million square feet of office space (*The Hindu*, 27 October 1997). Phase I of the project built over 6 acres was a 10-storey structure of 120 modular units and a large range of user-friendly features called Cyber Towers and the second phase is named Cyber Gateway (*Business Line*, 29 October 1999). The third phase is called CyberPearl and is a joint venture between L&T Infocity and Singapore firm Ascendas (*India Business Insight*, 11 September 2000). CyberPearl

Table 7.1: Technical and Layout Specifications of CyberPearl

| | |
|---|---|
| Type of building | 7-storey fully air-conditioned office building for IT and ITES. Office space for tenants to fit-out. |
| Super built-up Area | 250,000 sq ft (approximately) |
| Occupation | Multi-tenancy |
| Structure | Reinforced cement concrete columns structure with pre-stressed flat slab finished with Indian patent stone (IPS) |
| Parking | Available for car and motorcycles |
| Typical floor plate | 38,000 sq ft (approximately) |
| Typical column-to-column width | 11m × 11m |
| Floor-to-floor height | Ground floor—5.0m, 1st–6th floors—4.25m |
| Floor loading | Ground floor—5.0 Kilonewton (KN) psm, 1st–2nd floors—7.5 KN psm, 3rd–6th floors—5.0 KN psm |

Source: Ascendas newsletters.

was Ascendas' first business venture in Hyderabad and was expected to house about 5,000 people in IT and other high-tech industries. HITEC City has been completely taken up by demand for premium office space. Some of their tenants are Microsoft Inc, Oracle Inc and Tata Consultancy Services. Due to the strong demand for office space by IT companies attracted to Hyderabad, Ascendas has bought over Vanenberg IT Park from the Dutch Technology Group Vanenberg. The Vanenberg Park site has a total floor area of 850,000 sq ft and is 95%-occupied (*Business Times*, 24 December 2004).

### *CyberPearl—Ascendas*

Picture 7.3 shows CyberPearl. The multi-tenanted IT complex was built in two phases and provides 500,000 sq ft of business space on a five-acre plot. CyberPearl will have uninterrupted power with a diesel back-up generator and water supply, and will be equipped with telecommunications and fibre optic networks to maximise telecommunications at all times. CyberPearl is similar to the facilities available at Bangalore IT Park.

Similar to the IT Park Bangalore (ITPB) CyberPearl provides a work-live-play environment that caters to the young and dynamic professionals in the IT industry. CyberPearl has cafeterias, retail shops,

Picture 7.3: Exterior of CyberPearl at HITEC City, Hyderabad

automated-teller machines, fitness centres and a health club. CyberPearl also features a centralised air-conditioning system, smart lifts and an advanced security system. CyberPearl was officially opened on 18 October 2004 by the new Chief Minister of Andhra Pradesh, Dr Reddy, and Singapore Minister Lim Boon Heng.

### *Tamil Nadu—Chennai*

Apart from Bangalore and Hyderabad, the neighbouring city of Chennai is also emerging as India's next IT metro city. Situated in the southern Indian state of Tamil Nadu, Chennai has some 25 universities and 250 engineering colleges that produce about 60,000 engineering graduates each year, of which about 35,000 specialise in IT (*The Straits Times*, 4 September 2004). The major Indian IT companies—Wipro Technologies, Infosys Technologies, Tata Consultancy Services and Satyam Computer Services—have already invested in Chennai's IT expansion. These companies are building the world's biggest software development centre on a 53-hectare site that is part of the 687-hectare IT industrial park called Mahindra City. Approximately 35,000 jobs

Picture 7.4: Interior of CyberPearl

were created in Chennai in 2004, placing the city as the second-largest job creator after the National Capital Region around federal capital Delhi (*The Straits Times*, 4 September 2004). Eventually, the aim of constructing Mahindra City will be to create 70,000 jobs per year by 2008. The state government of Tamil Nadu has allocated land for an IT belt on the outskirts of Chennai; this area is known as Tidel Park and is shown in Picture 7.5 (Transport Policy, 12, 2005).

Picture 7.6 shows that the interior working environment of Tidel Park IT complex which is a landmark in Chennai, is similar to the IT Park in Bangalore and CyberPearl in Hyderabad (*Economic Times*, 17 October 2004). A number of MNCs such as Electronic Data Systems Ltd (EDS) have established operations at Tidel Park. The EDS facility will enhance application development, offer production support maintenance, and develop new solutions for the domestic market as well as the company's global customers (*Business Line*, 29 April 2001). Chennai also hosts BPO activities for big international banks such as Citibank, Standard Chartered, ABN Amro and the World Bank. Consultants CB Richard Ellis commented that there is a high requirement for Grade A office space in Chennai (*Economic Times*, 17 October 2004). Tidel

Picture 7.5: Tidel Park, Chennai, Tamil Nadu

Park I is fully occupied and, despite the strong commercial demand for high-end commercial space for IT and ITES space, the construction of Tidel Park II has been delayed by 15–18 months. The project appears to be back on track, with the company inviting bids from a consortium of design and construction firms for the Tidel Park II project.

The partnership between Singapore private companies and the state government of Tamil Nadu has been reinvigorated in the IT sector after the earlier 'Madras Corridor' proposal was shelved in 1993. In early 2001, both the Singapore and the Tamil Nadu state government parties, after a detailed feasibility study, had signed a Memorandum of Understanding (MOU) to develop an IT complex in Chennai for the second phase of Tidel Park IT complex (*Business Line*, 4 July 2002). The state government has allocated 40.19 acres of land adjacent to the existing Tidel Park I for the joint venture between Ascendas Pte Ltd and the Tamil Nadu Industrial Development Development Corporation (TIDCO). Although the MOU was signed at the downturn in global IT industry, the expected commercial demand for IT/ITES space in Chennai indicated a need for more IT infrastructure. In the project agreement for Tidel Park II, Ascendas could construct up to 1.5–2

Picture 7.6: Interior of Tidel Park

million square feet of built-up space depending on the demand for office space; Ascendas will be responsible for the overall implementation of the project including its management, assisting the special purpose for structuring its financing, and being the lead marketing agent for the project (*Business Line*, 14 November 2002).

The first phase of the five-acre IT complex was expected to be completed by the end of 2004 and was estimated to cost approximately S$52 million (*Business Line*, 18 June 2003). Both Ascendas and Tidco agreed on the specially structured equity holding. TIDCO has an 11% stake, with Ascendas holding the rest which is similar to the financial structure for CyberPearl in Hyderabad (*Business Line*, 14 November 2002). Ascendas was open to the idea of a third partner at the onset of constructing Tidel Park II or at the completion of the project, but this did not materialise.

Other IT infrastructures in place in Chennai include those undertaken by the Software Technology Parks of India (STPI). Similar to other IT parks across India, state-owned companies such as VSNL (Videsh Sanchar Nigam Limited), DoT (Department of Telecoms) and STPI are providing services to Tidel Park. For example, two dedicated

Picture 7.7: Indian IT Workers at Tidel Park Food Court

communication frameworks created for operation by VSNL and STPI have been provided. Each office space module at Tidel Park will have a facility for a bandwidth of 10–12Mbps. The Tamil Nadu Energy Board (TNEB) is also constructing a 110 Kilovolts (Kv) substation with a 10.5MVA diesel generator set for 100%. Tidel Park has also taken a long-term lease on 15 acres of land from neighbouring MGR Film City. This is to provide additional parking space, and recreation facilities like swimming pools and outdoor games. The state government has established the Chennai Metropolitan Development Authority (CDMA) to speed up the process and approve building applications for the state's IT infrastructure with the creation of an exclusive IT channel. The channel aims to clear any application in one to two weeks (*The Hindu*, 4 October 2004).

Tidel Park Phase II developed across from Phase I by Ascendas Land is known as Ascendas International Technology Park (Picture 7.9). Ascendas has invested in Chennai in a big way by completing the first phase of its International Technology Park Chennai (ITPC) for occupation by a range of software and IT-enabled companies from July 2005. Ascendas IT Park will have an overall area of 1.5 million square feet

Picture 7.8: Tidel Park II—Ascendas IT Park

that will be built in three phases, and has undertaken the project as a joint venture with the Tamil Nadu Industrial Development Corporation (TIDCO). The first phase of ITPC will consist of an 11-storeyed Grade A business space for IT, ITES, call centre, software, data centre and R&D units of large corporations (*News Today*, 15 April 2004).

The companies that have taken leases at the Ascendas IT Park Chennai include iNautix, Profit Logic Software, Fitness One, Paris Bijoux and Sumanas Florist. Although Ascendas IT Park has standby generators and its own telecommunications link, Chennai also needs to invest in infrastructure for the continued growth of its IT sector. Although electricity supply is of a lesser concern because Chennai is less populous than Bangalore, Chennai has to provide more suitable land for the expansion of the IT sector. According to real estate firm CB Richard Ellis, Chennai could only provide 0.6 million square feet of the 20 million square feet meant for IT firms in 2004. This is well below the 2 million square feet provided to IT firms in Bangalore in 2004. Nonetheless, the software output of Tamil Nadu has increased from Rs 3.9 billion in 1998 to Rs 8.1 billion in 2003. When completed, the International Tech Park Chennai (ITPC) will cover a space of 1.75 million square feet.

Picture 7.9: Interior of Ascendas IT Park, Chennai

As a result of the strong demand for more IT/ITES space on the outskirts of Chennai, Ascendas has signed another MOU with local joint venture partner, Mahindra Industrial Park (MIPL), to develop a million square feet of ready-built space at Mahindra City near Chennai to cater for the IT and BPO industries (*Economic Times*, 13 October 2004). Both companies also agreed that Mahindra City would adopt Ascendas Real Estate Management System (Arems) to enhance the quality of the Park management. Mahindra City will leverage on the Ascendas brand as a premier business solutions and space provider throughout Asia, and Ascendas will transfer its best practices and know-how in high-end real estate management to the Park. These include master plan review, asset management, marketing consultancy, property management, lease management and the use of its proprietary web-based Ascendas Integrated Management System (AIMS) (*Economic Times*, 13 October 2004). Ascendas and Mahindra have completed this IT Park called CyberVale in Chennai. CyberVale was inaugurated in September 2007 and was built in two phases in a Special Economic Zone (SEZ). CyberVale is spread across 18.5 acres of land. President and CEO of Ascendas, Ms Chong Siak Ching, said that, 'Ascendas'

Picture 7.10: Food Court at ITPC—Chennai

growth in Tamil Nadu is in response to the phenomenal growth of IT and ITES services in the state. CyberVale is the new member in the Ascendas family of IT Parks in Asia. With seven IT Parks in five Indian cities, India is one of our fastest-growing markets and we are here to stay' (*Ascendas Press Release*, 25 September 2007).

Besides the southern states of Karnataka, Andhra Pradesh and Tamil Nadu, Ascendas is also involved in developing IT Parks in the north of India in the state of Haryana at a place called Gurgaon, and in Kolkatta in the state of West Bengal (Transport Policy 12, 2005). Singapore, through GLC Ascendas, is expanding its investment in IT Parks across India. The latest state to attract Ascendas' attention is West Bengal, where Ascendas has announced plans to construct a S$150-million IT Park in its state capital of Kolkatta. Through Ascendas Land, the Singapore government has placed greater emphasis on the IT sector in India. The town of Rajarhat is a 15-minute drive from Kolkatta airport, and ITPK is within a 10,000-acre development site in Rajarhat demarcated for a new integrated township by the state government of West Bengal. The proposed ITPK will create 500,000 square feet of Grade A office space. To explain why Ascendas chose West Bengal for its next IT Park development, Ascendas' head for north India operations, Harminder Singh, explained that the IT industry in Kolkatta is growing at an annual compound rate of 119% against a national average of 36% in 2001–03. Moreover, West Bengal accounted for 14% (over 140,000) of the IT and ITES workforce in India. The ITPK, once fully completed, will provide 2 million square feet of business space for IT and software operations, making it one of the largest IT Parks in the state. However, this project has been put on hold by Ascendas because of the uncertain political climate in the state.

Nonetheless, Ascendas continues to initiate IT projects in other Indian states and has signed agreements with the Maharashtra state government to build two new IT Parks in that state. The company is in partnership with Maharashtra Industrial Development Corporation (MIDC) and Maharashtra Airport Development Company to build IT Parks in the cities of Pune and Nagpur, respectively. Both these proposed IT Parks are located within the government-approved and promoted SEZ areas (*Ascendas Press Release*, 18 April 2007). Ascendas is expected to invest about S$570 million in the two IT Parks until 2014 but in phases and depending on market demands. Both IT Parks will create an estimated 7 million square feet of high-grade IT space and could create employment opportunities for as many as 70,000 when fully completed. The International Tech Park Pune (ITPP) will be jointly developed with MIDC into a 2.5 million square feet office space over 25 acres as Phase 3 of the Rajiv Gandhi Infotech Park in Hinjewadi (*Ascendas Press Release*, 18 April 2007). To be developed in five phases, the first phase of ITPP will commence in mid-2007 and is expected to be completed a year later. The first phase is expected to generate employment for about 5,000 IT and ITES professionals. In Nagpur, Ascendas and MADC will both develop over 4.5 million square feet of space on a 63-acre site within the Multi-modal International Hub Airport (MIHAN) (*Ascendas Press Release*, 18 April 2007). The International Tech Park Nagpur (ITPN) is expected to be completed in six phases; construction of the first phase comprising 500,000 square feet began in mid-2007 and is projected to be completed by 2009. The first phase of the ITPN could accommodate about 5,000 professionals.

Both ITPP and ITPN will be developed and marketed under the well-known International Tech Park (ITP) brand in Maharashtra. These two IT Parks will likely benefit from the high-quality standards and branding attributed to Ascendas' IT Parks in Bangalore, Chennai and Hyderabad. The facilities available at ITPB in Bangalore will also be available at ITPP and ITPN (*Ascendas Press Release*, 18 April 2007). Ascendas launched a S$350-million Ascendas India IT Parks Fund in June 2005. The future of IT Parks in India remains positive because these high-tech parks overcame the impediments caused by India's inadequate infrastructure. The Singapore government is also aware that it has to work closely with and have the endorsement of the various state governments if its joint venture projects are to succeed. In the IT sector, Singapore's regionalisation policy is reaping benefits for both itself and India. Singapore and India have been able to leverage on each other's complementary economies to derive benefit from developing IT Parks across India.

The development of Ascendas' five IT complexes in India is an indication that its expertise in building high-end business space for software development and IT-enabled services (ITES) has strong demand in India. The formula for the development of these IT Parks seems to be adhering to the Bangalore IT Park (ITPL) model. Strong support of the host state government is a prerequisite and the projects have taken place on sites set aside as an enclave for high-tech companies or IT corridors. The state government authorities have to acquire the land, and Ascendas then signs an MOU with the state government and/or a local Indian partner to develop the IT Park. Basic infrastructure in terms of electricity, water and road links have to be worked out for these to remain secure and uninterrupted. The Ascendas projects so far have been multi-storey complexes and have a built space of 500–1.5 million square feet on a few acres but the ITPL in Bangalore is by far the largest. There has been a good amount of technology transfer from Ascendas to its local Indian partners and the financial structure is usually worked on some ratio, with Ascendas holding 40%–80% although this also varies through stages in the project.

After ITPL in Bangalore, the trend indicated that Ascendas was not using the conglomerate type approach to venture into other IT Park projects in India. Ascendas has either undertaken a joint venture alone with an Indian partner such as L&T or acquired already constructed IT Parks such as the Vanenburg IT Park, which has subsequently been renamed the 'V'. Moreover, having accumulated enough financial capital, Ascendas is not only constructing and marketing office space but has continued to retain ownership of its IT Parks. This strategy, given the acute shortage of premium office space in India, is likely to generate substantial income for Ascendas in the foreseeable future. Singapore companies like RSP Architects or Cesma International are also starting to bid for other Indian projects on their own. However, these above-named Singapore companies are GLCs; and Singapore SMEs are still finding it difficult to venture into the India market because of the lack of resources such as adequate knowledge of the Indian market and contacts with their Indian counterparts. Nonetheless, with more GLCs venturing into overseas markets such as in India, competition for SMEs in the various sectors in Singapore will probably ease.

CHAPTER EIGHT

# CONCLUSION: POST-CECA

## *Future Economy*

While the official illiteracy rate covers more than half of India's population of 1.1 billion, it is easy to forget that millions more Indians are literate, educated and talented. If Singapore is serious in its intent to be a knowledge-based economy, the source of foreign talent from India cannot to be ignored. The Indian education system is known to be rigid and to emphasise discipline, but it has built a strong foundation in mathematics and science, which largely explains the rich talent pool for the IT industry in India. The Singapore Minister for Education Tharman Shanmugaratnam commented that Singapore has a dream to be a 'global school house' of higher studies (*Hindu*, 8 August 2004). India plays a large role towards Singapore's ambition to be an education hub. The Singapore Tourism Board (STB) is involved in promoting Singapore as an education hub because of its extensive marketing channels and brand-building capabilities (*Hindu*, 8 August 2004). The Singapore Tourist Visitor Centre (STVC) in Chennai, in the southern state of Tamil Nadu, was opened in February 2004 and its staff is managed by the STB. The STVC is a 'one-stop shop' for disseminating information to travellers and aggressively markets the available educational opportunities in India (*Hindu*, 8 August 2004). The Singapore Tourism Board (STB) has campaigns for a whole range of educational needs in India—from basic education to higher leaning. One novel approach is to encourage overseas school trips from India to Singapore as 'learning in a fun environment'. The STB facilitates either a five-day or two-week educational tour in Singapore that includes the Underwater World and other scientific destinations. Another approach is to have educational roadshows in India's major cities such as Bangalore, Mumbai, Delhi as well as Chennai. The STVC in Chennai also covers the other southern states of Karnataka, Andhra Pradesh and Kerala.

The STB's approach in Chennai coincides with Singapore's strategy to pay closer attention to the four southern Indian states. In addition, tertiary institutions from Singapore, like the National University of Singapore (NUS), undertake yearly recruitment drives in southern India to attract bright undergraduates to NUS. Given the diversity and cosmopolitan outlook of Singapore, the presence of Indian students—whether in national schools or tertiary institutions—would positively add to this growing diversity and raise the benchmark for Singapore's education through competition. The universities in Singapore have signed a formal Memoranda of Understanding (MOU) with well-known Indian tertiary institutions such as Indian Institute of Technology, Bangalore (IIT-B), Indian Institute of Science, Bangalore (IISc), Indian Institute of Technology (IIT), Bombay, and Indian Institute of Technology (IIT), Delhi (*Hindu*, 8 August 2004). While Singapore has actively courted these Indian institutions to open offshore campuses in Singapore, there remained problems of convergence in mindsets. For example, the Indian Human Resources Ministry did not support IIM-Bangalore's plans to open a Singapore campus on the ground that it might dilute the Indian brand of IIM-Bangalore (*The Straits Times*, 24 January 2006). Nonetheless, during SM Goh's visit to India in January 2006, India's Human Resources Minister Arjun Singh mentioned that the ban on IIM-Bangalore opening a campus in Singapore was not indefinite and could be reconsidered.

The other advantages that Singapore offers to attract Indian talent to Singapore include: government and private funding for education and infrastructure, geographical proximity to India, a similar cultural identity among Singaporean Indians, and the relatively lower costs of tuition and living expenses (*Hindu*, 8 August 2004). Indian students are also eligible for a number of scholarships and grants, including postgraduate research. Some of the postgraduate scholarships available are Singapore-MIT Alliance Scholarship, Lee Kuan Yew School of Public Policy Graduate Scholarship, Temasek Scholarship, Research Scholarship and Studentships (*Hindu*, 8 August 2004). From the private sector, scholarships such as Singapore Airlines-NOL are available. Besides education, the drive towards encouraging entrepreneurship and attracting foreign talent has seen a growing group of Indian professionals in Singapore that numbered around 35,000 in 2004 (*Sunday Times*, 21 March 2004). Apart from the IT sector, the Singapore medical profession has also benefited from an inflow of doctors from India. There are around 129 India-trained doctors registered with the Singapore Medical Council (*Sunday Times*, 21 March 2004).

### *Asian IT Market*

India and Singapore are part of the rising wave of IT expansion in the Asia Pacific region. Apart from Japan, the East Asian region has already installed some 100 million personal computers and 400 million cellular phones. In addition, there are 165 million internet users in the region (*Economic Times*, 6 January 2003). As India moves slowly but steadily towards a services-oriented IT market structure, the country will continue to remain the preferred offshore outsource area for IT development (*Hindu*, 30 December 2002). The Indian IT brand name as reliability for outsourcing, took off towards the end of the 1990s, when Indian software solutions took an active part in developing Y2K solutions to remedy the Y2K (Year 2000) bug (*Business Times*, 21 August 2000). While uncertainties abound in the high-tech industries, industry observers noted that India's software industries remain one of the few high-tech areas, besides pharmaceuticals and telecommunications, to be on an expansionary phase in India. The optimism that pervades from India's late Minister for IT, Pramod Mahajan, is that despite India's shortcomings and failings to provide a continuous supply of power, lack of world-class telecoms facilities and low PC penetration, India has world-class human resources (*Time*, Asia, 16 October 2000).

For Singapore investors in IT, this represented a good opportunity to expand their interest in high-tech areas. For example, the Singapore-listed CMG Regional India Fund had a creditable return of 142% at end-1999 (*Economic Times*, 25 October 2000). Interest in Indian IT stocks has continued; in January 2003, Singapore Computer Systems (SCS) bought a 30% stake in Bangalore-based Kshema Technologies for US$9.2 million. Both companies have signed an agreement to this effect. SCS was incorporated in 1980 and is a leading Information and Communication Technology (ICT) service provider in the Asia Pacific region. SCS is a service provider for a range of IT services and business consultancy. By buying into Kshema's existing networks, SCS will then have the ability to establish a presence in both the US and Europe, and to extend its service providers (*Economic Times*, 8 January 2003). As the eighth-largest investor in India, Singapore had direct equity investments of some US$1.3 billion as at end-2001. According to the Infocomm Development Authority (IDA), in return, India's investments in Singapore has grown by 14% since the early 1990s (*Business Times*, 8 April 2002). At the end of 2005, Singapore became the third-largest foreign investor in India with a cumulative investment of more than S$3 billion. The major portion of Singapore's total investments in India is in IT Parks, the 'new temples' of India. In this context, the 'new temple' represented a new iconic symbol of India's emergence as a major economic power.

Singapore's then P.M., Goh Chok Tong said, 'I regard India as a country with great potential. The Prime Minister now is embarking on a second wave of reforms; I'm here to encourage him' (*The Straits Times*, 19 January 2000). Singapore has been instrumental in engaging India to look towards the Southeast Asian region. Senior Minister Goh has also urged the Indian government to change its mindset and to fully capitalise on its 'Look East' Policy. Since the mid-1990s, Singapore has urged Indian companies (numbering around 50 in 1996) to use Singapore as a base for their regional operations (*Hindu*, 7 January 1996). In 2000, the-then Prime Minister Goh reiterated the fact that Singapore would be an ideal launching pad for Indian e-business in the region and urged Indian companies to use Singapore as a regional platform (*Hindu*, 22 January 2000). The role that Singapore could perhaps play is to facilitate trade between the two Asian giants—China and India—and to encourage them to play a role in the Southeast Asian region (*Hindu*, 11 July 2000). In 2004, the number of Indian firms in Singapore increased to 1,400 which is more than Chinese firms that number 1,200, and of the 1,400 Indian firms, 450 are technology companies (*Sunday Times*, 21 March 2004). The Deputy Prime Minister of Singapore Professor Jayakumar in his speech as the chief guest at the Parvasi Bharatiya Divas (PBD) 2007 (the large gathering of NRIs and PIOs), which is held annually in India, also emphasised Singapore's role in encouraging India's growing interaction with the ASEAN region.[1]

### *Wooing Singapore's IT Investors*

The IT sector has highlighted the potential to strengthen economic ties between India and Singapore. In this regard, Chief Ministers from various states in India, other than Andhra Pradesh and Karnataka, have been trying to attract Singapore investors to IT sectors in their respective states. For example, the Chief Minister of Haryana Mr Om

[1] The author was present as a delegate at the Parvasi Bharatiya Divas 2007 in New Delhi from 7–9 January.

Prakash Chautala organised a 'roadshow' in Singapore to promote his investor-friendly state. Mr Chautala's message to Singapore investors was that other Indian states, especially those in the north, did not want to lag behind their southern counterparts (*Hindu*, 11 October 2000). On a larger scale, the-then Federal Finance Minister of India Yashwant Sinha and the late IT Minister Pramod Mahajan had planned an event to celebrate India-Singapore in October 2001. About 50 top Indian CEOs came for the event to explore joint venture opportunities in a range of services. The CII has been at the forefront of promoting bilateral ties; CII continues to collaborate with the IDA, the Singapore Chinese Chamber of Commerce and Industry (SCCCI), the Singapore Confederation of Industry (SCI) and IE Singapore (*The Straits Times*, 28 September 2001).

India's former High Commissioner to Singapore Prabhat P Shukla believed that the synergies between the two countries and their proximity should be emphasised (*The Straits Times*, 14 August 2001). This was despite the bleak picture painted for Asian economies after the Asian Financial Crisis of 1997–98 by the-then Singapore's Permanent Secretary at the Ministry for Trade and Industry Khaw Boon Wan and MTI's Chief Economist, Professor Tan Kong Yam. In this regard, the Indian economy will offer opportunities in a range of areas—from software to infrastructure development. While the Indian economy may not be as attractive as China's, there could possibly be less competition; in addition, Singapore is better placed than Hong Kong and/or the North Asian economies to leverage on the opportunities in India (*Business Times*, 11 August 2001). The-then Prime Minister Goh Chok Tong commented that Singapore had 'missed' the boat in China but greater economic cooperation with India was likely. Former Federal Finance Minister of India Yashwant Sinha opined that 'Singapore should take the early bird advantage of the new investment in India (*The Straits Times*, 15 May 2001).

Singapore's cumulative investments in India had amounted to S$2.2 billion by April 2002 (*Business Times*, 17 April 2002). Singapore and India had also signed an MOU agreeing to cooperate in harnessing the potential of IT for their mutual benefit. Both countries had also agreed to increase the IT trade between them from S$200 million in 2000 to S$1 billion by end-2003 (*Channel News Asia*, 29–30 March 2000). Singapore, through the EDB, has also openly canvassed Indian IT companies to establish operations in Singapore. The EDB has promoted Singapore as a meeting place for Indian IT companies and the 7,000 MNCs in Singapore (*Hindu*, 10 May 2001). Singapore is an ideal location for Indian companies that could leverage on Singapore's physical and IT infrastructure, its central location, cosmopolitan society and reputable IT industry for expansion into Asia (*Hindu*, 10 May 2001). According to the EDB, all of India's top 20 IT companies have established operations in Singapore.

To encourage more Indian IT companies to relocate or to establish subsidiary operations in Singapore, the Singapore government has developed its core values proposition on three areas. They include enabling India-based companies to establish a base in Singapore by facilitating the process of setting up operations. Singapore's extensive business connectivity to the region and the international market is a major attraction, and the availability of various funding sources increases the attraction to India-based companies (*Sunday Times*, 16 June 2002). One of India's largest software firms, Satyam Computer Services,[2] which has an estimated market capitalisation of US$4 billion, has opened it Asia Pacific headquarters in Singapore (*The Straits Times*, 17 April 2001).

Since the 9/11 terrorist attacks in the US, Indian software companies have been looking at overseas centres in which to base their disaster recovery centres. Clients of Indian software firms are also increasingly fearful that the frequent tension between India and Pakistan (besides terrorism) might damage their operations. Hence the need for the more than 1,000 indigenous software companies in India to create secure back-up facilities in safe locations (*The Straits Times*, 19 October 2002). In this regard, Singapore could attract at least 100 Indian software companies and generate more than US$100 million a year in business spending (*The Straits Times*, 19 October 2002). Singapore has come up on the list as a possible disaster recovery site. Mr Ashok Soota, then President of the CII, said, 'I cannot think of a better place than Singapore for such secure operations' (*The Straits Times*, 8 April 2002). Singapore is competing with other possible disaster recovery centres such as Mauritius. However, the concern over issuing bloc visas to some 2,000 software engineers was daunting because the number and type of visas are controlled by the Ministry of Manpower (MOM). Without being granted visas, Indian software engineers cannot move their

[2] Since 1987, Satyam has grown and expanded operations to 36 countries and employs more than 8,000 people that services 300 clients including 40 Fortune 500 companies: Hugh Chow, 'Satyam Computer creates idea-I model', *The Straits Times* (Singapore), 8 April 2002.

operations to Singapore. According to the MOM, it is supportive of the EDB's efforts to promote Singapore as a hub for disaster recovery and business continuity centres, however, some Indian companies such as Infosys did not apply for the bloc of 2,000 employment passes for the employees of their disaster recovery centres (*The Straits Times*, 26 October 2003).

### *Continuity*

In 1988, then Singapore Trade and Development Board (TDB) marked out four areas of cooperation between India and Singapore: electronics; marine and ocean engineering; tourism-related trade such as hotels and resorts; and, finally, the semi-processing of fruit products (*Xinhua News Agency*, 30 May 1998). By 1995, more than 42 joint ventures had been established between India and Singapore companies as bilateral trade grew between the two countries (*The Straits Times*, 28 April 1995). In 2000, India and Singapore established a bilateral task force to broaden economic ties and mooted the idea of a Free Trade Area (FTA). During the visit of Indian President KR Narayanan to Singapore, an MOU was signed between Singapore Trade and Industry Minister BG George Yeo and Indian Minister for Culture and Tourism Ananth Kumar. The task force would study how Singapore could be a catalyst for India's reform and look at measures to expand bilateral economic, financial sector and trade cooperation (*The Straits Times*, 11 November 2000). Singapore leaders also detected a renewed sense of dynamism among several states in India despite a change in state leadership in Karnataka from the Congress Party to the Janata Dal in December 2000. A sense of continuity in economic liberalisation has ensued in Karnataka which was vital for the continued development of Bangalore IT Park.[3] Despite the change in state governments in Andhra Pradesh and Karnataka in June 2004, there is expected to be more continuity than change in the IT industry. In 2006, there were 2,600 companies from India registered in Singapore and among them are several hundred IT companies. This proves that investments between India and Singapore flow in both directions.

[3] 'Singapore trade minister says business cooperation with India set to flourish', *BBC Summary of World Broadcasts*, 6 December 2000 and 'S'pore Minister Sees New Dynamism Among Indian States,' *The Hindu* (India), 18 December 2000.

Continuity in India's economic liberalisation has witnessed the spread of Software Technology Parks (STPs) across the Indian landscape. Bilateral linkages between India and Singapore in the IT sector continue to be strong, and India will continue to be a very important source of skilled and professional workers for Singapore in the short and medium term. India is likely to continue its dominance as an outsourcing hub for software developent but, as India produces more original software programs, that will gradually change to more value-added services. Indian professionals from Silicon Valley are starting to return to STPs in India to form their own start-ups and joint ventures to produce software programs. Venture capital firms are also establishing a base in Bangalore and major IT hotspots in India, looking at potential projects. While Singapore is actively pursuing JV projects with its Indian counterparts and investing in India, it sees a bigger role for India in regional development. As one of India's strongest supporters in ASEAN, Singapore's assistance was acknowledged by India when the first ASEAN-India Summit was inaugurated in Cambodia in November 2002.

### *Visit of DPM Lee to India*

Before taking office as Singapore's would-be Prime Minister, DPM Lee had toured India with his spouse, Ms Ho Ching, who is also Chairman of Temasek Holdings (investment arm of the Singapore government), for one of his longest state visits abroad amounting to 10 days. Just before his visit to India, BG Lee commented that besides the CECA which is more than a bilateral trade agreement, he would also be interested in seeking army-related training space in India. This was in addition to the already ongoing naval cooperation between the two countries (*Hindu*, 11 January 2004). While in India DPM Lee met a range of top Indian leaders and businessmen, and visited companies such as Satyam Computer Services, Infosys Technologies Limited and the Bangalore IT Park (*India News*, 2 February 2004). He also announced that the EDB would be establishing an office in Mumbai to facilitate Indian companies to invest in Singapore and the region. According to the EDB, India represents both a potential market and an investment source for Singapore (*The Straits Times*, 10 February 2004). Since then, the EDB has established an office in Mumbai. Singapore is also promoted as a hub for the Southeast Asian region and a place for Indian companies to raise capital in the form of debt and/or equity (*Economic Times*, 21

October 2004). According to Temasek Holdings, it was also exploring a range of business opportunities in sectors including telecoms. Other Singapore companies have also declared their interest, for example, the Port of Singapore Authority (PSA) has invested in Indian ports, the Development Bank of Singapore (DBS) has shown an interest in Indian banks, and CapitaLand is interested in India's real estate market. Temasek Holdings has acquired a 7% stake in India's ICICI Bank and manages the S$100 million Merlion Fund with Standard Chartered Private Equity. The Fund could invest in Indian ventures either directly or co-invest with non-Indian companies or co-invest with Indian companies into third countries. B.G. Lee expects Singapore investments to grow in India, which at end-2003 amounted to US$2 billion.[4]

The Bangalore IT Park is also being given a new role to enhance links between India and Singapore. In early June 2005, Ascendas announced the rebranding of the Bangalore IT Park with the 'A' brand, which reaffirms the long-term commitment of Ascendas to Bangalore as an investment location. The commonly used acronym for the Park, which was ITPL, has been revised to become the acronym ITPB (*Deccan Herald*, 10 June 2005). The rebranding suggests Ascendas' intention to widen its scope beyond the IT Park and assume a city-wide view to take on more projects and joint ventures with other companies (*Ascendas Press Release*, 9 June 2005). According to Chief Executive of Ascendas Ms Chong Siak Ching, 'the acquisition reflects the importance that Ascendas places on the International Tech Park Bangalore and the importance of Bangalore as an investment location in India for Ascendas' (*The Straits Times*, 13 April 2005). Ascendas has become the majority share owner of the International Tech Park by purchasing the 47% stake of the Park held by the Tata Group. Along with the acquisition of Venenburg IT Park in Hyderabad, Ascendas is building a portfolio of business space in India (*The Telegraph*, 13 April 2005). The repositioning of ITPB also paved the way for Ascendas to create a series of top-line International Tech Parks across India. Despite competition from other IT hubs in India such as Chennai and Hyderabad, Bangalore maintains its lead as the favourite choice for IT companies in India. As long as Bangalore continues to upgrade its infrastructure to keep pace with

[4] 'Lee Hsien Loong: Connecting India and Singapore', Standard Chartered Bank's Singapore Conference, Mumbai, India, 16 January 2004.

the strong demand for Grade A office space, it will likely continue to lead its competitors.

In June 2007, Ascendas launched a S$500 million fund to invest in property development projects in India. The fund is called Ascendas India Development Trust and has a target asset size of S$1 billion. This Trust would complement Ascendas India IT Parks Trust of S$250 million that was launched in June 2005 (*The Straits Times*, 14 June 2007). Ascendas would have a 26% stake in the fund and other investors include Bahrain-based Islamic investment bank Arcapita and ING Private Banking. Mr Jonathan Yap, the CEO of Ascendas India, has been appointed as the CEO of the company's India funds business. Mr Yap will manage all of Ascendas' India-focused funds including those in future. Mr Lim Sin Tiow from Ascendas will take over as CEO of Ascendas India (*The Straits Times*, 14 June 2007).

### *Reviewing CECA*

A ministerial review of CECA was conducted a year after the implementation of the agreement in June 2006. Under CECA, the IT sector comes under the services chapter and some of the key areas for concern are: improved market access for IT, national treatment of service providers in terms of no less favourable treatment vis-à-vis domestic service providers in the same sector, mutual recognition of qualifications, no restrictions on international transfers, and payment for current account transactions.[5] The benefits for the IT sector under CECA would also come in the form of national treatment of investors and institutionalised investment protection. Singapore and India were aiming to implement an improved Double Taxation Avoidance Agreement (DTAA). A number of issues have surfaced that is a growing concern for both countries. One of the main concerns from India is the relatively slow rate of investments flowing from Singapore into India, not necessarily in the IT sector but in terms of overall trends. From Singapore's perspective, despite CECA, investors from Singapore still prefer to route their investments to India via Mauritius because Mauritius continues

[5] Presentation by IE Singapore on 'Singapore-India Comprehensive Economic Cooperation Agreement (CECA), Overview of benefits', Connecting India Business Summit 2006, 12–13 April 2006, Singapore.

to enjoy preferential treatment by India. The post-CECA review will address this concern to determine why Singapore was not given the same preferential treatment as Mauritius. Another concern is the slow rate of disputes coming before the judiciary to be resolved.

Economic analysts view CECA as a possible model for India's economic integration into the ASEAN region. For Singapore, CECA was also an important tool to attract Indian-owned companies to situate a presence in Singapore. In strategic terms, Singapore's air connectivity, ports, logistics, infrastructure and telecoms make it an ideal location to be a regional distribution centre or overseas headquarters for Indian-owned companies in the Southeast Asian region. Thousands of skilled and professional Indians work in Singapore among the thousands of foreign MNCs. More than 50% of these firms also have their own regional headquarters (OHQ) in Singapore. Besides IT, significant numbers of skilled and professional talent from India are being employed in the financial sector, academia, oil and gas sector, as well as in other professions. Some of the factors that had attracted Indian foreign talent to locate themselves in Singapore included its proximity to India, enabling business ecology and shared culture with India. Similarly, these are strengths that Indian-owned companies will find attractive as a base for their regional operations. Singapore would also be an ideal partner for Indian-owned companies to branch out into third countries.[6] The CECA appeared to be an ideal business platform for Indian companies to ride on Singapore's brand name and networks with a number of countries. Furthermore, if stationed in Singapore, Indian companies could leverage on Singapore's one-stop network of international suppliers, partners, and end business in Singapore, to forge global alliances.

Future research on Singapore and India economic relations could encompass a wider study that would take into account different sectors where both economies are beginning to collaborate. The different sectors could include telecommunications, housing construction, banking, tourism and port development, among others. Indian companies are starting to have a growing presence in the economy and their impact as

[6] Presentation by IE Singapore on 'Singapore-India Comprehensive Economic Cooperation Agreement (CECA), Overview of benefits', Connecting India Business Summit 2006, 12–13 April 2006, Singapore.

foreign investors on the Singapore economy could also be examined. In the event that India and ASEAN successfully conclude their own CECA, studies of India's economic engagement with the ASEAN region would be timely. Potential bilateral FTAs between India and individual ASEAN members such as Malaysia are also areas for further research.

# BIBLIOGRAPHY


'A blend of eastern and western models', *The Hindu*, 8 August 2004.
'A new wing to fly higher', *The Straits Times*, 27 August 1997.
'A trade pact with ASEAN', *The Hindu*, 8 November 2002.
'An alternative destination for quality education', *The Hindu*, 8 August 2004.
'Andhra Pradesh Hitec City Phase 1 set to take off', *Business Line*, India, 19 November 1998.
'Andhra Pradesh launches third phase of Hitec City', *Express Computer*, 8 November 2004.
'Ascendas-Tidco's Tidel Park II project finally set to take off', *The Economic Times*, 17 October 2004.
'Ascendas signs pact with TIDCO for IT complex', *Business Line*, 18 June 2003.
'Ascendas' IT park woos Indian firms', *News Today*, NT Bureau (Chennai), 15 April 2004.
'Ascendas, MIPL to develop 1 mn sq ft for IT, BPO sector', *Economic Times*, 13 October 2004.
'Ascendas to embark on S$270 million expansion of International Tech Park Bangalore (ITPB)', *Ascendas Press Release*, 10 April 2007.
'Ascendas to invest in two IT park projects in Maharashtra, India', *Ascendas Press Release*, 18 April 2007.
'Ascendas to expand', *News Today* (Chennai), 10 June 2005.
'Ascendas launches S$350 million Ascendas India IT Parks Fund', *Ascendas Press Release* (Singapore), 16 June 2005.
'Ascendas launches IT parks fund', *The Hindu*, 18 June 2005.
'Asian IT market likely to bounce back this year', *The Economic Times* (India), 6 January 2003.
Aggarwal, N. 'S'pore is India's fastest-growing export market', *The Straits Times*, 25 July 2005.
——. 'ASEAN's trade with India to double to $36 billion', *The Straits Times*, Singapore, 26 September 2002.
——. 'Infosys may pick Mauritius over Singapore for disaster recovery site', *The Straits Times*, 23 October 2002.
——. 'Singapore-India Economic Ties', *The Straits Times*, 15 May 2001.
——. 'S'pore can draw 100 IT firms from India', *Straits Times*, 19 October 2002.
——. 'EDB woos Indian technology start-ups', *The Straits Times*, 9 April 2002.
——. 'S'pore—India free trade pact just weeks away', *The Straits Times*, 29 March 2005.
——. 'S'pore's external wing in full flight', *Sunday Times*, 13 April 1997.
——. 'Parameswara plans investment trip to India next month', *The Straits Times*, 24 November 1994.
——. 'Big corporate names in the bag for Bangalore IT Park', *The Straits Times*, 25 January 1997.
——. '30% of space sold for IT Park's first phase', *The Straits Times*, 4 April 1997.
——. 'Developers triple Bangalore park investment', *The Straits Times*, 8 September 1995.
——. 'Investors take up 30% of Bangalore IT Park's first phase development', *The Straits Times*, 24 January 1997.

——. 'Phase two of Bangalore IT Park gets underway', *The Straits Times*, 30 November 2000.
Aiyar, P. 'India-China trade: a long road ahead', *The Hindu*, 7 September 2006.
Akira, K. 'Seeking a Regional Framework for East Asia', *Japan Echo*, Vol. 32, No. 1, February 2005.
Allison, T. 'Software-the arrowhead of India's IT weaponry', *Asia Times*, 7 December 2000.
Anderson, S. W. and Lanen, W. N. 'Economic transition, strategy and the evolution of management accounting practices: the case of India', *Accounting Organisations and Society*, 24, 1999.
Ang, L. 'Focused on taking JTC into a new era', *Business Times* (Singapore), 3 April 2000.
Asher, M. and Srivastava, S. 'India and the Asian Economic Community', RIS, May 2003.
Asher, M. G. 'Economic Relations Between Singapore and India: Trends, Issues and Future Directions', Conference on 'Singapore-India: Emerging Linkages', National University of Singapore, 24 November 1993.
Asher, M. G. and Sen, R. 'India-East Asia Integration: A Win-Win for Asia', *RIS Discussion Papers*, RIS-DP # 91/2005, March 2005.
Austin, I. (2001) *Pragmatism and Public Policy in East Asia*, Fairmont International Private Limited, Singapore.
'Building the great Indian software brand', *Express Computer*, 24 March 2003.
'Building on the Singapore connection', *Business Times*, 17–18 September 1994.
Bajpai, R. 'Tata—led group pulls out of Indian airport project', *Business Times*, Singapore, 17 July 1998.
Bardhan, P. 'China, India Superpower? Not so Fast!', *YaleGlobal*, 25 October 2005.
Baru, S. (2006) *Strategic Consequences of India's Economic Performance*, Academic Foundation, New Delhi.
Baruah, A. 'Palm Oil Duty Cut', *The Hindu*, 28 July 2001.
——. 'Talks with ASEAN will ease tension: PM', *The Hindu*, 17 May 2001.
——. 'Consensus in ASEAN for Summit in India', *The Hindu*, 10 January 2001.
——. 'Selling "Cyberyana" in S'pore', *The Hindu*, 11 October 2000.
Basu, I. 'Indian IT: Not just talk, substance too', *Asia Times*, 30 October 2004.
——. 'Chinks in India's IT armor', *Asia Times*, 8 September 2005.
BG George Yeo. 'India and Singapore', *Speeches*, Vol. 17, No. 1, January–February 1993.
BG Yeo. Minister of Information and the Arts 'Let Others Learn From Singapore, But Keep Fire of Creativity Burning Bright To Stay Ahead', Speech to the Singapore International Chambers of Commerce, *The Straits Times*, 5 June 1993.
BG (NS) George Yeo. Minister of Information and the Arts, Singapore, 'The Singapore-India Link', Speeches, Vol. 18, No. 4, July–August 1994.
——. Minister for Information and the Arts and Second Minister for Foreign Affairs, 'India and Singapore: Partners in Progress', Speeches, Vol. 17, No. 1, January–February.
Biers, D. and Sidhva, S. 'Life in the Slow Lane', *Far Eastern Economic Review*, 21 August 1997.
Boey, D. 'Creating a buzz in India,' *Business Times*, Singapore, 17 April 2002.
——. 'Full occupancy at S'pore-link tech park in India', *Business Times* (Singapore), 30 November 2000.
Bradnock, R. W. (1990) *India's Foreign Policy Since 1971*, Royal Institute of International Affairs, Pinter Publishers, London.
'Can Indian software firms hold their own against MNCs', *Express Computer*, 11 February 2002.

Chairman's Statement of the Fifth ASEAN + India Summit Cebu, Philippines, 14 January 2007.
'Chennai grows a major IT hub', *The Straits Times*, 4 September 2004.
'China, India to reopen border trade', *Asia Times*, 20 June 2006.
'Contribution of Government-Linked Companies to Gross Domestic Product', Singapore Department of Statistics, March 2001.
Correspondent, 'Karnataka, top BPO destination in India', *Rediff.com*, 9 June 2004.
Cadene, P. and Holstrom, M. (eds.) (1998) *Decentralized Production in India*, Sage Publications, New Delhi.
Castells, M. (1996) *The Rise of the Network Society*, Blackwell Publishers, UK.
Castro, I. 'Big Brother China Woos ASEAN', *Asia Times*, 6 November 2002.
Chang, H. 'Indian Chamber incorporates holding company for investments in India,' *Business Times*, 15 April 1993.
Chaze, A. (2006) *India: An Investor's Guide to the Next Economic Superpower*, Wiley.
Chellam, R. 'India offers a US$7b IT opportunity,' *The Business Times*, 8 April 2002.
Cheow, T. C. Eric. 'Strategic Relevance of Asian Economic Integration', *RIS Discussion Papers*, RIS-DP # 90/2005, March 2005, p. 3.
Chia, S. Y. et al. (2001) *Growth and Development of the IT Industry in Bangalore and Singapore*, Stirling Publishers, Singapore.
Chiang, Y. P. 'SM: S'poreans Must Now Build Up External Economy', *The Straits Times*, 16 November 1992.
Chirathivat, S. 'ASEAN-India Cooperation in Trade and Tourism: Trends and Prospects,' *Journal of Asian Economics*, Vol. 7, No. 4, Winter 1996, pp. 743–757.
Chong, V. 'Ascendas buys Vanenberg IT Park in India', *Business Times*, 24 December 2004.
Choong, W. 'Temasek to focus on 3 tasks', *The Straits Times*, 13 December 2001.
Chorafas, D. N. (2003) *Outsourcing, Insourcing and IT for Enterprise Management*, Palgrave, MacMillan, UK.
Choudhury, A.R. 'Is India's IT just a bubble?' *The Business Times* (Singapore), 21 August 2000.
Chow, H. 'Satyam Computer creates idea-I model', *The Straits Times*, 8 April 2002.
Chowdhury, D. R. 'Free Trade for Thailand, free fall for India', *Asia Times*, 14 June 2005.
Chua, P. M. 'Government can help companies go regional', *Business Times*, 25 September 1992.
Chun, W. C. (1997) 'IT2000: Singapore's Vision of an Intelligent Island', *Intelligent Environments*, Peter Droege (ed.).
Contractor, F. J. and Kundu, S. (2004) 'The role of export-driven entrepreneurship in economic development: A comparison of software exports from India, China and Taiwan', *Technological Forecasting & Social Change*, 71, pp. 799–922.
Contractor, F. J. and Lorange, P. (2002) August, 'Growth of Alliances in the Knowledge Based—Based Economy', *International Business Review*, 11(4) 485–502.
Cox, J. 'As economy expands, India on verge of something big', *USA Today*, 2 August 2004.
Cua, G. 'Goh urges S'pore companies to spread regional investments', *Business Times*, 22–23 May 1993.
'Delay in launch of IT Park', *The Hindu*, 3 November 1998.
'Dhana is chairman of SICCI investment company', *The Straits Times*, 7 April 1993.
Damodaran, R. 'Fast track to success', *New Straits Times*, 26 January 2005.
De Silva, G. 'Dhana: Parameswara not restricted to India', *The Straits Times*, 26 November 1994.
Dhanabalan, S., Minister for Trade and Industry, 'Go Regional Push Must Bring Spin-Offs for Singapore', *The Straits Times*, 23 May 1993.

Dieter, H. and Higgott, R. 'Exploring alternative theories of economic regionalism: from trade to finance in Asian co-operation', *CSGR Working paper* No. 89/02, January 2002.

DPM Tony Tan (1997) 'Global City, Best Home', *National Day Rally Speech*, Singapore.

Dubey, S. 'Goh Urges India Executives To Look East to Singapore,' *Business Times*, 26 January 1991.

Dunning, J. H. (1997) *Alliance Capitalism and Global Business*, Routledge, New York

——. (ed.), (2000) *Regions, Globalization, and the Knowledge-Based Economy*, Oxford University Press, Oxford, New York.

*Economic Development in India: Achievements and Challenges*, (1995) A World Bank Country Study.

'EDB to open first office in India soon', *The Straits Times*, 10 February 2004.

'EDS opens centre at Chennai Tidel Park', *Business Line*, 29 April 2001.

'ERC panel calls for cluster approach in helping Singapore firms venture abroad', *Channel News Asia*, Singapore, 13 September 2002.

Editorial 'Sustain the interest', *The Hindu*, 24 January 2000.

Editorials 'Work with other nations to tap business openings', *The Straits Times*, 22 May 1993.

Excerpts from the Singapore Lecture by Indian Prime Minister Narasimha Rao, 'Rao extends his hand of partnership', *The Straits Times*, 9 September 1994.

Excerpts of speech by Madam Ho Ching, Temasek Holdings Executive Director, 'Looking into the future of GLCs', *The Straits Times*, 18 July 2002.

Extract of transcript of Interview By BG George Yeo, Minister for Trade and Industry with Arnaud Rodier of Le Figaro, (2001) *Singapore Government Press Release*, MITA, 11 October.

Edna, K. 'Top 14 S'pore brands worth $7.6b', *The Straits Times*, 22 October 2002.

——. 'Backsliding on services: Act fast or lose out', *The Straits Times*, 17 September 2002.

Engardio, P. 'A New World Economy', *BusinessWeek*, 6 September 2005.

——. (2007) *Chindia. How China and India Are Revolutionizing Global Business*, McGraw-Hill, UK.

——. *Friends and Neighbours, India & ASEAN, Dialogue Partnership* (1997) Indian Ministry of External Affairs, Paper presented at ASEAN Ministerial Meeting in Kuala Lumpur, Malaysia, July.

'FTA will boost India—Thailand trade', *The Hindu*, 11 July 2004.

Furman, J. L., Porter M. E. and Stern, S. (2002) 'The determinants of national innovative capacity', *Research Policy*, 31.

'Gathering to harness diversity of communities; Overseas Indians a Force to Reckon with', *The Straits Times*, 19 June 1996.

'Germany woos Indian IT', *BBC News*, 17 May 2000.

'Global City, Best Home', National Day Rally Speech, 1997, Ministry of Education.

'Go global with TDB', *Business Times*, 20 November 2001.

Galbraith, Craig S. and Alex F. De Noble. 'Competitive Strategy and Flexible Manufacturing: New Dimensions in High-Technology Venture-Based Economic Development', *Journal of Business Venturing* 7, 1992, 387–404.

Ganguly, S. (2003/4) 'India's Foreign Policy Grows Up', *World Policy Journal*.

Ghosh, N. 'JTC to cash in on India dotcom fever', *The Straits Times*, 24 January 2000.

——. 'India govt should try to change its mindset,' *The Straits Times*, 20 January 2000.

——. 'Phase Two: JTC to expand tech park in Bangalore', *The Straits Times*, 6 June 2000.

——. 'Singapore, India set high-tech tie-up in motion', *The Straits Times*, 22 January 2000.
——. 'Tech Park a symbol of joint effort', *The Straits Times*, 22 January 2000.
——. 'PM Goh urges India to look towards S-EA', *The Straits Times*, 19 January 2000.
——. 'India's show of confidence in S'pore', *The Straits Times*, 28 September 2001.
——. 'S'pore-India IT park gets thumbs up', *The Straits Times*, 18 January 2002.
Giridharadas, A. 'India's Mini-Multinationals Make Waves in Western Markets', *The International Herald Tribune*, 2 September 2005.
Goh, S. N. (2002) 'China gobbles up $87 billion in investments', *The Straits Times*, 28 December.
Green, D. J. (1994) 'Convergence and Cohesion within the ASEAN-4,' *Journal of Asian Economics*, Vol. 5, No. 1.
Haley, U. (1998) 'Virtual Singapores: shaping international competitive environments through business-government partnerships', *Journal of Organisational Change Management*, Vol. 11, No. 4, 1998, pp. 338–356.
Hamid, H. 'India-ASEAN summit to further define ties', *Business Times*, Malaysia, 24 September 2002.
Han, F. K. 'India Celebrates in Grand Style', *The Straits Times*, 27 January 1994.
——. 'India hopes co-operation with S'pore will help to boost its ties with region', *The Straits Times*, 26 January 1994.
——. '$150m fund to help firms go abroad', *The Straits Times*, 26 January 1994.
Hardgrave, R. L. and Kochanek, S. A. (1986) *India: Government and Politics in a Developing Nation*, 4th Edition, Harcourt Brace Jovanovich Publishers, London.
Heng, C. (2003) 'Economic Contributions of Singapore's Creative Industries, Ministry of Trade and Industry', Singapore Ministry of Trade and Industry, First quarter.
Heng, T. C. (2002) 'Mapping Singapore's Knowledge Based Economy, Economic Survey of Singapore—Third Quarter', Ministry of Trade and Industry, Singapore.
Hoge, J. F. 'A Global Power Shift in the Making', *Foreign Affairs*, July/August 2004.
Hutton, W. and Giddens, A. (eds.) (2000) *On the Edge Living With Capitalism*, Jonathan Cape, London.
'India—a password for outsourcing', *The Hindu* (India), 30 December 2002.
'India and the ASEAN', *The Hindu Index* (New Delhi), 20 December 1995.
'India and China to double trade', *BBC News*, 21 November 2006.
'India and Silicon Valley: Now the R&D Flows Both Ways', *Businessweek*, 8 December 2003.
'India trade think-tank launched', *Today News*, 21 June 2007.
'India for Increased Technological Cooperation With ASEAN', *The Hindu*, 28 July 2001.
'India: Foreign Trade Challenges', *Business Line*, India, 14 June 2001.
'India: Look East, Look ASEAN', *Business Line*, 2 June 2001.
'India outsourced services worth US$11bn in 2003–04', *Times of India*, 3 December 2004.
'India special: The next knowledge superpower', *New Scientist*, 19 February 2005.
'India takes up Arun Jain's arrest issue with Indonesian government', *Hindustan Times*, 17 December 2002.
'India: Over 90 PC of Cyber Towers Space Sold Out', *Business Line*, 29 October 1999.
'Indian IT isn't Hype at All', *Time Asia*, Vol. 156, No. 15, 16 October 2000.
'Indian IT firm opens Singapore haven', *BBC News*, 7 August 2002.
'India's IT market to be US$25 billion by 2004: survey', *Business Times*, 11 July 2000.
'India's strength: Knowledge resources', *Rediff.com*, 28 November 2005.

'India's exports of outsourcing to hit US$23.4b', *Business Times*, 11–12 February 2006.
'India can use S'pore as base to crack S-E Asia', *The Economic Times*, 21 October 2004.
'Indian cos get entry point to Europe', *Economic Times*, 25 August 2003.
'Indian Chinese Civilisations Should Focus on Similarity', *The Straits Times*, 10 September 1994.
'Indian firms now free to tap funds overseas', *Business Times*, 21 January 2000.
'Indian software giant targets Europe', *BBC News*, 30 August 2001.
'Indonesia frees Indian software boss', *BBC News*, 20 December 2002.
*Information Technology Park, Bangalore* (1993) Economic and Development Board, EDB Publication, Singapore.
'Infosys: a hint of the future of India's economy', *Business Times*, 21 January 2000.
'Insurer moves 1100 jobs to India', *BBC News*, 11 October 2004.
'Intel to Hire More in Bangalore', *Economic Times*, 13 April 2004.
'International Technology Park, Bangalore gets new brand identity and positioning', *Ascendas Press Release*, 9 June 2005.
'IT services, BPO cos need to tap new lines: Nasscom', *Business Line*, 13 February 2003.
'ITPL gets new brand identity', *Deccan Herald*, 10 June 2005.
Ian, B. 'A potent brand of steel and silk,' *The Straits Times*, 27 September 2002.
Ibrahim, Z. 'Just 0.5% talent loss will hit S'pore hard: SM', *The Straits Times*, 15 March 2007.
——. 'S'pore gears up for new growth wave,' *The Straits Times*, 13 October 1998.
Jayanth, V. 'S'pore PM to focus on South,' *The Hindu*, India, 2 January 2000.
Jayaram, P. 'India gets Thai help to develop north-east', *The Straits Times*, 17 April 2007.
'Kashmir threatens India's IT sector', *BBC News*, 5 June 2002.
Katyal, K. K. 'Bringing economies of India, S'pore close', *The Straits Times*, 16 April 1993.
Khan, J. A. (1999) *India and West Asia. Emerging Markets in the Liberalisation Era*, Sage Publications, New Delhi.
Khanna, T. 'India Needs to Encourage Trade with China', *Harvard Business School*, 6 December 2006.
Khanna, V. 'Tapping India's tech boom', *The Business Times*, 25 October 2000.
——. 'Preparing for dawn while it's dark', *The Business Times*, 11 August.
——. 'Network launched to foster S'pore-India trade links', *Business Times*, 19 October 2002.
Khosla, I. P. (ed.) (2006) *Economic Diplomacy*, Konark Piblishers Private Limited, Delhi.
Kitazume, T. 'Political power plays cloud East Asian economic community vision', *The Japan Times*, 13 December 2005.
Klein, A. 'AOL to Open Netscape Office in India's Tech Center', *Washington Post*, 6 March 2001.
Knoke, D. (2001) *Changing Organisations, Business Networks in the New Political Economy*, Westview Press, Colorado, US.
Koh, E. 'GLC success shows where Singapore firms can go', *The Straits Times*, 18 July 2002.
Koh, F., Toh W. and Tschang F. 'An Analytical Framework for Science parks and Technology Districts with an Application to Singapore', *Journal of Business Venturing*, Special Issue, 25–27 April 2003.
Koh, L. 'Reinventing the Singapore economy', *The Straits Times*, 24 November 2001.
Kotkins, J. (1992) *Tribes: How Race, Religion and Identity Determine Success in the New Global Economy*, Random House, New York.

Krishna, M. 'Indian IT firms look to Gulf as business in US slows', *Indo-Asian News Service*, 18 October 2002.

Krueger, A. O. (ed.) (2002) *Economic Policy Reforms and the Indian Economy*, Oxford University Press, New Delhi, India.

Kumar, N. 'Towards a Broader Asian Community: Agenda for the East Asia Summit', *RIS Discussion Papers*, RIS-DP # 100, November 2005.

Kumar, V. R. 'Over 90 PC of Cyber Towers Space Sold Out', *Business Line*, India, 29 October 1999.

Kundu, S. L. 'The business of knowledge in India', *Asia Times*, 9 September 2005.

Kuppuswamy, C. S. 'India's Policy: Looking Eastward', *South Asia Analysis Group*, Note No. 151, 29 April 2002.

Kwan, W. K. 'Seek Business Openings Throughout Region: PM Urges S'pore Investors', *The Straits Times*, 10 May 1993.

'Lee Hsien Loong: Connecting India and Singapore', Standard Chartered Bank's Singapore Conference, Mumbai, India, 16 January 2004.

'Long-term investments,' *Financial Times* (London), 18 February 1997.

Landler, M. 'A New Kind of Software Company for India', *The New York Times*, 26 March 2001.

Larson, V. 'Offshoring is a high-tech trend. More companies are exporting computer jobs. The impact is smaller in Nebraska, but big firms are shifting work to India and elsewhere', *Omaha World Herald* (Nebraska), 11 August 2003.

Latif, A. 'Business panel to strengthen S'pore-India ties', *The Straits Times*, 4 February 2005.

Lavoie, M. et al. (2003) 'A growing trend toward knowledge work in Canada', *Research Policy*, 32.

Lee, B. G. 'Holds talks in India aimed at boosting trade ties', *The Straits Times*, 24 March 1992.

Lee, R. 'Indian IT giant picks Singapore as headquarters', *The Straits Times*, 17 April 2001.

——. 'Indian IT picks Singapore as headquarters', *The Straits Times*, 17 April 2001.

Lee, S. H. 'Fast-growing India seeks to become bigger world player', *The Straits Times*, 21 June 2007.

——. 'S'pore-India ties get boost with launch of two forums', *The Straits Times*, 20 June 2007.

Lee, S. S. 'S'pore working to draw more Indian firms here', *Sunday Times* (Singapore), 16 June 2002.

Lee, T. Y. (ed.) (1991) *Growth Triangle, The Johor-Singapore-Riau Experience*, Institute of Policy Studies, Singapore.

Lian, D. 'Temasek Charter authorises external economy mission of GLC', Morgan Stanley, 8 July 2002.

Lien, J. 'Silicon Valley S'poreans propose a 10% solution', *Business Times*, 8 April 2002.

Lim, L. 'Govt to retain control of seaports, airports', *The Straits Times*, 4 July 2002.

——. 'Parliament to debate role of GLCs', *The Straits Times*, 27 August 2002.

Lim, R. 'S'pore unveils blueprint for knowledge-based economy', *Business Times*, 21 January 1999.

Leow, A. J. 'Group plans to expand IT park project in Bangalore', *The Straits Times*, 26 November 1993.

Leung, E. 'Southeast Asia—China: Threats, opportunities', *Asia Times*, 2 August 2003.

Liaw, W. C. 'Firms vie for the best as global talent war hots up', *The Straits Times*, 12 March 2007.

Loh, H. Y. 'India Beckons', *Business Times* (Singapore), 17 April 2002.

Long, S. 'The tiger in front', *The Economist*, 5 March 2005.
Low, E. 'Property ownership, tariff structure among issues brought up to Indian officials,' India trip allowed business team to raise concerns: Das,' *Business Times*, 24 January 2000.
Low, I. 'Temasek Sharpens Its Focus', *The Straits Times*, 4 July 2002.
Low, L. and Johnston, D. M. (eds.) (2001) *Singapore Inc.*, Asia Pacific Press, Singapore.
Luo, Y. and Tan, J. J. (1998) 'A comparison of multinational and domestic firms in an emerging market: A strategic choice perspective', *Journal of International Management*, Vol. 4, No. 1, pp. 21–40.
'Making an impact in Singapore', *Business Times* (Singapore) 31 December 1991.
'Message By Shekhar Datta, President CII, *Tradespur*, International Enterprises, Singapore, June–July 1996, p. 16.
'MNCs occupy 95 pc in HITEC City phase-II', *The Hindu*, 25 June 2001.
'More tie-ups likely as trade increases', *The Straits Times*, 28 April 1995.
Motion on Temasek Charter and EISC's Recommendations on Government in Business, Parliament of Singapore, (2002) Notice Paper No. 140.
Mahizhnan, A. 'Corporate networking: Where to next', *Business Times*, 27–28 February 1993.
Mahiznan, A. and Lee, T. Y. (eds.) (1998) *Singapore Re-Engineering Success*, Institute of Policy Studies Singapore and Oxford University Press, Singapore.
Mani, S. (2002) *Government, Innovation and Technology Policy*, Government of India, India.
Mathews, J. A. (2002) *Dragon Multinational. A New Model for Global Growth*, Oxford University Press, New York.
Mehra, K. and Dhawan, S. K. (2003) 'Study of the process of organisational learning in software firms in India', *Technovation* 23.
Mehta, R. 'Economic Co-Operation Between India and Singapore: A Feasibility Study', *RIS Discussion Papers*, RIS-DP # 41/2003, February 2003.
Mehta, R. and Narayanan, S. 'India's Regional Trading Arrangements', *RIS Discussion Papers*, RIS-DP # 114, August 2006.
Meine, Pieter Van Dijk and Roberta Rabellotti (eds.) (1997) *Enterprise Clusters and Networks in Developing Countries*, Frank Cass, London.
Menkhoff, T. and Gerke, S. (eds.) (2002) *Chinese Entrepreneurship and Asian Business Networks*, Routledge Curzon, London and New York.
Menon, A. K. and David, S. 'Hitech Hardsell Hyderabad Wants to Lure Investors from Bangalore', *India Today*, 15 April 1997.
Mirza, H. (ed.) (1998) *Global Competitive Strategies in the New World Economy*, Edward Elgar, UK.
Mohan, C. R. 'Bill Clinton arrives to a warm welcome', *The Hindu*, 20 March 2000.
Mohanty, S. K. 'Possibility of Close Economic Cooperation between India and Singapore', *RIS Discussion Papers*, RIS-DP # 45/2003, April 2003.
Mohanty, S. K., Pohit S. and Roy, S. S. 'Towards Formation of Close Economic Cooperation among Asian Countries', *RIS Discussion Papers*, RIS-DP # 78/2004, September 2004.
Mukta, M. 'Exploring export markets', *Financial Express*, 2 August 2000.
Murray, G. and Perera, A. (1996) *Singapore The Global City-State*, China Library Folkstone, Kent, UK.
*National Conference on Software and Telecom Industries*, 11 January 1997, Windsor Manor Sheraton, Bangalore, India.
'New CEO of Ascendas India', *The Hindu*, 4 March 2006.
'New economic strategy dates back to '86', *The Straits Times*, 30 May 1993.
'New chief takes over at Bangalore IT Park', *The Straits Times*, 13 March 1996.
'New problems hit country's software industry', *Economic Times*, 22 April 2003.

Naik, S. D. 'India and ASEAN: Towards enhancing economic partnership', *Business Line*, 16 October 2002.
Narayana, P. M. P. 'Aiming to Become Kings of Software', *Business Times*, 13 May 2002.
Nirmala, M. 'Ties with India entering new chapter, says BG Yeo', *Straits Times Weekly Edition*, 16 July 1994.
Nirmala, N. 'Ho Ching as leader, wife and mother', *The Straits Times*, 27 June 2002.
'Outsourcing moves to knowledge arena', *Deccan Herald*, 20 June 2005.
Ohmae, K. (1995) *The End of the Nation State, The Rise of Regional Economies*, Harper Collins, London.
O'Reilly, B. 'Your New Global Work Force', *Fortune*, 14 December 1992.
Ong, K. Y. 'Advancing the ASEAN-India Partnership in the New Millennium', *RIS Discussion Papers*, RIS-DP # 96/2005, May 2005.
'Passage to India: High-Tech Job Moving Abroad, Lured by Country's Low Costs, Skilled Labour', *Rocky Mountain News*, (Denver, Colorado), 12 July 2003.
'Plenty of opportunities in India for enterprising investors: BG Yeo', *The Straits Times*, 8 March 1997.
'Police detain top Indian businessmen after fraud complaint,' *The Jakarta Post*, 18 December 2002.
Presentation by IE Singapore on 'Singapore-India Comprehensive Economic Cooperation Agreement (CECA), Overview of benefits', Connecting India Business Summit, Singapore, 12–13 April 2006.
Press Statement on the Second Meeting of the Singapore-India Task Force on Information Technology, Communications and Services, Singapore Government Press Release, MITA, 2 July 2001.
Press Statement from the Prime Minister's Office: Official Visit of Prime Minister Goh Chok Tong to India, Ministry of Information and the Arts, Singapore, 17 January 2000.
'Profits boost for India's Satyam', *BBC News*, 24 October 2001.
Parameswara Holdings Limited, *Shareholders Report*, 10 July 1997.
Patibandla, M. and Petersen, B. (2002) 'Role of Transnational Corporations in the Evolution of a High-Tech Industry: the Case of India's Software Industry', *World Development*, Vol. 30, No. 9, pp. 1561–1577.
Patni, A. (1999) 'Silicon Valley of the East', *Harvard Business Review*, Cambridge, Fall.
Pereira, D. 'PM Goh happy that Rao has raised Indian fever', *The Straits Times*, 18 September 1994.
Phar, K. B. 'Southeast Asia losing FDI fight to China', *Asia Times*, 8 October 2002.
Phua, K. K. 'Forward and Outward together', *The Straits Times*, 30 May 1993.
PM Goh Chok Tong. 'Singapore Must Plug Into Thriving Economies And Grow With Them', *The Straits Times*, 22 May 1993.
——. 'Staying competitive through regionalisation', *Speeches*, May–June 1993, Vol. 17, No. 3.
——. 'Prospects for India in the New World Economic Order', *Speeches*, January–February 1995.
Porter, M. E. 'Clusters and the New Economics of Competition,' *Harvard Business Review*, Nov./Dec. 1998, Vol. 76(6).
Preer, R. W. (1992) *The Emergence of Technopolis*, Praeger, Westport.
Pucher, J., Korattyswaporam, N. et al. (2005) 'Urban transport crisis in India', *Transport Policy* 12.
*Regionalisation*, Economic Development Board, Singapore, April 1997.
'Riding on the Singapore brand name', *The Straits Times*, 16 October 2001.
Rajan, R. S. *Trade Liberalization and the New Regionalism in the Asia-Pacific: Taking Stock of Recent Ongoings*, University of Adelaide, School of Economics, February 2003.

Rajan, R. S. and Sen, R. A. 'Decade of Trade Reforms in India', *World Economics*, Vol. 3, No. 4, October–December 2002.

Rajawat, K. Y. 'Global IT firms target chip designers from India', *Economic Times*, 30 September 2002.

Rajendra Prasad, 'Another Silicon Valley', *The Hindu*, 27 October 1997.

Ram-Prasad, C. (1994) 'Culture and Complementarities: Implications of the Singapore-India MOU on Culture, Heritage and the Archives', Yong, M. C. and V. V. Bahanoji Rao (eds.), in *Singapore-India Relations A Primer.*

Ramachandran, K. 'IT infrastructure boom in Chennai', *The Hindu*, 4 October 2004.

Ramakrishnan, N. 'Ascendas to market space to ITES firms', *Business Line*, 14 November 2002.

Ramesh, M. 'Indo-Thailand trade pact to go live from September', *Business Line*, 11 July 2004.

Ramirez, C. D. and Ling, H. T. 'Singapore, Inc. Versus the Private Sector: Are Government-Linked Companies Different?' *IMF Working Paper*, International Monetary Fund, July 2003.

Ranade, S. 'India-China trade: Win-win situation or zero sum game', *Business Line*, 16 April 2005.

Rao, B. V. V. (1996) 'Indian Economic Reforms and ASEAN-India Economic Relations', *Journal of Asian Economics*, Vol. 7, No. 4, pp. 759–768.

Rao, G. 'Singapore to ink IT pact with Karnataka today', *The Economic Times*, 21 January 2000.

Ratti, R., Bramanti A. and Gordon R. (eds.) (1997) *The Dynamics of Innovative Regions: The GREMI Approach*, Ashgate, Aldershot, UK.

Ravichandran, R. 'India-ASEAN Business Summit to Boost Trade and Investment TIE', *Malaysia Economic News*, 16 October 2003.

Ray, A. 'BPO and new protectionism', *Business Line*, 4 July 2003.

Rekhi, S. 'India all out to woo S'poreans', *The Straits Times*, 14 August 2001.

——. 'S'pore and India eye free-trade area', *The Straits Times*, 11 November 2000.

Reuters, A. F. P. 'India and the US set up group to boost trade and investment', *Business Times* (Singapore), 22 March 2000.

Rodan, G. (1989) *The Political Economy of Singapore's Industrialization*, Forum, Kuala Lumpur.

Root, F. R. (1994), *Entry Strategies for International Markets*, Lexington Books, New York.

Rosenberg, D. (2002) *Cloning Silicon Valley, the next generation high-tech hotspots*, Reuters, Pearson Education, London, New York, Singapore.

'Sanctions, currency crisis may slow India tech park growth', *Business Times*, 22 June 1998.

'SAP to double Indian headcount', *BBC News*, 11 February 2004.

'Second Phase of Hitec City Begins', *India Business Insight*, 11 September 2000.

'Share benefits with hosts: PM', *The Straits Times*, 22 May 1993.

'Singapore firm picks up 20% in Kshema Tech,' *The Economic Times* (India), 8 January 2003.

'Singapore trade minister says business cooperation with India set to flourish', *BBC Summary of World Broadcasts*, 6 December 2000.

'S'pore Minister Sees New Dynamism Among Indian States', *The Hindu*, 18 December 2000.

'Singapore businessmen eye India', *The Straits Times*, 22 September 1993.

'Singapore as a catalyst for investment in India', *The Hindu*, 7 January 1996.

Singapore Defence Minister Teo Chee Hean 'The little red dot that signifies our hopes and dreams', *The Straits Times*, 20 April 2007.

'Singapore pact is a step towards India-ASEAN FTA', *Business Line*, 1 July 2005.

'Singapore, India agree to launch study on bilateral free trade area', *BBC Worldwide Monitoring*, 8 April 2002.
'Singapore Must Plug Into Thriving Regional Economies and Grow With Them', *The Straits Times*, 22 May 1993.
'Singapore and India to cooperate in Information Technology sector', *Channel News Asia*, Singapore, 29 March 2000.
'Singapore and India click to up IT trade to S$1 billion by 2003', *Channel News Asia*, Singapore, 30 March 2000.
'S'pore bullish on Indian IT companies', *The Hindu*, 10 May 2001.
'Singapore's tech park sets the benchmark', *The Straits Times*, 12 April 2007.
'Singapore shaping up as disaster recovery hub', *Business Times*, 3 March 2003.
'Singapore to promote investment and trade in India', *Xinhua News Agency*, 30 May 1988.
Singapore Trade Minister BG George Yeo 'Building a Silicon Valley in Singapore', *International-Asian Business*, 19 June 2000.
'Singapore trade minister says business cooperation with India set to flourish', *BBC Summary of World Broadcasts*, 6 December 2000.
'S'pore Minister Sees New Dynamism Among Indian States', *The Hindu*, 18 December 2000.
'S'pore needs to tap region, go offshore and stay competitive', *The Straits Times*, 29 October 1992.
'S'pore firms should focus on region: BG Lee', *Business Times*, 29 October 1992.
Special Correspondent 'India has potential for increasing trade with ASEAN', *The Hindu*, 18 October 2002.
Special Correspondent 'Ascendas buys Tatas' stake in ITPB', *The Hindu*, 13 April 2005.
Special Correspondent 'Singapore ideal launching pad', *The Hindu*, 22 January 2000.
Speech by Deputy PM and Chairman of the Monetary Authority of Singapore, Lee Hsien Loong, at the Credit Suisse First Boston seminar, Singapore, 26 October 1999.
Speech by George Yeo, Minister for Trade and Industry, TDB International Day, Singapore, 9 January 2001.
Speech by PM Goh Chok Tong at the Singapore-India Business Forum on Monday, 8 April 2002, Singapore Government Press Release, Ministry of Information and the Arts.
Speech by PM Goh Chok Tong at Official Opening of the International Tech Park Bangalore, 21 January 2000, Bangalore, India-MITA Press Release.
Speech by Singapore PM Goh Chok Tong at the Singapore-India Business Forum, Singapore, 8 April 2002.
Speech by Singapore Prime Minister at the Official Opening of the International Tech Park Bangalore on 21 January 2000, Bangalore, India, Singapore Ministry of Information and the Arts.
'Spreading information about the Lion City', *The Hindu*, 8 August 2004.
Staff Reporter, 'A Historic Moment', *The Hindu*, 20 March 2000.
'Survey—India: Information Technology', *Financial Times*, London, 1 December 1999.
Sarma, A. and Mehta, P. K. (2002) *Exploring Indo ASEAN Economic Partnership in Globalising World*, Bookwell, New Delhi.
Saywell, T. 'Interview George Yeo: India Deserves Better', *Far Eastern Economic Review*, 25 January 2001.
Saywell, T. and Plott, D. 'Re-Imagining Singapore', *Far Eastern Economic Review*, 11 July 2002.
Schein, E. (1996) *Strategic Pragmatism*, MIT Press, US.
Schmitter, P. C. and Lehmbruch (1979) *Toward Corporatist Intermediation*, Sage, London.

Seshagiri, N. (1991) 'The Informatics Policy in India', *Information Systems Frontiers* 1:1, pp. 107–116.
Shafaeddin, S. M. (2004) 'Is China's accession to WTO threatening exports of developing countries?' *China Economic Review*, Vol. 15, Issue 2, pp. 109–144.
Shanker, V. 'Towards an Economic Community: Exploring the Past', *RIS Discussion Papers*, RIS-DP # 47/2003, April 2003.
Shaumian, T. L. (1988) 'India's Foreign Policy; Interaction of Global and Regional Aspects', *Asian Survey*, Vol. XXVII, No. 11, November, pp. 1161–1169.
Shiva, R. S. (1995) *The Dragons of Asia: Asia Pacific Rim Countries and Their Multinationals*, Wheeler Publishing, New Delhi.
Sikes, J. 'Singapore: Making the Indian Connection', *Asian Business*, May 1993.
Singh, D., Member of Parliament and Chairman of India Regional Discussion Paper, India Strategy Paper in *The Report Of the Regional Business Forum*, September 1995.
Sisodia, N. S. and Bhaskar, C. U. (eds.) (2005) *Emerging India, Security and Foreign Policy Perspectives*, Institute for Defence Studies and Analyses, New Delhi.
Sridhar, V. 'China's proposal for a free trade agreement with India meets with resistance from Indian industry', *Frontline*, Vol. 22, Issue 10, 7–20 May 2005.
Srinath, M. G. 'Infrastructure reforms holding back India's economic progress,' *Deutsche Presse Agentur*, 6 August 1997.
Srinivasan, G. 'Asian Economic Community—Potential to unleash regional growth', *The Hindu*, 25 November 2005.
Srivastava, S. 'India, China reach new trade heights', *Asia Times*, 22 June 2006.
Stremlau, J. 'Bangalore: India's silicon city', *Monthly Labor Review*, November 1996.
——. 'Dateline Bangalore: Third World Technopolis,' *Foreign Policy*, No. 102, Spring 1996, pp. 152–168.
Suleri, A. Q. and Sharma, B. 'The SAFTA mirage', *Himal*, February 2004.
Sunil, M. (2002) *Government, Innovation and Technology Policy: An International Comparative Analysis*, Edward Elgar, Cheltenham, UK.
Suryanara, P. S. 'Economic, defence cooperation between India, Singapore vital', *The Hindu*, 11 January 2004.
——. (1997) 'A treaty and a message', *Frontline*, Vol. 22, Issue 15, 16–29 July 2005. Affairs, Paper presented at ASEAN Ministerial Meeting in Kuala Lumpur, Malaysia, July.
——. 'We can play catalyst to reforms: Goh', *The Hindu*, 11 July 2000.
——. 'World calls India, says Singapore Minister', *The Hindu*, 10 July 2004.
Sussman, G. and Lent, J. A. (eds.) (1998) *Global Productions Labour in the Making of the 'Information Society'*, Hampton Press Inc, New Jersey, US.
Talking Points by Mr Tharman Shanmugaratnam, Singapore Senior Minister of State, Ministry of Trade and Industry and Ministry of Education, ASEAN Business Summit, New Delhi, 17 October 2002.
'Tatas pull out from airport project', *The Statesman* (India), 16 July 1998.
'Tatas exit Bangalore tech park', *The Telegraph*, 13 April 2005.
'Thakral earmarks $14–21m for its Direct Investment Division', *The Straits Times*, 6 January 1997.
'The Indian brain gain', *Sunday Times*, 21 March 2004.
'TDB's Strategic Approach to Accessing the Indian Market', *Tradespur*, June–July 1996.
'Temasek's role that of a catalyst', *The Straits Times* (Singapore), 28 June 2002.
'Thailand, India sign FTA agreement to boost trade', *Kyodo News International, Inc*, 9 October 2003.
'The India Business Group—Expanding Investment and Trade Links with India', *Tradespur*, June–July 1996, p. 4.
'The Bangkok Summit', *The Hindu*, 11 March 1996.
'The Indian brain gain', *Sunday Times*, 21 March 2004.

'Tidel Park still awaits Tidco, Ascendas JV', *The Economic Times*, 17 October 2004.
'Tidco in pact with JTC arm for software park', *Business Line*, 4 July 2002.
Tan, A. 'India vying with China to be Asia's red hot economy', *The Straits Times*, 2 April 2004.
Tan, C. H. (1995) *Venturing Overseas; Singapore's External Wing*, McGraw Hill, Singapore.
Tan, E. C. 'Look at Bangalore, Madras when Investing in India', *The Straits Times*, 27 February 1993.
Tan, J. 'Infosys did not apply for empoyment passes', *The Straits Times*, 26 October 2002.
Tan, L. H. (ed.) (1993) *Regional Economic Integration In The Asia-Pacific*, Institute of Southeast Asian Studies, Singapore.
Tan, S. 'Make the world our economic hinterland', *The Straits Times*, 30 May 1993.
——. '10 local-based Indian firms make pledges to Indian chamber's investment group', *The Straits Times*, 9 June 1993.
Teo, A. 'Govt may finance consortiums working on big projects abroad', *Business Times*, 25 August 1993.
——. 'Panel urges govt financing for S'pore business going abroad', *Business Times*, 18 May 1993.
Teo, C. C. 'Strategic Relevance of Asian Economic Integration', *RIS Discussion Papers*, RIS-DP # 90/2005, March 2005.
Teo, J. 'Ascendas sets up $500m fund for Indian properties', *The Straits Times*, 14 June 2007.
——. 'Ascendas buys Tata's 47% stake in Bangalore tech park', *The Straits Times*, 13 April 2005.
Thakur, R. (1994) *The Politics and Economics of India's Foreign Policy*, Oxford University Press, Delhi.
Thant, M., Tang M. and Kakazu H. (eds.) (1994) *Growth Triangles in Asia, a new approach to regional economic cooperation*, Oxford University Press, Oxford.
Thornton, T. P. 'India Adrift: The Search for Moorings in a New World Order', *Asian Survey*, Vol. 32, No. 2, December 1992, pp. 1063–1077.
Toh, M. H. and Low, L. Singapore-India Conference on 'Emerging Linkages and Spore's Rationale for Tapping Emerging Market', Department of Business Policy, National University of Singapore.
'UK relaxes visa norms for Indian ventures', *Business Line*, 13 February 2003.
Urban, S. (1998) *From Alliance Practice to Alliance Capitalism*, Gabler Press, Germany.
'Vajpayee to talk to Megawati for Polaris chief's release' *The Economic Times*, 18 December 2002.
Vaghul, N. 'Liberalization of the Financial Markets in India', *The Columbia Journal of World Business*, Spring 1994, p. 44.
Van Gils, A. and Zwart, P. 'Knowledge Acquisition and Learning in Dutch and Belgian SMEs: The Role of Strategic Alliances', *European Management Journal*, Vol. 22, No. 6.
Vasuki, S. N. 'Ratan Tata takes charge', *Business Times*, 17–18 September 1994.
Vellor, R. 'India identifies two southern cities for Singapore investments', *The Straits Times Weekly Edition*, 16 July 1994.
Velloor, R. 'India stands firm on FTA list', *The Straits Times*, 18 April 2007.
——. 'Troika Approach gets the nod', *The Straits Times*, 9 September 1994.
——. 'Bangalore Tech Park ready for operations in September', *The Straits Times*, 18 July 1997.
——. 'Singapore stake in Bangalore park to go up', *The Straits Times*, 14 December 1998.
——. 'Take-up seen improving to 50% in next three months', *The Straits Times*, 18 July 1997.
——. 'Litte red dot grows larger on face of India', *The Straits Times*, 31 March 2007.

——. 'Indian state's chief eyes closer ties', *The Straits Times*, Singapore, 19 May 1997.
——. 'Frank talk among old friends', *The Straits Times*, 24 January 2006.
Venu, M. K. 'An Asian economic community?' *The Economic Times*, 20 September 2005.
Venugopal, K. 'Thailand removes India's misgivings—Coast is clear for free trade pact', *Business Line*, 31 July 2004.
Vohra (ed.) (2003) *Emerging Asia: Challenges for India and Singapore*, India International Centre, Manohar, New Delhi.
'When will software products take off?' *Economic Times*, 2 November 2004.
Willner, J. 'Ownership, efficiency, and political interference', *European Journal of Political Economy*, Vol. 17, 2001, pp. 723–748.
Yap, J., CEO, Ascendas India, 'The Ascendas IT Park Story', at Conference on 'Connecting India', Asia Pacific Business Summit, 12–13 April 2006, Singapore.
Yasheng, H. and Khanna, T. 'Can India overtake China?' *Foreign Policy*, July/August 2003, pp. 74–81.
Yeoh, C., Lau G. Theng, Goh M. and Richardson J. (eds.) (1992) *Strategic Business Opportunities in the Growth Triangle*, Longman, Singapore.
Yeung, W. C. (2000) 'State intervention and neoliberalism in the globalizing world economy: lessons from Singapore's regionalization programme', *The Pacific Review*, Vol. 13, No. 1.
Yong, M. C. and Rao, B. (1995) (eds.) *Singapore-India Relations: A Primer*, National University of Singapore Press, Singapore.
Zhang, Y. 'Effecting Science park management for Economic development: Tracing the 20 Year History of the Singapore Science Park for Experience and Lesson', University of Waikato, New Zealand (unpublished).
Zoher, A. 'The Singapore Connection', *Asian Business*, February 1994.

# INDEX

www.ingramcontent.com/pod-product-compliance
Lightning Source LLC
LaVergne TN
LVHW080652011026
849160LV00014B/1391
*9789004170643*